SLOW TRAVEL

North & Mid Devon

Local, characterful guides to Britain's special places

Hilary Bradt
Gill & Alistair Campbell

EDITION 1

Bradt Guides Ltd, UK
The Globe Pequot Press Inc, USA

First edition published May 2022
Bradt Guides Ltd
31a High Street, Chesham, Buckinghamshire, HP5 1BW, England
www.bradtguides.com
Print edition published in the USA by The Globe Pequot Press Inc,
PO Box 480, Guilford, Connecticut 06437-0480

Text copyright © 2022 Bradt Guides Ltd
Maps copyright © 2022 Bradt Guides Ltd; includes map data © OpenStreetMap contributors
Photographs copyright © 2022 Individual photographers (see below)
Project Managers: Anna Moores and Emma Gibbs
Cover research: Ian Spick

ISBN: 9781784778842

British Library Cataloguing in Publication Data
A catalogue record for this book is available from the British Library

Photographs © individual photographers credited beside images & also those picture libraries credited as follows: Alamy.com (A); awl-images.com (AWL); Shutterstock.com (S); Superstock.com (SS); Wikimedia Commons (WC)

Front cover Stunning countryside near Crediton (Adam Burton/AWL)
Back cover Horse-drawn barge along the Great Western Canal (dcurzon/S)
Title page The beach at Croyde (Ian Woolcock/S)

Maps David McCutcheon FBCart.S
Typeset by Ian Spick, Bradt Guides
Production managed by Zenith Media; printed in the UK
Digital conversion by www.dataworks.co.in

AUTHORS

Hilary Bradt co-founded Bradt Travel Guides in 1974 and now lives in semi-retirement in Seaton, East Devon. After 45 years of writing guidebooks to Madagascar and South America, she has embraced her chosen home to the extent of insisting that such a large, varied and beautiful county deserved three Slow guides, not just one. A keen walker, she has hiked many miles of the South West Coast Path and the Devon Coast to Coast trail. Most Saturdays see her taking part in

one of Devon's parkruns (5km, but she's appropriately slow); during the summer, a swim in the sea – just a few minutes away from where she lives – is always a pleasure. Hilary is a productive member of the South West Sculptors association and lectures regularly on travel-related topics at libraries and literary festivals, both in Devon and further afield.

Gill and Alistair Campbell have lived in the West Country for more than 17 years. During that time they have walked extensively in the area, often leading walks for local residents, tourists and foreign tour groups. They have hiked the entire South West Coast Path, the Two Moors Way and the Macmillan Way West, and hope to finish the Tarka Trail in 2022. They are both volunteer workers for the National Trust (NT) and Exmoor National Park, where they restore ancient stone

walls, repair footpaths and help visitors get the most out of their visit to the southwest. Gill and Alistair also love to travel. In 1971, Gill joined an exploratory overland expedition from London to Singapore and she has not stopped travelling since. Alistair's early travels were often business related, working in cities all over Europe and Asia, but whenever not at work, he was walking, talking, eating and drinking with local people. Still exploring today, they are always looking for that new place to visit; that new person who has stories to tell.

CONTRIBUTORS

Claire Barker lives in rural North Devon, where she writes children's books in an iron wagon. She is the author of two series: *Knitbone Pepper Ghost Dog* (Usborne) and *Picklewitch and Jack* (Faber and Faber). Her boxes are on pages 84, 122 and 136.

Janice Booth settled in Devon in 2002 and considers it her 'home county' after many decades living in other parts of the UK. She's fascinated by Devon folklore and history, and has co-written (with Hilary) Bradt's *East Devon & the Jurassic Coast* and *South Devon & Dartmoor*. Her boxes are on pages 19, 55, 190 and 232.

Joanna Griffin is an open-water swimmer and travel writer who has written about numerous swimming adventures throughout the UK and Europe. She won Bradt's 'My Perfect Day' competition in 2016 with her description of wild swimming in East Devon, has been published in *Outdoor Swimmer* magazine and has won *The Telegraph*'s 'Just Back' competition on two occasions with accounts of swims in Lapland and Copenhagen. She has researched wild swimming throughout Devon and Exmoor for Bradt's Slow series. Her contributions are on pages 22 and 154.

Siân Scott was working for the National Trust when she visited Lundy in 2017 as a winter break but was stranded for a further five days by Storm Doris. During that forced stay she fell in love with the island and applied successfully for the post of Assistant Warden and Education Officer, a post she left in 2019.

ACKNOWLEDGEMENTS

Apart from all our beloved contributors, who slaved away in their free time for no recompense, and to whom we owe a debt that we cannot ever repay, we would like to thank (in alphabetical order): Alan Clark of the Tarka Rail Association; Alison Holmes of Dingles Fairground Heritage trust; Annette Dennis of Holsworthy Amateur Theatrical Society (HATS); Barny Butterfield of Stanford Orchards; Briony Clinch of Lapford Community Church; David Nation of Crediton Area History & Museum Society; Ian Ripper and Maggie Watson at Wheatland Farm; Jax Williams of Tarka Pottery; Lyndsey Green of the Landmark Trust and Rosie Ellis, National Trust Education Officer, for their meticulous work on our Lundy chapter; Michael Downward of Eggesford Church; Rebecca Catterall of the Devon and Cornwall Rail Partnership; Sally Everton and Tina Veater of Visit Devon; Tim Gowan at Torview Wine; and finally all the staff and volunteers at museums and tourist information centres (TICs) whose enthusiasm for their towns and regions is so infections, particularly all at Combe Martin TIC and Charles Dumpleton at Hatherleigh TIC.

FEEDBACK REQUEST

At Bradt Guides we're aware that guidebooks start to go out of date on the day they're published – and that you, our readers, are out there in the field doing research of your own. So why not tell us about your experiences? Contact us on ✆ 01753 893444 or ✉ info@ bradtguides.com. We will forward emails to the author who may post updates on the Bradt website at ⟲ bradtguides.com/updates. Alternatively, you can add a review of the book to Amazon, or share your adventures with us on social:

 BradtGuides BradtGuides BradtGuides

SUGGESTED PLACES TO BASE YOURSELF

These bases make ideal starting points for exploring localities the Slow way.

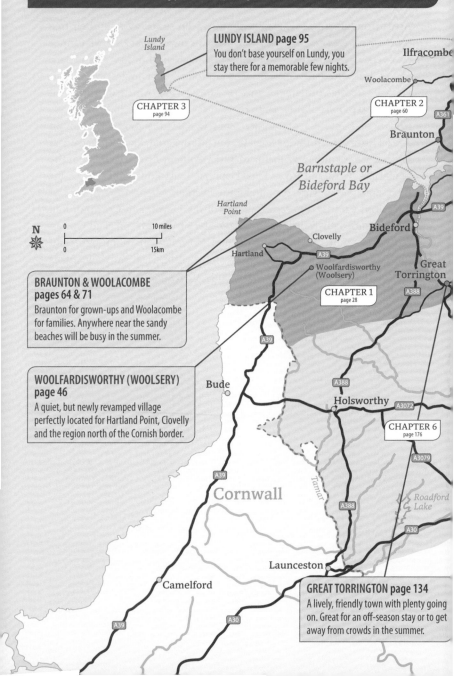

LUNDY ISLAND page 95
You don't base yourself on Lundy, you stay there for a memorable few nights.

CHAPTER 3
page 94

CHAPTER 2
page 60

Barnstaple or Bideford Bay

CHAPTER 1
page 28

CHAPTER 6
page 176

BRAUNTON & WOOLACOMBE pages 64 & 71
Braunton for grown-ups and Woolacombe for families. Anywhere near the sandy beaches will be busy in the summer.

WOOLFARDISWORTHY (WOOLSERY) page 46
A quiet, but newly revamped village perfectly located for Hartland Point, Clovelly and the region north of the Cornish border.

GREAT TORRINGTON page 134
A lively, friendly town with plenty going on. Great for an off-season stay or to get away from crowds in the summer.

N

0 ___ 10 miles
0 ___ 15km

Lundy Island

Ilfracombe
Woolacombe
Braunton
Hartland Point
Clovelly
Bideford
Hartland
Woolfardisworthy (Woolsery)
Great Torrington
Bude
Holsworthy
Cornwall
Tamar
Roadford Lake
Launceston
Camelford

A361
A39
A388
A3072
A3079
A30

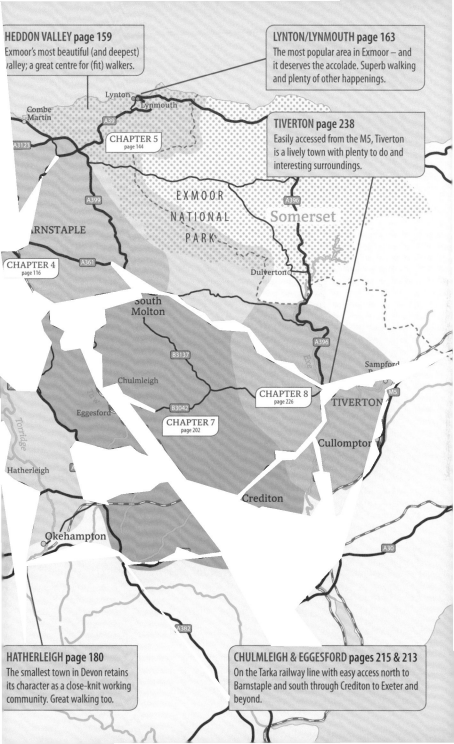

HEDDON VALLEY page 159
Exmoor's most beautiful (and deepest) valley; a great centre for (fit) walkers.

LYNTON/LYNMOUTH page 163
The most popular area in Exmoor – and it deserves the accolade. Superb walking and plenty of other happenings.

TIVERTON page 238
Easily accessed from the M5, Tiverton is a lively town with plenty to do and interesting surroundings.

Lynton
Combe Martin
Lynmouth
A39
A3123
CHAPTER 5
page 144
A399
EXMOOR
NATIONAL
PARK
Somerset
A396
ARNSTAPLE
CHAPTER 4
page 116
A361
Dulverton
South Molton
B3137
A396
Eye
Sampford
M5
Chulmleigh
CHAPTER 8
page 226
TIVERTON
Eggesford
B3042
CHAPTER 7
page 202
Cullompton
Torridge
Hatherleigh
Crediton
Okehampton
A30
A382

HATHERLEIGH page 180
The smallest town in Devon retains its character as a close-knit working community. Great walking too.

CHULMLEIGH & EGGESFORD pages 215 & 213
On the Tarka railway line with easy access north to Barnstaple and south through Crediton to Exeter and beyond.

CONTENTS

NORTH & MID DEVON

This is a county of sudden surprises, spendthrift in its contrasts. It is richly agricultural, richer in its virgin red soil than perhaps any other county in England, and then, suddenly, it is maritime, and the pastures give place to the blue sea, the second home of Devon men since history became articulate.

L du Garde Peach, *Unknown Devon*, 1927

When asked by a travel magazine to list my five favourite places in the world, I included North Devon. I'd just come back from a research trip for the previous incarnation of this book, walking some of the coastal paths in glorious sunshine and discovering new (to me) churches and unsung villages, and my heart was full of how lucky I was to live in the southwest and to be sharing my enthusiasm for the pleasures that constitute Slow travel: cliff paths, hidden coves and wonderful Exmoor with its heathery hills and combes. Slow food is part of Slow travel, and this region lends itself to time spent lingering over a meal or cream tea.

For this new title – not just a new edition – the coverage has changed, embracing my enthusiasm for the whole county of Devon. So we have lost Somerset's part of Exmoor – the national park now has its own volume – but gained the infinitely rewarding though little-known area of Mid Devon and two new, indefatigable authors, Gill and Alistair Campbell. All of Devon is now covered in our three Slow guides, just as it should be: *East Devon & The Jurassic Coast*; *South Devon & Dartmoor*; and this new Slow guide to North and Mid Devon.

I want locals who thought they were familiar with the region to say 'I didn't know that!' And I want visitors from afar to learn that there's more to Devon than the beaches and commercial places that get into the tourist brochures (although they're also included here). After all, that's what Slow is all about.

A TASTE OF NORTH & MID DEVON

This part of Devon is exceptionally appealing to foodies. The abundance of fresh produce and excellent restaurants is largely due to the farming heritage of the region, which encourages free-range animals and organic methods.

DAIRY TREATS

The taste of Devon is undoubtedly that of clotted cream. A Devon cream tea is as integral a part of a visit to this region as rain (indeed, the one often leads to the other). Clotted cream is quite unlike any other sort of cream, being as thick as butter and almost as yellow; it contains more fat (around 63%, while double cream is 48%), and traditionally was made by gradually heating fresh milk using steam or hot water, and allowing it to cool very slowly. The thick cream that rises to the top was then skimmed off. The original term was clouted cream, clout being the word for patch, referring to the thick crust that forms when the cream is heated.

Clotted cream is only made in Devon and Cornwall, and we Devonians are not only convinced that ours is better but that we got there first. After all, it was one of the wives of the Dartmoor giant, Blunderbus, who won her husband's affection by bringing the knowledge of clotted-cream-making to his kitchen. The story is slightly spoiled by the fact that Jennie was exiled to a cave in Cornwall at the time for being a lousy cook, and it was a Phoenician sea captain who taught her the process as a reward for saving his ship from wreckers.

Clotted cream is served with fresh scones, which should be warm from the oven not the microwave; purists prefer plain scones but others, myself included, love the fruit ones. In Devon we spread the cream on the scone first, instead of butter, and add jam on top; in Cornwall it's the opposite: jam first, then clotted cream. Either way it's utterly delicious – and very filling. The Victorian prime minister William Gladstone was right when he called clotted cream 'the food of the gods'.

Talking of jam, an Exmoor speciality is whortleberry jam. Whortleberry is the Exmoor name for bilberry, a heather relative, which grows on the moor.

◄ Clovelly's main street, Up-a-Long and Down-a-Long, leading to the harbour.

THE SLOW MINDSET

Hilary Bradt, Founder, Bradt Travel Guides

We shall not cease from exploration
And the end of all our exploring
Will be to arrive where we started
And know the place for the first time.
T S Eliot, 'Little Gidding', *Four Quartets*

This series evolved, slowly, from a Bradt editorial meeting when we started to explore ideas for guides to our favourite part of of the world – Great Britain. We wanted to get away from the usual 'top sights' formula and encourage our authors to bring out the nuances and local differences that make up a sense of place – such things as food, building styles, nature, geology or local people and what makes them tick. Our aim was to create a series that celebrates the present, focusing on sustainable tourism, rather than taking a nostalgic wallow in the past.

So without our realising it at the time, we had defined 'Slow Travel', or at least our concept of it. For the beauty of the Slow Movement is that there is no fixed definition; we adapt the philosophy to fit our individual needs and aspirations. Thus Carl Honoré, author of *In Praise of Slow*, writes: 'The Slow Movement is a cultural revolution against the notion that faster is always better. It's not about doing everything at a snail's pace, it's about seeking to do everything at the right speed. Savouring the hours and minutes rather than just counting them. Doing everything as well as possible, instead of as fast as possible. It's about quality over quantity in everything from work to food to parenting.' And travel.

So take time to explore. Don't rush it, get to know an area – and the people who live there – and you'll be as delighted as the authors by what you find.

As you would expect in a beachy region, there is a proliferation of ice-cream parlours and locally made ice cream.

MEAT

Meat eaters are in for a treat in this region. Some hotels convert to shooting lodges in the winter so pheasant, partridge, woodcock and venison feature on many country menus.

The native cattle could claim to produce the best steak in England. The nickname for the North Devon breed of cattle, Red Ruby, is appropriate: these animals are a beautiful chestnut red, the colour of a ripe conker. They are prized for their docility, hardiness and ability to convert grass to succulent, marbled meat. Most of the herds you will see grazing in the North and Mid Devon fields are grown slowly, outdoors (though the climate is such that they need to be brought inside during the winter), with the calves staying with their mothers until they are weaned.

Another native breed, the Exmoor horn sheep, has adapted to the conditions on Exmoor over the centuries. And Exmoor has adapted to the sheep, so the landscape you enjoy today owes as much to the grazing of these animals as it does to nature. The sheep are all-white and, as the name suggests, both rams and ewes have horns. They are dual-purpose animals, raised for wool as well as meat – in the days when mutton was regularly eaten they were considered to have the finest meat of any breed. Devon closewool sheep are another breed from Exmoor favoured for meat and hardiness.

Pigs, the original domestic meat animal, do well on Exmoor, and rare-breed Berkshire and Middle White pigs are raised outdoors (mostly) to provide succulent pork.

BOOZE

North and Mid Devon has 14 breweries listed by the Campaign for Real Ale (CAMRA). They are: Artbrew (Holsworthy); Barum (Barnstaple); Buckland (Bideford); Clearwater (Bideford); Combe (Ilfracombe); Country Life (Abbotsham); FatBelly (Lynton; page 169); Grampus (Lee; page 75), GT Ales (Barnstaple); Holsworthy Ales (Holsworthy; page 183); Magical Craft Brewery (Hele Bay); Tally Ho! (Hatherleigh); Taw Valley (North Tawton; page 183); and Yelland Manor (Barnstaple). Quite a collection! See ⬩ northdevoncamra.org.uk for further details.

There are also some interesting local ciders. Sandford Orchards in Crediton and Sam's Cider in Winkleigh both produce excellent ranges – it's fun finding your favourite. Cider making is seasonal, so if you are in Devon in late autumn you may see apples being collected for pressing. The juice is then fermented for 14 days and blended, which can take up to two years; Devon's cider makers don't hurry, they just want to make great cider. Similarly, there are a number of small vineyards that produce excellent English wine.

You'll find ales, ciders and wines in most farm shops and stores selling local products as well as in the producers' own on-site shops.

If it's the stronger stuff you're after, there's a number of excellent local gin distilleries in the region. Exmoor's **Wicked Wolf Gin** is making a

DEVON SQUAB PIE

Clotted cream is, surprisingly, the accompaniment to a traditional savoury recipe, Devon squab pie. Medieval dovecotes are still found in the grounds of the great West Country estates, so it's not surprising that squab, or young pigeon, should feature in an ancient recipe. Except that it doesn't. Devon squab pie is made with mutton. The likely explanation for this misnomer is that until the 17th century, squab – a luxury food – could be consumed only by the lord of the manor and the parish priest; perhaps the mixture of fruit and mutton tasted something like the sweet meat of a real squab. Be that as it may, this is a tasty dish composed of layers of mutton or lamb alternating with apples, prunes and spices. Some recipes add onion or leek. It's easy to make and, to add the authentic Devon touch, you need to serve it with clotted cream on the side. Below is the recipe I used for my 2021 Christmas lunch. I can affirm that it is delicious!

Devon squab pie recipe

Ingredients

2lb 3oz lamb or mutton, cubed
Plain flour
Oil for frying
2 leeks cut into rings and/or 1 chopped onion
1 eating apple, 1 cooking apple
    and 10 pitted prunes
Thyme and bay leaves if available

Pinch each of cinnamon and
    nutmeg, and/or all spice
16 fluid oz lamb or chicken stock
9 oz shortcrust pastry
1 egg
1 tbsp milk
Clotted cream

Method

Preheat the oven to Gas Mark 3/170°C.

Toss the lamb in some flour and salt and pepper, then heat a little oil in a frying pan and brown the meat thoroughly. Transfer to a bowl. Add more oil to the pan if needed, then fry the leeks and onion until both are soft. Arrange the lamb, leeks and onion in layers in a pie dish along with the peeled and sliced apples, prunes, thyme, bay leaves and spices. Some recipes call for a teaspoon of brown sugar at this stage. Pour the stock over the combined ingredients.

Roll out the pastry on a floured board until it is large enough to cover the pie. Mix the egg and milk to make an egg wash and dampen the edge of the dish. Place the pastry on top of the dish, then trim off any excess pastry and press and crimp the edges to seal. Brush with the egg wash and cook in the oven for about an hour until golden brown.

Serve with Devon vegetables and clotted cream on the side.

name for itself ($\oslash$ wickedwolfgin.com); it's run by a husband-and-wife team in Brendon who are proud of the eleven premium botanicals that go into it. Likewise, the **Atlantic Gin** distillery ($\oslash$ atlantic-spirit.co.uk) on the North Devon coast uses 'locally foraged botanicals' including samphire and laver for their distinctive tastes. In a tiny distillery near Winkleigh, Dawn and Mark make **Gotland Gin** ($\oslash$ gotlandgin.co.uk) and they will happily show you how they do it, before you do some tasting in their outdoor, covered bar. Gin making is one of Britain's fastest-growing industries so you will no doubt find other distilleries during your travels.

FOOD FESTIVALS

Before the Covid-19 pandemic, several North and Mid Devon market towns held food festivals. One that has endured is the **Clovelly Lobster & Crab Feast** in September, with live music, a variety of food and craft stalls, and an abundance of lobster and crab. Another is the **Crediton Food and Drink Festival** in June, with opportunities to sample local food and drink, and to watch demonstrations by local chefs. **Cullompton** holds its Autumn Festival of Food and Crafts in October, and others are sure to restart, so keep an eye on Visit Devon's listings ($\oslash$ visitdevon.co.uk).

FESTIVALS

North and Mid Devon have some of the most eccentric and interesting festivals in England. Most were cancelled during the Covid-19 pandemic, so always check their websites to be sure they have resumed.

Hunting the Earl of Rone $\odot$ Spring bank hol. Combe Martin's annual craziness (see box, page 88).

GoldCoast Oceanfest Croyde $\odot$ Jun. Three days of music and sport (see box, page 69).

Holsworthy's St Peter's Fair $\odot$ Jul. This week-long fair includes ale tasting, the rather strange crowning of the Pretty Maid, and the Furry Dance, a version of the Flora Dance (see box, page 196).

Chulmleigh Old Fair $\odot$ late Jul. Over 30 events spread over four days, starting with a money scramble at the Town Hall (see box, page 215).

Birdman Festival Ilfracombe $\odot$ Aug $\oslash$ visitilfracombe.co.uk. Who can fly furthest off the pier in their homemade contraption? Thrills and spills (page 79).

Clovelly Herring Festival ☉ Nov. Celebrating the 'silver darlings' (page 43).
Hatherleigh Annual Carnival ☉ Nov. A day that starts and ends with tar barrels being dragged, ablaze, through the streets (see box, page 184).

NGS GARDENS & OPEN STUDIOS

Each year householders from all over England and Wales open their gardens for charity as part of the National Garden Scheme (NGS) (⊘ ngs.org.uk). There are now more than 3,700 participants with homes of every size, from manor houses to semi-detached cottages. Since this guide aims to get under the skin of North and Mid Devon, a visit to one of these open gardens is the perfect way to understand the locals or – if you are a visitor from overseas – the English. We consider ourselves the most passionate gardeners in the world, and the West Country, with its rich soil and mild climate, makes enthusiasts out of even reluctant horticulturists.

And it's not just the gardens you'll enjoy. Almost every householder taking part in the scheme adds to the money raised by offering coffee and tea with a wonderful array of home-baked cakes.

Gardens open at different times throughout the year, although more, of course, in spring and summer. Some open only for one weekend so you need to plan ahead; the website has a good map and details of more than 60 open gardens in Devon. The NGS annual publication, the Garden Visitor's Handbook (known as 'the yellow book'), gives a complete countrywide list and can be bought via the NGS website, but there are separate county lists too. The Devon one can usually be picked up free at tourist offices or accessed through the website.

"Throughout the county, artists open up their studios to show their work and to talk to art enthusiasts."

A somewhat similar scheme, in that it brings you into contact with the locals, is the Open Studios fortnight which takes place annually in September in Devon. It is an initiative of the Devon Artist Network (⊘ devonartistnetwork.co.uk) and participating studios are listed on its website. Throughout the county, artists open up their studios to show their work and to talk to art enthusiasts. Some exhibit in groups, in galleries, others set aside a room in their homes. For art lovers it adds a hugely enjoyable element to their visit to Devon.

CAR-FREE TRAVEL

The mode of lionising the neighbourhood is on pony or donkeyback, or, far better, on foot. The roads are ill-equipped for carriages, being steep and circuitous.
A Handbook for Travellers in Devon and Cornwall, 1872

The Slow traveller prefers to get around under his or her own leg power or by bus, but the latter can be quite a challenge in this region of poor public transport. Detailed information on getting around without a car is given in each chapter, but do bear in mind that bus timetables change and buses are being withdrawn with an unnerving frequency. If you are relying on public transport for any part of your visit in Devon you should check the excellent website *⊘* traveldevon.info, which has an interactive bus map. It also covers self-powered travel: cycling and walking.

HORSERIDING

Exmoor, the home of one of Britain's most distinctive native ponies, is perfect for riding, but there are stables in other parts of North and Mid Devon which are equally scenic. There are also several accommodation providers, some included in this book, who will also provide a field or stabling for your own horse, so a riding holiday using the information in this book plus a bit of additional research is entirely realistic.

Stables
Boldtry Riding Stables Chulmleigh *⊘* 01769 580366 *⊘* boldtrystables-chulmleigh.co.uk
Brendon Manor Stables Lynton *⊘* 01598 741246 *⊘* brendonmanor.com
Collacott Equestrian Centre Umberleigh *⊘* 01769 572725 *⊘* collacott.co.uk
Dean Riding Stables Parracombe *⊘* 01598 763565 *⊘* deanridingstables.co.uk
Easter Hall Park Petrockstowe *⊘* 01837 810350 *⊘* easterhallpark.co.uk
Exmoor Riding Centre Lynton *⊘* 01598 753967 *⊘* exmoorcoastholidays.co.uk
Follyfoot Equestrian Centre Northam *⊘* 07759 182242 *⊘* follyfootequestriancentre.co.uk
High Mainstone Equestrian Ashford, Barnstaple *⊘* 01271 817407 *⊘* highermainstoneequestrian.co.uk
Mullacott Riding Centre Ilfracombe *⊘* 01271 866685 *⊘* mullacott.com
Thinking Horses Muddiford *⊘* 01271 850864 *⊘* ridinglessons.co
Woolacombe Riding Stables Woolacombe *⊘* 01271 870260 *⊘* woolacomberidingstables.co.uk

CYCLING

Mike Harrison, compiler of Croydecycle maps (see box, page 20), writes: 'Cycling in North Devon is a pleasure, being far from cities so most of the rural lanes are quiet. The Tarka Trail (NCN3 and 27) on the old railway lines around the Taw and Torridge estuaries is ideal for families and there are other quiet and level lanes around Braunton. Coastal roads can be busy at peak times and often a bike is the quickest way round the narrow lanes but be wary of cars.'

Each chapter gives local cycling information, and you'll find helpful information on ⊘ traveldevon.info.

WALKING

The **South West Coast Path** (SWCP) is the most popular long-distance national trail in this region. It begins in Minehead and follows the coast, with occasional forays inland, for 124 miles to the Cornish border before completing its 630-mile journey round the Cornwall peninsula to Poole Harbour in Dorset. The North Devon section is considered by many to be the most beautiful, as well as the most challenging, of the entire route. All keen walkers who visit Devon will do parts of the coast path, most utilising the inland footpaths to make a circular trip or doing one of the 'bus-assisted walks' suggested in this book. However, there are several inland long-distance footpaths, including the **Two Moors Way** which runs from Ivybridge on the southern edge of Dartmoor to Lynmouth on the North Devon coast. There is now an extension to the Two Moor Way that links it to the south coast at Wembury near Plymouth, the whole walk being 117 miles and called **Devon's Coast to Coast**. Other paths include the **Macmillan Way West** from southeast Exmoor to Barnstaple; the **Samaritans Way South West**, from Bristol to Lynton; and the **Coleridge Way** from the Quantocks to Lynmouth.

I (Hilary) walked Devon's Coast to Coast (still mostly signed as The Two Moors Way) in 2020 and can highly recommend it, even for oldies like me. It was so varied and so beautiful, I hardly noticed my tired legs. The longest stretch – and it is indeed a tough one – is a little over 13 miles across Dartmoor with no escape route, but after that you can always arrange shorter days. The Mid Devon section is particularly enjoyable because so few walkers do it. From Drewsteignton, on the northeastern fringe of Dartmoor, you walk through farmland, with some woodland, through Witheridge and Knowstone and into Somerset to meet Exmoor at Tarr Steps.

These are just the named trails; a network of minor footpaths and excellent maps allow you to devise your own walk. Suggestions and detailed walk descriptions are given in each chapter, and chapter maps include the ♀ symbol to indicate that there is a described walk in that area.

WALKING MAPS & GUIDES

Walkers and cyclists have a bonus in this region – Mike Harrison's marvellous pocket-sized Croydecycle maps (see box, page 20). There are two 1:15,000 maps just for the South West Coast Path, but it's the 13 maps that cover the entire North Devon and Exmoor coast at a scale of 1:12,500 or five inches to a mile, which are such a joy. It's not just the scale that makes them special, it's Mike's snippets of explanatory or helpful text. So footpaths may have the warning 'may be muddy after rain' or the reassuring 'sheep grazed' or 'firm grass'. Places of historical or geological interest will have a little block of explanatory text, and any other bit of empty space is filled with hard information on buses, phone numbers and other tourist information. The maps are regularly updated and an added bonus is the street plans of some of the larger towns. All this for £3.

In addition to the series of walking maps there are larger-scale cycling maps at 1:30,000, also North Devon and Exmoor & Taunton at 1:100,000

GOOD TIDINGS

Janice Booth

North Devon and Exmoor's beautiful stretches of coastline are a huge delight for visitors fascinated by cliffs, beaches and the shore. However, lifeboats are all too often called out to rescue people trapped by the incoming tide. These potentially dangerous and costly call-outs can be avoided by always checking the tide tables (available in local shops and TICs) before a seashore wander.

Non-seawise visitors don't always realise how much the extent and timing of a tide's ebb and flow vary with the phases of the moon. The fact that you could walk round the tip of that promontory yesterday at midday and return safely doesn't mean you can do the same tomorrow, even if you calculate the time difference correctly: the tide may ebb less far or rise higher, and more deeply, and you'll be cut off.

These variations apply year-round and on every stretch of Britain's coastline, so – better safe than sorry!

MIKE HARRISON, MASTER MAP-MAKER

Mike Harrison is certainly a popular person in Devon and Exmoor. Not that most users of his Croydecycle maps even know his name – they just know that these are by far the best walking maps of the area.

I visited Mike in his centuries-old stone-built cottage next to the church in Croyde. 'It belonged to my great grandmother,' he told me. 'She bought it in 1900 for £150 and it's been in the family ever since.' When Mike was made redundant from his teaching job in Hereford, he had little idea that, at an age when most men have retired, he would be selling tens of thousands of maps, produced by himself in Rose Cottage. I asked him how it all started. 'I met a Russian in Greece in 2002 with a beautiful, large-scale map which actually turned out to be useless when it came to knowing where to find water.' Mike's locally bought, smaller-scale map had bits of text giving vital information for walkers – such as the location of water supplies. 'I thought, we don't have anything like this at home and, as a keen cyclist, I also found the size of existing maps unwieldy.'

A venture into producing cycling maps of Devon and Cornwall had limited success, but 'I produced my first large-scale walking map – for Croyde – in 2006 and suddenly here was a product that was popular.' Popular is an understatement. Once you've used a Croydecycle map (the original name stuck, even though walking rather than cycling is now the emphasis) you feel dissatisfied with anything else. It's the way Mike squeezes all the information you could possibly want on to a pocket-sized map. Despite his output, with a total of 50 maps on Devon and Exmoor, north Cornwall and west Dorset, this is still a one-man show. When researching a new map, Mike will walk up to 20 miles a day, checking out all the footpaths, in both directions, and taking notes on every feature of use or interest to the walker. The base map comes from six-inch-to-the-mile Ordnance Survey maps published in 1880 and 1905. 'Not that much has changed, but I add information from satellite pictures. Remember, a plan is accurate, a map is about giving the right impression.' An example is that if a map showed roads in their real width in relation to the scale, they would be the thickness of a hair. Junctions may need to be exaggerated for clarity.

Each map takes about two months to create. The profit from this venture is modest for one who works seven days a week. 'But it's fun, isn't it?'

which are more useful to car drivers than any other maps I've found. The maps are widely available in the region but you can also order them direct from ⌀ croydecycle.co.uk.

For inland areas not covered by Croydecycle you'll need the Ordnance Survey Explorer maps. The OL9 double-sided one covers all of Exmoor at a scale of 1:25,000, so is ideal for walking, though its size makes it unwieldy. At the same scale are two single-sided Explorer maps, 126 and 139, covering the North Devon chapters of this book.

A number of guidebooks detail walks in the area. *Shortish Walks in North Devon* by Robert Hesketh are easy to follow with clear maps. Other regional self-published walking guides are listed in each chapter.

For walkers doing the South West Coast Path one guide stands out: *Exmoor & North Devon Coast Path* by Henry Stedman and Joel Newton, published by Trailblazer. This has the hallmark of all Trailblazer's walking guides: clear, hand-drawn maps, masses of background information, accommodation and eating suggestions. As an added bonus it's written with wit and observation.

WILDLIFE

From spotting puffins on Lundy to watching rutting red deer on Exmoor, the region offers some wonderful wildlife viewing. The range of habitat from moorland to farmland, woodland to coast, and river to wetlands brings a diversity of insects and their predators. Butterflies and moths are particularly well represented, with the rare heath fritillary and even rarer marsh fritillary present on their favourite habitat.

The iconic mammal of Exmoor is undoubtedly the red deer; you are more likely to see them here than in any other part of England. If you're lucky you may also spot smaller creatures, such as otters and hares.

The North Devon coast is particularly blessed with rock pools; several TICs – such as Lynmouth and Combe Martin – have microscopes so you can study your finds. They also organise tide-pooling expeditions for youngsters.

Lundy Island is exceptional, not only for its birdlife, but for the marine environment. It is the nation's first Marine National Statutory Reserve, and draws divers from far afield for its rare corals and other marine specialities. It is also known for its unusual lichens.

FURTHER READING & MEDIA
NEWSPAPERS & MAGAZINES

If you buy a local newspaper while in Devon make it the *Western Morning News* (⊘ thisiswesternmorningnews.co.uk). Published since 1860, it is an excellent paper with lots of information and reports on

WILD SWIMMING IN NORTH DEVON & EXMOOR

Joanna Griffin

In recent years, swimming in the wild has increased in popularity. Perhaps it is the sheer sense of freedom, the adventure, and the thrill of exploration that is drawing us to wilder waters. Or maybe it is the uniquely sensory experience of an open-water swim; the pull of a current, the subtle change in light, the brush of weeds or the chill of the water after the rain. Wild swimming enables us to reconnect with the natural world, and with each other, allowing us to travel through our landscape from a different viewpoint.

Whatever it is that is drawing us away from our local swimming baths towards our rivers and lakes, we can be sure that no two swims are ever the same. From deep, shady woodland pools to the more exposed waters of the open moor, wild swimming in North Devon is an experience as varied as the landscape. Whether you're more of a 'dipper' or looking for something longer, wild swimming enables you to experience this lovely region from a different perspective.

Although some swim spots can be accessed more easily than others, the more remote stretches of water are quieter, and locating them is all part of the adventure. There is nothing quite like trekking across open moorland until suddenly an elusive swimming hole comes into view; or finally spotting that hidden stretch of river, long and deep enough for a decent swim. I describe wild swims in the region on pages 154 and 173, but these are just a sample of what's available.

And of course, there is the sea. This beautiful stretch of dramatic coastline – wild and secluded in parts – offers up deserted bays, family-friendly coves with gently shelving access, and tidal pools, presenting quite a different experience to swimming in fresh water. Here, there are tides to consider as well as wildlife of a different kind, including seals. Although some stretches of coastline can be busy, particularly the sandy beaches to the west of the region, there are still many opportunities for a truly wild swim. Even if it might involve a scramble down a steep rocky slope with the aid of a rope, or a long trek down rickety steps, swimmers are rewarded by secret beaches and interesting swims through gullies and caves.

As always when wild swimming, it is important to make sure that the water is safe and that swimming is permitted. A good way of doing this is to use the crowd-sourced wild swim map detailed below, or to join a friendly group of local swimmers with lots of local knowledge and good company.

Further reading & wild swimming resources

Wild Swimming, Daniel Start, Wild Things Publishing, second edition, 2013

⌖ wildswimming.co.uk

local events as well as politically unbiased international news. Taking the longer view is the monthly magazine *Devon Life* (⊘ devonlife.co.uk), with in-depth articles on a range of town and country issues.

Scene (⊘ northdevongazette.co.uk) is a free magazine focusing on North Devon that can be picked up in TICs and other outlets, and *North Devon Visitor*, an A3-sized magazine listing all events in the region, is widely available and published yearly.

RADIO

Radio Devon (103.4MHz FM), broadcast from the BBC studios in Plymouth, is one of the most listened-to of the BBC's local radio stations. Tune in to hear traffic news as well as local-interest stories and interviews.

BOOKS

The area has a strong literary heritage, with probably more book-inspired place names than anywhere else in the country. Starting with the Victorians, North Devon has Charles Kingsley's *Westward Ho!* (the only town in the world named after a book) then Henry Williamson made his mark with *Tarka the Otter*, which has lent its name to a railway and a trail, and strongly evokes the region's landscape.

Children will love the pony books written by Victoria Eveleigh, farmer at West Ilkerton (page 168) and Exmoor pony breeder. *A Stallion Called Midnight* vividly describes the landscape and way of life on Lundy Island, as well as North Devon.

SOURCE MATERIAL

I have drawn on the information in several out-of-print books by inspirational authors. These include:

The Coasts of Devon and Lundy Island: their towns, villages, scenery, antiquities and legends Page, John Lloyd Warden. Originally published in 1895 by Horace Cox, reprinted in facsimile by Ulan Press. Page travelled, observed, listened and wrote exhaustively about Devon. His fat book is stuffed with observations, legends and history.
Devon Hoskins, W G, Collins 1954; reprints 2003 & 2011, Phillimore & Co. Hoskins is *the* authority on Devon. No place is too small or insignificant to merit an entry in the gazetteer.
Devon (Architectural Guide) Pevsner, Nicholas, Yale University Press, 1989. The definitive guide, full of acerbic and insightful comment. Part of a series that covers all of England,

ALEXEY LOBANOV/S

NORTH DEVON PHOTOGRAPHY/S

VISIT DEVON

TOMHOLDERIMAGERY/S

which is said to be 'the greatest endeavour of popular architectural scholarship in the world'.

Devon: A Shell Guide Jellicoe, Ann & Mayne, Roger, Faber & Faber 1975. The erudite research and literary style that you would expect in a Shell Guide.

Early Tours in Devon and Cornwall Pearse Chope, R (ed), James G Commin, 1918; reprinted 1967, David & Charles. A fascinating look at how early travellers in Devon saw the county. The writers include John Leland (travelling 1534–43), Celia Fiennes (1695), Daniel Defoe (1724), W G Maton (1794–6) and Robert Southey (1802).

Glorious Devon Mais, S P B, Great Western Railway Company, 1932. A warm and human account, in Mais's masterly style, bringing the scenery and the people enjoyably to life.

A Handbook for Travellers in Devon and Cornwall (no author credited) John Murray, 1872. Extraordinarily detailed information on how and where to travel around using horse-drawn carriages and 'post buses'.

The King's England: Devon Mee, Arthur, Hodder and Stoughton. Various editions since 1928. Mee's descriptions of the places are affectionate and his style is very readable. He includes some unusual details and a sprinkling of old tales and legends.

Unknown Devon du Garde Peach, L, Bodley Head, 1927. An entertaining and interesting account of an exploration of Devon by motor car.

HOW THIS BOOK IS ARRANGED

MAPS

The map at the front of this book shows the area covered in each of the eight chapters, along with suggestions on where to base yourself for a holiday in this region. Each chapter then begins with a sketch map of the area, highlighting the places mentioned in the text or in the accommodation section. The numbers on the map correspond to the numbers against the headings or emboldened names in the text. The ♀ symbol on these maps indicates that there is a walk in that area. There are also sketch maps for some of these featured walks.

FOOD, DRINK & ACCOMMODATION

We've listed some of our, and local people's, favourite pubs, cafés, restaurants and farm shops – anywhere supplying particularly good

◄ 1 Kayaking along the rugged North Devon coast. 2 Traffic-free cycling on the Tarka Trail. 3 Horseriding on North Devon's hills. 4 Catching a wave off Woolacombe Sands, part of the World Surfing Reserve.

or unusual food or drink, or because they're in a convenient location. Just be aware that such places close or change ownership frequently so check before setting out for that special meal. This is by no means intended to be an exhaustive list, and readers will find excellent places for themselves. Do let us know, on the update website, if you have found an eatery you'd like to recommend.

The last chapter of this book lists a few recommended **places to stay** – or camp – out of the many hundred in this region. The hotels and B&Bs are indicated by 🏠 under the heading for the town or village in which they're located. Self catering is indicated by 🏠; campsites 🅰 and glamping by ⛺.

One self-catering provider that differs from the others is the Landmark Trust, which leases Lundy Island from the National Trust. This charitable organisation's role is to rescue historic buildings in danger of dereliction, restore them, and rent them out as holiday accommodation. Apart from those on Lundy, there are seven Landmark Trust places in North Devon. Three are included (pages 247, 248 and 250).

Prices change regularly so are not mentioned, but we have tried to suggest whether a place is an upmarket option or more suited to the budget-conscious. Some accommodation providers keep their prices consistent all year but many, especially those by the coast, charge peak rates in July and August.

For full listings see ⊘ bradtguides.com/midnorthdev.

ATTRACTIONS

When useful, we have given contact details for attractions – it is always worth checking websites for any changes in advance of any visit, however. We have not listed admission fees as they change regularly; always check them beforehand to avoid an unpleasant shock. If a description does not say admission is free, you should expect to be charged.

Note that no charge has been made for the inclusion of any business in this guide.

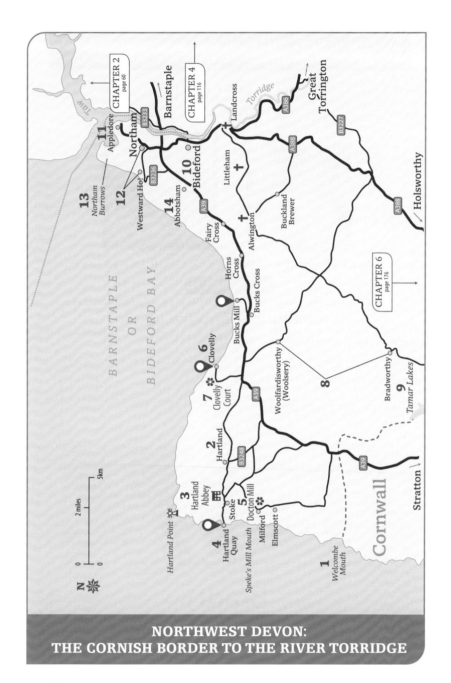

NORTHWEST DEVON:
THE CORNISH BORDER TO THE RIVER TORRIDGE

1

NORTHWEST DEVON: THE CORNISH BORDER TO THE RIVER TORRIDGE

**This remote north-western corner of Devon is a place to dream in ...
The deserted coast is backed by a rich hinterland, full of sleepy little
villages which have never awakened for long enough to find a place
in the history books. They are still fast asleep, just perhaps turning
and muttering a little if they happen to lie by the great highway along
which the purposeful motorist does his thirty or forty miles in the hour
towards Cornwall.**
L du Garde Peach, *Unknown Devon*, 1927

This 'wild west' of the county is perhaps my favourite part of North
Devon. Here there are few sandy beaches but the ever-changing wood
and cliff scenery from the coast path is sublime, as are the sand dunes
and salt marsh of Northam Burrows. The region's most charming **fishing
villages** are here (Clovelly and Appledore), as are the splendid **Hartland
Abbey**, some good **gardens** (Clovelly Court, Docton Mill) and a clutch
of villages whose churches are crammed with carved bench ends and
other curiosities.

Charles Kingsley and Sir Richard Grenville share the honour of being
the region's favourite son. Kingsley's name is everywhere, though few
21st-century readers appreciate his flowery, moralistic prose (he wrote
The Water Babies and *Westward Ho!*), while Grenville, who met his
death when his ship, *The Revenge*, tackled a vastly superior Spanish fleet,
is mainly celebrated in his home town of Bideford.

 WET-WEATHER ACTIVITIES

Burton Art Gallery and Museum Bideford (page 50)
Exceptional churches (page 56)
Hartland Abbey (page 33)
North Devon Maritime Museum Appledore (page 52)

GETTING THERE & AROUND

Few Slow travellers will grumble that the region is so poor in transport infrastructure – for there lies the secret of its wildness. The nearest railway station is Barnstaple, from where regular buses run to Bideford and Westward Ho!. The only main road is the A39 (the Atlantic Highway), which runs close to the coast until a few miles from Clovelly where it loses its nerve and takes a short cut to Bude in Cornwall. However, the 319 bus does a pretty good job of servicing this road every two hours or so, with diversions to the impressively named Woolfardisworthy and Clovelly before finishing in Hartland.

SELF-POWERED TRAVEL

There are no dedicated **cycle paths** here and, although the network of lanes carries little traffic, they are narrow and visibility is poor so cyclists need to take particular care.

Walkers, on the other hand, can enjoy the splendidly rugged section of the South West Coast Path above the layered and crumpled rocks of Hartland Quay and Hartland Point, heaved up by geological forces millions of years ago and cut by streams and waterfalls. This is reckoned, by some, to be the finest coastal walking in Devon. There are also numerous inland footpaths where you won't meet a soul.

Walking maps & guides

Ordnance Survey's 1:25,000 Explorer series 126 covers the region, along with Croydecycle's 1:12,500-scale walking maps, *Hartland & Clovelly* and *Bideford, Appledore & Westward Ho!*.

For the South West Coast Path, you're well set up with Trailblazer's *Exmoor & North Devon*.

THE HARTLAND HEARTLAND

It is not the height of Hartland Point that makes it so striking, it is the perpendicular wall of rock, dark and forbidding, with nothing but a few clumps of heather to soften its grimness; its wild and indeed mountainous appearance, which gives it a look of grandeur shared by no other headland in the Bristol Channel.
J L W Page, 1895

The area west of the A39 is the wildest corner of North Devon – literally a corner, since the coastline makes a right-angle turn at Hartland Point. There's no better place in Devon to see the effects of a mighty collision of tectonic plates around 300 million years ago, which folded the rock like an accordion or pushed it up on its side. Different types of rock erode at varying rates so they tip and slide forming cliffs and sea-stacks.

To experience these remarkable formations fully you need to walk a stretch of the coastal path; but there are three car access points, at Hartland Quay, Hartland Point and Welcombe Mouth near the Cornish border, where the less mobile can admire the seascape. There are no bus-assisted walks here – the A39, and therefore the bus, runs too far from the coast.

1 WELCOMBE MOUTH

⋏ **Koa Tree Camp** (page 247)

Close to the border with Cornwall is this other-worldly beach of furrowed rocks worn smooth by the tides and surrounded by high grassy cliffs over which the coastal path climbs. One sandy channel leads into the sea and I was assured by a local that it was safe for swimming, but I wouldn't try it at high tide when the hidden rocks could be dangerous. There is a carpark above the steep path down to the beach.

Walkers can do a lovely stretch of the South West Coast Path from here to Hartland Quay, just under five scenic miles away.

2 HARTLAND

🏠 **Downe Cottages** (page 247), ⋏ **Loveland Farm** (page 247)

The main settlement in the area has a long history. Hartland was a gift from King Alfred to his son Edward, and passed down a line of kings until Canute and eventually William the Conqueror. Seven hundred years later, however, it was described by W G Maton as having 'an air of poverty that depresses it to a level with a Cornish borough'. These days it has regained its confidence and has much to offer visitors, including a range of galleries and potteries, as well as cafés and pubs, a village store that stays open late and a free carpark. The 319 bus passes every two hours or so, enabling you to do a fair amount of sightseeing even without a car.

The two principal sights are some distance from Hartland, but both conveniently in the direction of Hartland Quay. The glorious **Hartland**

Abbey is about a mile away (see opposite) and **St Nectan's Church**, whose tower – at 128ft the highest in Devon – provides a landmark for walkers, is a mile further on at Stoke.

You enter the church via an unusual swivel lych-gate with a counter-balance weight to keep it closed. Inside are numbered pews from the days when parishioners had to pay 'pew rent' for their seat in church, a huge, intricately carved screen with typical Devon fan vaulting and carved bench ends. The font is interesting, not only for its carved sides but for the heads that glare at each other from the base and below the bowl. The ones on the base are gloomy grotesques, while their opposites – visible only if you lie on the floor – are wise old bearded men. You can draw your own conclusions as to what they mean.

In the south chapel are some stone fragments from the original Hartland Abbey, including a (decapitated) angel.

The graveyard, which has the headstones of members of the Lane family who founded Penguin books, once served as pasture for the vicar's horse. A neighbouring cleric commented that 'he cherishes for his horse the grain that grows from out the bosoms of the dead.'

✳ ✳ ✳

⅄ AROUND HARTLAND POINT

❀ OS Explorer map 126 or Croydecycle *Hartland & Clovelly*; start: Hartland Quay EX39 6DU; 5 miles; strenuous

Local walks expert Bryan Cath warned me: 'It may look short, but there are five up and downs and no escape route; it's more than some people can cope with.' Indeed, it looks easy to follow the coastal path round Hartland Point to the lighthouse and beyond, but it is certainly strenuous. However, I've known worse elsewhere on the South West Coast Path and the scenery is superlative, so the above is a warning not a deterrent. And it's easy to make it a circular walk, with a chance to see St Nectan's Church and Hartland Abbey too. If you plan to visit Hartland Abbey you can park there and take the private path to Blackpool Mill, thus cutting out one of the hills. Or achieve the same objective by parking at Stoke and taking the path that follows the south bank of Abbey River.

1 From Hartland Quay, take the path round Warren Beach. After meeting and leaving the road, start your first climb, admiring the pleated and puckered cliff rocks as you go, to Dyer's Lookout.

2 Follow the path as it curves east and drops to River Abbey and its bridge. You'll see Blackpool Mill Cottage ahead. Another few ups and downs and you'll be at Hartland Point with its lighthouse (closed to visitors) sitting coyly at the base of the cliff and the big radar 'football' on the hill, used during World War II to track enemy vessels and aircraft. The hills are hard work but from every summit there's a splendid view. The steeply sloping rock faces here are used for **climbing** and **abseiling** activities run by Skern Lodge (⏁ skernlodge.co.uk).

3 At the end of the track there's a carpark and welcome refreshment kiosk. After a reviving cuppa, take the road out of the carpark and follow the lanes south through Blegberry and Berry to Stoke. Here, keep ahead on the road signposted to Hartland Quay, passing the church on your right. You will reach the carpark in just over half a mile.

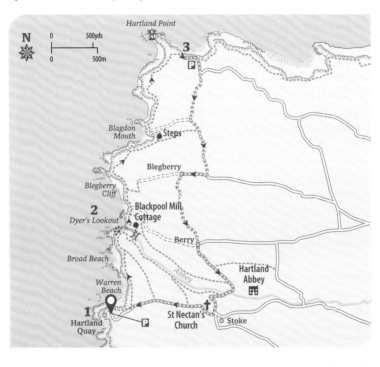

✳ ✳ ✳

3 HARTLAND ABBEY

EX39 6DT ✆ 01237 441496/441234 ⏁ hartlandabbey.com ☉ May–Oct, times vary, but generally gardens & tea room 11.00–17.00, house 14.00–16.00 Sun–Thu. Check website or phone before visiting.

W G Maton may have had a poor view of Hartland, but he loved the house, which stands in the location of an old abbey, now disappeared.

> Every advantage has been taken of the spot to create a picturesque and agreeable scene, the slopes on each side being planted very judiciously, and the intermediate lawn opened to a little bridge that crosses a swift, bubbling brook... Though built in a monastic fashion, with Gothic windows, the Priory [sic] is wholly modern, no remains of the old structure being left. It is at present the residence of Colonel Orchard.

The house was indeed wholly modern when Maton saw it in the 1790s; Paul Orchard had completely rebuilt it only 20 years earlier. Nothing remains of the original abbey, which survived longer than any other monastery in England. When Henry VIII finally got round to dissolving it in 1539 he gave it to the appropriately named William Abbott, who was Sergeant of his Wine Cellar at Hampton Court (nice job; nice perks!). In 1583 Prudence Abbott married into the Luttrell family of Dunster Castle who retained ownership until the house passed, again through marriage, to Paul Orchard. The Orchards held it for a hundred years before it passed to the Stucleys in the mid-1800s; it has been with their family ever since. The Orchards and the Stucleys demolished, rebuilt and altered parts of the house over the centuries, so the current building is a hodgepodge of different designs – but it works, perhaps thanks to architects like Sir George Gilbert Scott who was commissioned by Sir George Stucley to design the entrance and front hall, which give the arriving visitor such a positive impression.

Hartland Abbey is gorgeous: far superior to most other great Devon houses, which sometimes struggle to justify their entrance fee. This is undisputedly grand, with magnificent fireplaces, splendid furniture and paintings, many of them from Poltimore House near Exeter (the heiress of Poltimore married a Stucley), and stunning views from the huge windows. The quality of the contents is one of the advantages of a house that has never been sold, but passed down through the centuries by inheritance. Families do not always respect good furniture, however. In 1933 one of the twelve Chippendale chairs was found to be missing; it was discovered in St Nectan's church with the lower part of its legs sawn off to make it the right height for Marion Stucley to play the organ.

1 Folded rock formations, Welcombe Mouth. 2 Hartland Abbey. 3 Hartland Quay. ▶

MILESTREVELYAN/S

VISIT DEVON

PETER TURNER PHOTOGRAPHY/S

VISIT DEVON

PABLO FERNANDEZ VILLOCH/S

STEVE HEAP/S

A similar, but less drastic, fate befell the heroic murals in the Drawing Room, commissioned by Sir George Stucley in the mid 19th century. They show historical events in which his ancestors played a part, only to be covered a generation later with white paper to make the room brighter in the years before electricity. The paper was stripped away and the paintings revealed in 1992.

The library was built within the walls of the original abbey and is hung with portraits, including one by Sir Joshua Reynolds and two by Gainsborough. And there are quite a few books. Before the war it used to have a lot more – 8,000 more, in fact. In 1939 these books were found to be surplus to requirements and taken to the local tip. A canny farmer intercepted the cart and decided they would be just the thing for building a boundary wall: cheaper than bricks. This literary wall contained such rarities as a copy of a Hebrew grammar from 1597. There will have been some erudite cows in North Devon.

"This literary wall contained a copy of a Hebrew grammar – there will have been some erudite cows in North Devon."

Scattered around the house are laminated newspaper cuttings that add snippets of intrigue: Princess Margaret in a bath wearing a tiara, for instance. The stewards are enthusiastic and knowledgeable and will tell you the background to these photos – and demonstrate how the unique circular dining room table can be adjusted in size.

The **gardens** are as rewarding as the house, and the lived-in, or rather worked-in, feeling is even stronger since almost all of the work has been done by the Stucley family themselves. They only employ 1½ gardeners, so to have achieved this amount of order in such a vast garden is an inspiration to us inept amateurs. The information leaflet describes this challenge in detail; make sure you pick up a copy before setting out to explore. In the spring the Shrubbery is a must, a blaze of warm colours from the mature rhododendrons and azaleas. Rewarding at any time of year is the Bog Garden where narrow paths wind around huge stands of giant rhubarb, *Gunnera manicata*, and more delicate ferns and other water-loving plants. Some way from the house is the lovely

---

◄ **1** Accessible only to walkers, Speke's Mill Mouth waterfall plunges dramatically into the sea in a series of falls. **2** St Nectan's church provides a landmark for sailors. **3** This tranquil woodland is part of Docton Mill gardens.

Walled Garden and productive Kitchen Garden, which helps to feed the present-day family.

Special events such as open-air theatre productions are held regularly in the Abbey grounds.

Beyond the carpark is a path signed 'to the beach'. It joins the South West Coast Path at Blackpool Mill and, since it misses out the first up and down of the Hartland Point walk (page 32), makes a sensible alternative to starting the walk at Hartland Quay if you are visiting the Abbey. The walk is full of interest. On a high point, just before meeting the coast path, is the Stucley's restored gazebo with a super view over the sea to Lundy Island. Blackpool Mill Cottage, in the valley, has starred in several films and TV dramas, most recently *The Night Manager*.

4 HARTLAND QUAY

🏠 **Hartland Quay Hotel** (page 247)

Hartland Quay is the focal point of the region, with its hotel and restaurant, beach and dramatic scenery. I have been there in stormy weather and on warm sunny days and it's always visually rewarding – and with the promise of coffee, soup or a full meal for tired walkers. Indeed, it is so popular you may be asked to pay a £2 toll for access and parking during peak holiday times.

Opposite the Hartland Quay Hotel is a gift shop with a small shipwreck museum upstairs, a good reminder of the days when this was a busy port. In the late 18th century W G Maton commented that 'Hartland-quay consists of about a dozen decent cottages, and has a commodious little pier, at which commodities of various kinds, for the supply of this part of the country, are landed from Bideford and Barnstaple; and here the fishermen and coasters find good shelter against the south-westerly winds, by mooring under the eminences.' The quay was still in use 50 years later when Hartland Abbey's Sir George Stucley landed a load of Maltese stone from his yacht, destined for the fireplace in the billiard room.

"I have been there in stormy weather and on warm sunny days and it's always visually rewarding."

Warren Beach (no dogs), dramatically backed by high cliffs, is accessible via the concrete slipway.

✳ ✳ ✳

🚶 HARTLAND QUAY TO SPEKE'S MILL MOUTH & DOCTON MILL

❃ OS Explorer map 126 or Croydecycle *Hartland & Clovelly*; start: carpark, Hartland Quay EX39 6DU ♀ SS22572474; 4 miles; moderate

The terrain of this walk from Hartland Quay's carpark is very varied, with easy, level stretches and some steep, uneven climbs. The first half of the walk is along a wonderful part of the coastline, with craggy rock formations and many wildflowers, while the return route visits Docton Mill, which has lovely gardens and an opportunity for refreshments.

1 From the carpark, follow the Coast Path sign (to Speke's Mill) along a fairly wide path. There are views of spectacular rock formations – high cliffs and jagged peaks jutting out into the might of the Atlantic Ocean – unsurprisingly, many ships have been wrecked here. At low tide, the black finger-like reefs are visible far below you. At your feet you may spot yellow bird's-foot trefoil, pale blue sheeps-bit, pink thrift and, in the spring, early purple orchids.

The path continues south towards St Catherine's Tor, once the site of a Roman villa or chapel; it then runs behind the tor, where a lovely waterfall tumbles to the beach below. Cross the stream via the stepping stones; there are spectacular views up the coastline and beyond to Lundy Island. After a short while this easy path gently climbs before dropping steeply into Speke's Mill Mouth. Here, two streams cascade down a sheer rock face and through a series of smaller falls to the sea below. In *The Coasts of Devon and Lundy Island* (published in 1895), J L W Page describes this with his usual enthusiasm: 'This, perhaps the finest cascade on the coast, is at least 50ft high, and against the black glistening wall of rock, the spray shows white as snow.'

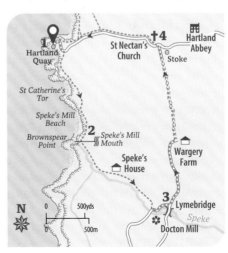

2 At Speke's Mill Mouth, turn left on to the footpath signed to Lymebridge. Stay on the main path, keeping the river on your right and ignoring the first fork left to Speke's House, to reach the road at Lymebridge after about a mile.

3 Turn left at the lane, which brings you to a staggered crossroads. To the right is Docton Mill, with its appealing gardens and excellent food (see below). Turn left up the steep hill and then continue straight, following the track past Wargery Farm. As the track curves, there are more views of Lundy Island and, ahead, the church tower in Stoke.

4 When you reach Stoke, turn left and then left again, passing some enticing tea rooms and the 14th-century St Nectan's Church, the 'Cathedral of North Devon'. Its tower is the second tallest tower in Devon and inside the church is an original wooden rood screen. Walk through the churchyard and over the steps in the far right corner to then pick up the public footpath running in front of the coastguard cottages. This path runs parallel to the road, eventually joining the Coast Path back to the carpark. Next to the carpark, the Hartland Quay Hotel (page 247) has a view to cherish, and is a nice place to end the walk. Drinks, snacks or full meals are available from the hotel's Wrecker's Retreat bar.

✳ ✳ ✳

5 DOCTON MILL

Lymebridge, Hartland EX39 6EA ✆ 01237 441369 ⌗ doctonmill.co.uk ◷ Apr–Oct 10.00–17.00 daily (check website for exact dates)

This delightful place combines an excellent tea room with a beguiling garden full of winding mossy paths through mature woodland, a bog garden and lawns bordered by the little River Speke, which later cascades over a slab of rock at Speke's Mill Mouth. When there is sufficient water in the river it runs the mill, which is still operating. Both the tea room and the gardens have won awards, and plenty of people come here for lunch or cream tea without visiting the garden – which is a pity. There is so much variety here in a relatively small area, including streams, lawns and an orchard, and always something to see whatever the time of year. Lana and John Borrett, the owners, have been here for 18 years and are responsible for creating the Magnolia Garden and many of the herbaceous borders, and for bringing the tea room up to its present high standard, with indoor and outdoor seating.

The carpark is small, so the owners ask you not to leave your car there while you go walking; it is for tea room and garden visitors only.

If using a sat nav to reach Docton Mill, be careful not to follow it blindly up the narrow lane to Milford, as I did, but keep an eye on the signs, which direct you to the entrance on your right just after the bridge. On the other side of this road is an extension of the gardens, a narrow path that leads to the weir, providing a wonderful display of bluebells and wild garlic in the spring.

THE CLOVELLY AREA

At Clovelly is a little pier for vessels, and the harbour is noted for the herring-fishery. The land, as it juts out into the promontory of Hartland, is by no means remarkable for fertility, nor is it either novel, or varied enough to be pleasing to the eye.

W G Maton, travelling during 1794–96

6 CLOVELLY VILLAGE

🏠 **New Inn Hotel** Clovelly (page 247), 🏚 **Bridge Cottage** Peppercombe (page 247)
Tourist information: EX39 5TA ✆ 01237 431781 🖊 clovelly.co.uk ⊙ 10.30–17.00 daily.
The visitor centre at Clovelly deals with all enquiries, including accommodation in the village.

The village has certainly changed since Maton's visit, but it took another century for its charms to become widely known. The man credited with this is Charles Kingsley who, in 1885, described Clovelly in typically overblown fashion in his novel *Westward Ho!*. Visitors began arriving by boat and, as the herrings – which had provided the village with income for centuries – declined in number, so the tourists increased. After Kingsley came Christine Hamlyn, who ensured that this tiny fishing village remained in the time-warp that you see today. It has no cars, two hotels, and 2,000 visitors a day in summer.

Clovelly has been owned by one family since Zachary Hamlyn, a wealthy lawyer, bought the estate from the last of seven generations of the Cary family in 1738. Christine married Frederick Gosling in 1889, persuading him first to change his name, and secondly to earmark a portion of his large fortune for improving the estate. Many of the cottages were run down, so they and the entire village were restored and prettified according to Christine's taste. Her initials and the date of restoration can sometimes be spotted above a doorway. It was she who ensured that the village remained car-free, the only transport up and down its stepped, cobbled main street being donkeys and sleds. Tourist sentiment has put paid to the pannier-laden donkeys that used to carry supplies and mail; the animals now live in a sanctuary and pose for photos or give rides to children. But the sleds are still used, and you'll see them tied up outside the cottages. Souvenir shops are restricted and all cottages must be leased as the primary home of the tenant; prospective residents are interviewed to make sure they will be an asset to the village. Thus, although Clovelly is extraordinarily picturesque, it is a lived-in, working village, but with about 70% of its inhabitants commuting to the real world. In the 1920s

VISIT DEVON

THE CLOVELLY ESTATE COMPANY

THE CLOVELLY ESTATE COMPANY

OLIVER STONE

the author S P B Mais wrote: 'Clovelly has been overphotographed. It cannot be overpraised. It bears no resemblance to any other place in the world. With its one street full of tourists, you might as well not try to see it, because it is no longer there to see. Its whole virtue goes when full.' That sentiment still holds partly true so plan to spend as much Slow time in the area as possible; walk into Clovelly in the evening if you can, or stay the night (page 247) so that you can see the village when it is there to see. And, away from the crowds, you cannot help but be enchanted by the little whitewashed cottages with grey slate roofs and flower-crammed gardens, stacked almost on top of each other. The cobbled road is called Up-a-Long and Down-a-Long, and is so steep, and so slippery after rain, that for centuries visitors – and locals – have grumbled about it. A local remarked to the author J L W Page: 'The folks do only dare get tight at one inn – the one at t'bottom o' the hill. Them as lives three doors away must keep always sober.'

"You cannot help but be enchanted by the little whitewashed cottages and flower-crammed gardens."

If you arrive the conventional way, by car, you will be processed through the visitor centre, paying an entrance fee before watching a film about the village's history. Then you're funnelled down the narrow cobbled street to peer into the windows of private houses, choose a few souvenirs, and buy a beer and Cornish pasty from the Red Lion pub, before returning to your car. If the steep climb back up is too daunting a Land Rover service will help you out. But stay longer and get your money's worth. There is plenty to see: a Kingsley Museum, a Fisherman's Cottage showing life as it was in the 1930s, and craft workshops. And, if you still resent paying the entrance fee, bear in mind that it is this income that keeps the village as it is, free from fast-food outlets and amusement arcades.

Each year, in mid November, the Clovelly Herring Festival is held; it focuses on everything herring, including traditional sea shanties and plenty of local beer and cider. And in September there's the annual Lobster & Crab Feast.

Fishing trips and **sightseeing boat trips** operate from the quay. Check with the visitor centre for operators.

◀ 1 Clovelly harbour. 2 Clovelly Herring Festival: a traditional smokehouse turns the fish into kippers. 3 Clovelly Court Gardens. 4 In times past donkeys were Clovelly's only transport option.

WALKS TO OR FROM CLOVELLY

If you arrive in Clovelly on **foot** you will avoid the feeling of entering a theme park and see it for what it is: an extraordinarily picturesque working village. There's a circular walk from the carpark at Brownsham (see below) or a bus-assisted walk from Bucks Mills (see opposite); each is around five miles. The **319 bus** running along the A39 from Barnstaple makes some useful sorties away from the road, including to Clovelly Visitor Centre and Hartland, but a linear walk between these two points doesn't really work since Hartland is 2½ miles inland from the South West Coast Path, making it a tough 12 or so miles.

✳ ✳ ✳

🅰 A CIRCULAR WALK TO CLOVELLY
FROM BROWNSHAM

❄ OS Explorer map 126 or (better) the Croydecycle *Hartland & Clovelly*; start: NT carpark at Brownsham EX39 6AN ♀ SS2852325973; 5½ miles; easy

Leave your car in the National Trust carpark at **Brownsham** and take the path through Beckland Woods, following the signs to Mouth Mill; it has some ruined buildings from the old lime kiln in which you can shelter if it's raining, and a pebble beach with the sea-sculpted Blackchurch Rock in view. The rock formations are splendid, like multi-tiered sandwiches laid on their sides. You are now less than an hour from Clovelly, walking through Brownsham Wood, which is owned by the National Trust. About a third of the way along you'll pass the beautifully carved 'Angel Wings' seat, put there by Sir James Hamlyn Williams in 1826. It is one of several shelters he constructed around the estate. This location was particularly special to him as, from it, he could look across the bay to where his daughter, Lady Chichester, lived.

Soon you'll get glimpses of Clovelly tucked into the cliffs and have a choice of routes into the village: either the footpath that leads you to the centre of the village or the road, or a steep walk downhill, to emerge near the Red Lion hotel by the quay. The Red Lion has two bars, both serving local food and drinks.

Returning takes about an hour, and is straightforward except for one confusing bit. Walk out along the road to the main gate of the estate, and pass through the side gate, past the church, then follow the bridleway. Once you see the cottage marked Snacksland on the Croydecycle map (or Snaxland on the OS map), leave the track and bear right across the field. The bridleway is signposted where it enters Brownsham Wood; after that simply follow it to the carpark.

* * *

🚶 BUS-ASSISTED WALK FROM BUCKS MILLS TO CLOVELLY

❋ OS Explorer map 126 or Croydecycle *Appledore & Westward Ho!* plus *Hartland & Clovelly*; start: Bucks Mills carpark ♥ SS358232; EX39 5DY; approx 4½ miles; moderate

If you have a car it makes sense to leave it at Bucks Mills and take the bus back from Clovelly carpark. However, a lovely alternative in the summer is to do this walk in the early evening, have dinner in Clovelly, either at the New Inn or the Red Lion, and see the village when the visitor masses have gone home. However, the last bus back to Bucks Cross (for the lane down to Bucks Mills and your car) is currently at 18.26, so unless you opt for a very early dinner, you should leave your car at Clovelly and take the bus to Bucks Cross to start your walk. Note that the bus does not currently run on Sundays.

The coast path is clearly signposted throughout this walk so you won't go wrong. Bucks Mills is a scatter of white houses above a very steep hill to the beach and a ruined lime kiln. If the weather is fine and you have the energy, it's well worth paying a visit to this lovely pebble-and-sand beach with its eroded rocks and a little waterfall. In the 18th century limestone and coal were transported here by boat from south Wales . The coal was used to heat the limestone in the kiln to create quicklime; this was used for limewash, mortar and fertiliser. On the way down you'll pass a tiny cliff-top studio, the Cabin, used from 1920 until 1971 by two artists, Mary Stella Edwards and Judith Ackland. It is now owned by the National Trust, who have kept it just as it was in the 1970s; the interior looks as if the ladies have just gone out for a walk. It is sometimes open to the public (☏ 01237 441976). Mary and Judith's paintings are now displayed in Bideford's Burton Art Gallery (page 50).

Returning to the signposted SWCP, you can follow it without difficulty to Clovelly. Initially it has some steep and often muddy ascents and descents before levelling off and passing between some magnificent beech trees in Barton Wood, with carpets of bluebells in the spring. It comes as something of a relief to meet the former carriageway of Hobby Drive. This was constructed – as a hobby – by James Hamlyn during the Napoleonic Wars, perhaps using the labour of French prisoners of war. During those times of high unemployment, land owners thought up schemes to provide work for their labourers, and carriageways were popular projects.

It's now an easy three-mile stroll into Clovelly, with arresting views of the village and its harbour, and handy seats to rest on. You emerge at the top of the village, not far from the New Inn, where you deserve at least a drink and perhaps a meal.

7 CLOVELLY COURT GARDENS & CHURCH

Clovelly EX39 5SY ✆ 01237 431781 ⌗ clovelly.co.uk/village/clovelly-court-gardens
⊘ year round, 10.00–16.00; admission charge to village includes visit to the garden.

Clovelly Court is the original seat of the Cary family (their manor burned down in 1796) and now the Hamlyn descendants live here. The house is private but the **kitchen garden** is well worth a visit. It is mostly given over to growing food. And what food! The combination of a sheltered walled garden in a warm climate, and splendid glasshouses, allows the harvesting of peaches, apricots, grapes, oranges and lemons, peppers, tomatoes… and so on. There are plenty of flowers and shrubs to provide colour, but organically grown fruit and vegetables are the main thing here and there is generally a good selection offered for sale.

All Saints' Church is old, as can be guessed by the Norman arch above its door. The tower is also Norman. The graveyard is full of Cary family tombstones, and there are several memorials to them inside. Charles Kingsley is also commemorated – his father was a popular rector here.

SOUTH OF THE ATLANTIC HIGHWAY

Between the A39 and the A388 is a maze of narrow lanes passing through farmland. You can feel delightfully cut off pottering through this very rural region towards Cornwall. The main attractions are the serene and lovely **Upper and Lower Tamar Lakes**, which provides a surfaced walk of three miles round the lake (half in Devon, half in Cornwall) and plenty of opportunity for watery activities.

8 WOOLFARDISWORTHY & BRADWORTHY

More of a curiosity because of its name – surely one of the longest unhyphenated village names in England – than because it has anything of spectacular interest, but **Woolfardisworthy** is a pleasant, large village with a handy store, an excellent fish and chip shop, and an interesting church. There is a lovely, recently refurbished pub, The Farmer's Arms, and a new hotel converted from the Manor House will soon be open. All this is thanks to multi-millionaire American benefactor Michael Birch, who has adopted the village in which many of his forebears are buried. It also has the advantage of being on the 319 bus route, making a variety of visits and walks possible without a car.

For convenience, and fitting on signposts, the name is often shortened to (and pronounced) Woolsery.

The church has a Norman doorway, with carved heads that make a convenient shelf for the swallows that nest there, and a floor slab in the porch dated 1684. The interior is airy and spacious, with some carved bench ends and an effigy of Richard Cole (1614), in full armour, propped uncomfortably on one elbow and showing traces of polychrome; it would once have been brightly coloured.

Bradworthy, 14 miles south of Woolsfardisworthy, is the largest village in the region, with several shops, including a huge hardware store, and wears its history with pride: a display board tells us that it was an early Saxon development and has the largest village square in the West Country.

9 TAMAR LAKES

Snug against the Cornish border are these two tranquil lakes, ideal for gentle walks to observe nature. Fortunately, both are pushchair and wheelchair friendly.

The two lakes comprising Tamar Lakes (EX23 9SB) straddle the Devon–Cornwall border and are managed by the South West Lakes Trust (⊘ swlakestrust.org.uk). The reservoir was created in the early 19th century to provide water to Bude. Various water-based activities are available on Upper Tamar Lake, such as paddleboarding, kayaking, canoeing, sailing, windsurfing and rowing. You can bring your own equipment or hire from the trust; wet suits and buoyancy aids are included as part of the hire packages.

This lake is also a great coarse fishery, with learner sessions available (⊙ Wed–Sun) – all equipment is provided and they guarantee that you will catch a fish. There is good level walking around the **Upper Lake** (three miles) or down to the **Lower Lake** (two miles return). On both lakeside walks there are benches and bird hides – more than 200 different species have been seen on the lakes. The Lower Lake is predominantly managed as a nature reserve and is an excellent place to see wildfowl in winter, including the rather striking goosander.

After all this activity, you may like to visit the **café** next to the carpark, where Sophie and Luisa serve good coffee, homemade cakes and Uncle Tom's ice cream (from his farm just a few miles away). There is a campsite on the shore.

BIDEFORD & AREA

The Bridge at Bedeforde is a very notable Worke... A poore Preste began thys Bridge; and, as it is saide, he was animated so to do by a Vision. Then al the Cuntery about sette their Handes onto the performing of it, and sins Landes hath bene gyven to the maintenaunce of it. Ther standith a fair Chapelle of our Lady at the very ende of it, and there is a Fraternite in the Town for perservation of this Bridge; and one waitith continually to kepe the Bridge clene from al Ordure.
John Leland, travelling during 1534–43

Bideford's Long Bridge over the River Torridge is still its most notable 'worke' although an even longer modern one carries most of the traffic from Barnstaple. The old bridge has linked the town with its neighbour across the Torridge, East-the-Water, since about 1280. Two hundred years later the wooden structure was reinforced with stone; the original wooden arches varied in width, and this irregularity has been preserved with each rebuilding. Leland's 'fraternite in the Town', the Bideford Bridge Trust, continued to maintain the bridge until 1968 when the western arch collapsed; the Department of Transport then decided that enough was enough and took over responsibility.

"The old bridge has linked the town with East-the-Water, since about 1280."

The Grenville family owned Bideford from Norman times until 1744, but until the late 16th century it was mainly a centre for shipbuilding, and largely overshadowed by Barnstaple. After Sir Richard Grenville's 1585 voyage to establish colonies in Virginia and Carolina, trans-Atlantic trade took off, along with Bideford's fortunes. The quay was built in 1663 and quantities of tobacco and Newfoundland cod were landed there. The town's surge of prosperity began towards the end of the 17th century when it was the main port for the transport of goods to and from the American colonies. Tourists are now transported to Lundy Island from here – when the tides are right.

Downriver is the still-charming town of Appledore, and, turning west, the uniquely named resort of Westward Ho! and its older neighbour Northam (page 54).

---

1 View across the Torridge Estuary towards Bideford's medieval Long Bridge. **2** Appledore, once the centre for Devon's shipbuilding industry. **3** Westward Ho! Beach. **4** Sheep racing at The Big Sheep. ▶

SARAH2/S

NORTH DEVON PHOTOGRAPHY/S

NORTH DEVON PHOTOGRAPHY/S

THE BIG SHEEP

10 BIDEFORD

⌂ **Hoops Inn** Horns Cross (page 247)

Tourist information: Burton Art Gallery, Kingsley Rd, EX39 2QQ ✆ 01237 477676

⌂ visitdevon.co.uk/northdevon. Unmanned.

Generally accepted as being the most attractive town in northwest Devon, Bideford has its Long Bridge, a rich maritime history, good shops and restaurants, and the excellent Burton Art Gallery and Museum. This is beyond the statue of Charles Kingsley at the north end of the quay, set in Victoria Park. Also in this peaceful, flowery place are eight guns captured from the Spanish by Grenville or his contemporaries. The entrance to the **Burton Art Gallery and Museum** is through the popular Café du Parc. Here you'll find quality ceramics and other arts and crafts. The shop has a particularly good selection of cards. One interesting exhibit in the very good **museum**, in the same building, is a model of the Long Bridge from 1280 to 1925, showing its gradual evolution. Unusual and intriguing is the display of visiting-card cases used by upper-class Victorians and ships made by Napoleonic prisoners of war (there was a small camp in Bideford). A separate room houses the Burton Ceramic Collection – locally made slipware using red clay and decorated with nautical scenes. The oldest is dated 1691.

Of the narrow streets rising steeply from the quay, the most interesting architecturally is Bridgeland Street; you can pick up leaflets from the TIC that guide you along the Bideford Heritage Trail. The best shops and restaurants are along the pedestrianised Mill Street, which runs parallel to the Quay. Here you'll find an appealing second-hand bookshop, **The Book Relief**, which rescues damaged books and funds various literary projects. Annie, who was working in the shop when I visited, told me that she loved reading so much that as a teenager she made a bed out of books. For new books, go to **Walter Henry's Bookshop** on the High Street. Cafés and restaurants in this area are listed on page 51. Above Bridge Street, which leads up from the old bridge, is the elegant 1884 building that houses the pannier market from Tuesdays to Saturdays.

St Mary's Church (⊙ 10.00–noon daily), nearby, is crammed with maritime memorials. The Norman font is one of the few old things in the church, and it is here that the first Native American to be brought to England was baptised in 1588. His name was Raleigh, in deference to Grenville's contemporary, and he was from the Algonquin tribe. He only survived a year, dying, presumably, of an infection against which he would have had no immunity.

¶¶ FOOD & DRINK

Café du Parc Victoria Park ✆ 01237 429317 ⊘ 10.00–16.00 Mon–Fri, 11.00–16.00 Sun. French café specialising in crêpes. Occasional seafood dinners.

Number Eight 8A Allhalland St, EX39 2JD ✆ 01237 237589 ⬦ numbereightrestaurant.com ⊘ 18.30–late Thu–Sun. Run solely by Joshua and Chloe, this small fine-dining restaurant serves food from locally sourced produce. The seven course tasting menu changes weekly.

Secret Garden Café 45A Mill St ✆ 07763 239378 ⊘ 08.00–17.00 Mon–Sat. It has indeed got a secret garden at the back, with enticing alcoves, and is dog friendly. The food is very good, too.

11 APPLEDORE

Reminiscent of Clovelly, with its car-free streets sloping steeply down to the long, curved quay, this still feels like a working maritime village – as indeed it is. Once the centre of North Devon's ship-building industry, with a large dry dock, it was building frigates and other ships until declared uneconomic and closed in March 2019, despite an Appledore shipbuilders' protest outside the Houses of Parliament.

This region was once thought to be the site of a fierce battle between the local Saxon population and Hubba the Dane in the first millennium (see box, page 55). A plaque marking the spot where the battle supposedly took place can be seen at the bend in the road still known as Bloody Corner, between Appledore and Northam. In fact, this is much more likely to be the site of a battle between the native Saxons and the Norman invaders in 1069. But never mind, the defeat of Hubba the Dane is a good story and one that Appledore clings on to. On Western Green stands a

POLACCA

Unique to North Devon were the little boats that plied the Bristol Channel in the 18th and 19th centuries bringing coal and limestone for the many lime kilns that are a feature of this part of the county, where 'burnt lime' or quicklime was needed to improve the fertility of the acid soil. Polacca were small vessels that could be sailed backwards to navigate the tricky Bideford Bar. The name was also spelled poleacre, referring to the single pole mast, which allowed the sail to be hoisted or lowered quickly in an emergency.

hunk of Lundy granite, the **Hubbastone**, erected in 2009 and carved with Nordic designs to commemorate this battle. The cherry on this slice of historical cake is that the local stonemason who worked on the modern memorial was named – appropriately – Gabriel Hummerstone.

The **North Devon Maritime Museum** (Odun Rd ✆ 01237 422064 ⌂ northdevonmaritimemuseum.co.uk ⊙ summer 10.30–17.00 daily, check website for off-season openings) is an exceptionally rewarding museum that is all about Appledore's relationship with the sea, but the exhibits are so varied that it is never dull. Even if you're not normally a museum person, do visit this one, especially if you have children in tow. There are pirates and smugglers, interactive exhibits for kids, and plenty to engage adults such as the adventures of the shipwrights who took the little ship *The Peter and Sarah* to Prince Edward Island in 1818 to start a lucrative timber – and migrant – trade between Canada and North Devon. In fact, it's surprising to learn how much trade there was between North Devon and North America, with fleets of boats going all the way to Newfoundland for cod. One room is given over to the town's history, including the exploits of Hubba the Dane, and other rooms contain intricate models of historically important ships, as well as the rather surprising fact that a collar and cuff factory in the town once employed a hundred women. The museum also sells the *Appledore Heritage Trail* booklet which describes and illustrates buildings and places of interest in the village.

ROPE-MAKING

In Appledore's maritime museum is a working model of how rope was made when every seaside village had its Ropewalk. A straight stretch of at least 300yds was needed to make the rope that was an essential part of the shipping industry. The process was similar to the way a sheep's fleece is turned into yarn, but on a much larger scale.

The hemp, usually grown locally, was dried and then 'heckled' or 'hatchelled' with iron spikes to separate the fibres, called 'streaks'. To twist the fibres, the spinner walked backwards, feeding streaks from the bundle round his waist into the 'yarn', while another worker turned the handle of a simple device which twisted the yarn into 'strands', their length depending on the length of the Ropewalk – anything up to 800yds. Spinners worked 12-hour shifts and in the course of a working day could walk 18 miles – backwards.

The name Ropewalk is retained in many British towns and cities, as is Ropery. They are both throwbacks to the traditional skill of rope-making.

Good shops abound, including the **Appledore Crafts Company** (5 Bude St ✆ 01237 423547 ◌ appledorecraftscompany.co.uk ◔ summer 11.00–17.00 daily, check website for off-season openings), a co-operative of craftspeople selling a range of work, from ceramics and textiles to jewellery and furniture. Hidden away in the Old Glove Factory on New Quay Street is the workshop and gallery of **Sandy Brown**, a celebrated ceramics artist; her work has been exhibited in the Victoria and Albert Museum, in Chatsworth House and in museums around the world. Sandy opens her workshop every Friday (◌ sandybrownarts.co.uk ◔ 11.00–17.00), or at other times by arrangement. Here you can see her at work as well as admire what she describes as, 'a constantly evolving exhibition' with many pieces here available to buy. She has recently been working on 'Earth Goddess', a 12-metre high ceramic sculpture for St Austell's sculpture trail, but she also sells more modest pieces including cups, saucers and plates.

Six pubs provide plenty of choice for refreshment and a multi-award-winning café/delicatessen, **Johns** (✆ 01237 429065 ◌ johnsofinstow. co.uk), has a range of delicious take-away picnics, pastries and fresh produce for sale as well as being a café. It is also the village post office and has some tourist information leaflets. For a good meal, **The Royal George** (page 55) is your best bet.

The village turns literary in late September for the **Appledore Book Festival** (◌ appledorebookfestival.co.uk), a week-long event with big-name authors.

The **ferry service** to Instow (◌ appledoreinstowferry.com) across the river is run by volunteers, operating a few hours each side of the high tide. Look for the signs on the quay. Bicycles can be taken if there's room.

You can also walk along the Torridge to Northam, with the help of the Croydecycle *Bideford, Appledore & Westward Ho!* map. It's a pleasant walk, mainly along footpaths, with a good bus service to take you back to Appledore.

12 WESTWARD HO! & NORTHAM

Writing at the end of the 19th century, J L W Page quoted a contemporary journalist as saying that **Westward Ho!** was 'a tedious place, that no one would visit had they anywhere better to go to.' Over a hundred years later, some visitors might still agree with him, but give it a chance. Beyond the usual seaside amusements the town has a surprising lot to offer: a huge beach, the leafy heights of Kipling Tors, named after the town's more erudite literary connection who was at school here, and some pleasant walks.

This is the only town to be named after a book rather than the other way round, and also the only one to have an exclamation mark. It is entirely the creation of a 19th-century development company which saw the benefits of cashing in on Kingsley mania; his book was actually set in Bideford.

The village of **Northam** is altogether more tranquil than its brash neighbour, Westward Ho!, tightly contained with some good shops and restaurants, and an interesting monument. On Bone Hill, opposite the church tower, is a tall **flag pole**/ship's mast that is a memorial to the sailors who died in Queen Elizabeth I's time, helping Britannia rule the waves. It was created in 1897 to commemorate Queen Victoria's Diamond Jubilee and is formed of 60 stones from Bideford Bay, each representing a sailor as well as the 60 years of Victoria's reign. It includes Drake, Raleigh and Grenville, and is surprisingly moving. And there's a splendid view over the Bristol Channel.

¶¶ FOOD & DRINK

Marshford Organic Foods Churchill Way, Northam EX39 1NS ✆ 01237 477160 ⊘ marshford.co.uk ◷ 11.00–17.00 Tue, Wed, Fri & Sat, 13.00–17.00 Thu. Situated just off the A386, this farm shop is jam-packed with organically grown vegetables, meat, baked treats and a host of other goodies. You can order online for deliveries in the area, so it's ideal if you are self-catering.

Memories 8 Fore St, Northam ✆ 01237 473419 ⊘ memoriesrestaurant.co.uk ◷ 19.00–23.00 Thu, Fri & Sat. This outstanding restaurant is unique in its approach to dining. Run by a husband and wife team, Brett and Naomi, it is only open three evenings a week ('We like to do other things as well' Naomi told me), can only seat 12 people and only has one sitting. The dishes, cooked by Brett, are marvellous, there's a good wine list and Naomi treats all her customers like special guests. On Thursdays there's a set menu, the other two days it's à la carte. Locals come here again and again, and for that special treat it's hard to beat it anywhere in North Devon.

Pig on the Hill Pusehill, Westward Ho! EX39 5AH ✆ 01237 459222. This is *not* part of the well-known, upmarket Pig chain, it's a regular family- and dog-friendly pub in a lovely location high above Westward Ho!.

There's a cheerful bar and the meals are substantial and mostly meat based. Tables inside and out. A good choice for Sunday lunch.

The Royal George Irsha St, Appledore EX39 1RY ✆ 01237 424138 ⌾ trgpub.co.uk
⊙ 11.00–23.00, food noon–14.30 & 18.00–21.00 daily. Renovated to a high standard in
2018, and making the most of their wonderful views over the water, this is now the best
restaurant in Appledore with a skilfully cooked, upmarket menu. Rooms available too.

13 NORTHAM BURROWS

EX39 1XS ⌾ torridge.gov.uk/northamburrows ⊙ walkers year-round; cars Mar–Oct
07.00–22.00 daily; Nov–Feb 07.00–18.00 daily

Walk north from Westward Ho! on the path and boardwalk that heads
along the coast and you quickly enter Northam Burrows, a world away
from the town's seaside amusements. More than two miles of sand dunes

HUBBA THE DANE

Janice Booth

Hubba the Dane and Bloody Corner (between Northam and Appledore) are so tangled up in legend and conflicting historical reports that 'facts' about them need to be treated with a degree of caution. In the 17th century Tristram Risdon (1580–1640, author of *A Chorographical Description or Survey of the County of Devon*) and Thomas Westcote concluded that the 9th-century battle of Cynuit had taken place at Henniborough near Northam and that Hubba (who died in it) was buried at Wibblestone – which was renamed Hubbastone in his honour. The story was embraced locally and expanded over the years, as happens with such things. A plaque erected at Bloody Corner by one Thomas Chappell in 1890 instructs: 'Stop stranger stop/Near this spot lies buried/King Hubba the Dane/Who was slayed in a bloody retreat/By King Alfred the Great'.

However, current research suggests that the battle in which Hubba died took place elsewhere (probably near Beaford) and that he wasn't slain by Alfred. He was indeed a 9th-century Viking leader, possibly named Ubba Ragnarsson; tradition claims that in AD878 he landed his ships at Boathyde with conquest and pillaging in mind, and marched on Kenwith, where he was defeated and killed. A version of this story appears in Thomas Cox's *Devonshire* (1738):

In this place [Appledore] it was that Hubba the Dane, having wasted South Wales with fire and sword, landed in the days of King Alfred with 33 sail of ships, and laid siege to the castle of Kenwith, now called Hennaborough. The Devonshire men bravely opposed their ravagers, and having slain Hubba, their general who lies buried at Hublestone, and many of his followers, obliged them to fly to their ships and make their escape.

and pebble ridge protect a large area of low-lying grasslands, salt marsh and mudflats from the Atlantic Ocean, and the whole area is now part of the North Devon UNESCO Biosphere Reserve and a Site of Special Scientific Interest. The great attraction of the Burrows is that so many different habitats co-exist in an area that can easily be walked around.

The vast sandy beach is more than two miles long and, at low tide, over 100yds wide. That may mean it's a long walk if you want to swim

SOME EXCEPTIONAL CHURCHES

Dotted around the area are some wonderful little churches with that hallmark of Devon, carved bench ends. So if you love these storehouses of history and folk art, it's worth making a diversion.

ALWINGTON

The little church of St Andrew (EX39 5DA) is famous for its complete depiction of the Bible, Old and New testaments, carved into the bench ends. Not all these are old – many were carved by a local man, Reuben Arnold, in the early 20th century, but some date from the 16th century and the carving, and subject, is exceptional. The name associated with Alwington from these times is Coffin. There is a wall memorial to Richard and Elizabeth Coffin and their 15 children. The Coffins married into the Pine family and became – almost unbelievably – the Pine-Coffins.

The church is kept locked but the address and phone number of the nearby key-holder are on the porch noticeboard.

LITTLEHAM

The church of St Swithun or Swithin (EX39 5HR) sits on its own, nearly a mile from the village but well signposted. I was lucky to find the warden, Andrew Tregoning, mowing the graveyard. He gave me a guided tour: 'I'll show you the walrus.' Not an animal you expect to find carved into a church screen, but it was a pun on the name of the rector who, in 1892, took on the tremendous task of restoring the dilapidated church. His name was the Reverend George Morse, and morse (or something similar) is the Nordic name for walrus. The striking bench ends are in light-coloured oak so are the first thing you notice on entering the church. Some of the subjects of these carvings defy description. There are men whose faces are starting to morph into foliage, some with long tongues (I guess) disappearing into some sort of vessel. And is that an eagle wearing a horned headdress? One can only agree with Andrew when he says 'Of course a lot of the carvers were high on LSD' (it is known that mould – ergot alkaloids – growing on rye bread could produce hallucinations).

At the back of the church is a chest hollowed out from a solid oak trunk. Dominating the south side is the huge tomb of General Crealock, who lived and died in Victorian times. The tomb is topped by

(there is a lifeguard here in summer), but it is just perfect for sandcastle building and games. Dogs are banned from the southern half of the beach during the summer but they are allowed year-round further up. In the dunes at the rear of the beach live some quite rare plants like water germander, which looks like mint and smells like garlic.

The grassland in the centre of the country park is both a golf course and a common. In 1701 'Potwallopers' – local people who had boiled

a beautifully carved effigy of the general, who evidently did not die in poverty. Or modesty. His descendants spared no expense on the memorial; he is surrounded by 12 angels, with female figures representing the virtues of Truth, Hope, Faith, Justice, Fortitude and Wisdom. The latter has a man's face carved at the back of her head; make of this what you will.

There is an old (but restored) painting of St Swithun on the wall, which probably dates from the 14th century. He was an Anglo-Saxon bishop of Winchester (and later, patron saint of the cathedral) who went out of his way to help the poor. His humility decreed that he be buried outside the church so under the feet of passers-by and subject to the rain falling from the cathedral roof. The story goes that when his remains were dug up and reburied in a shrine within the cathedral, he showed his anger through a downpour that persisted for 40 days. Hence the belief that if it's raining on St Swithun's Day (15 July) it will continue for 40 days.

LANDCROSS
In the same parish as Littleham, the sweet little Holy Trinity Church (EX39 5JA), which

lost its tower to lightning over a hundred years ago, sits high above the River Torridge. There is plenty here to engage the visitor, with medieval tiles on the floor and some carved bench ends, including two contortionists. The pulpit is also made up of old carvings.

ABBOTSHAM
The church, St Helen's (EX39 5AP), is joined to the old school, which suggests it played an important part in education. It has a quaint, stubby little tower, a high, white wagon roof with painted bosses, and some wonderful bench ends, although – even with the lights on – a torch is useful to see the detail. These are a mixture of religious pictures, some of which were defaced during the parliamentary wars, along with workmen's tools, and 'village art', which is open to interpretation, although the chained ape is supposed to represent drunkenness. Here, also, is a contortionist similar to the ones in Landcross. A useful walk-around information board identifies each one.

Near the altar is a fine chair carved with scenes from the crucifixion and, on a secular note, there is often local honey for sale.

their own pot in the parish for six months – were given grazing rights to this land. Today, locals still have those rights and their sheep, ponies and horses can be seen wandering the grassland, presumably trying to avoid the flying golf balls.

A short walk along the coast, and around the point, brings you to **The Skern** (you could also use the northern entrance to the Burrows (EX39 1NL) to drive there). This area of mudflats and salt marsh is protected by the point from the Atlantic rollers and is a haven for birdlife including the rare avocet. In winter The Skern is home to hosts of golden plover; seeing them take off in their hundreds is an unforgettable experience. Hunting around the mudflats, you may also discover ragworms, lugworms and cockles.

There are three roads into the Burrows; a toll for cars is charged from April to October. This is also when the excellent **visitor centre** is open (☉ Easter–Oct 10.00–15.00 daily) which is a good place to start your visit, with knowledgeable staff and lots of information. Their blackboard will tell you the wildlife to look out for – when we visited there was a long list of birds and small animals including slow worms and green shore crabs. They can also explain their three walking trails – there are interpretation boards, too, or you can download the walks from their website. The centre also has a tank that is regularly restocked with sea creatures from the tidal pools – but it is perhaps more fun to see what you can find yourself along the shore.

14 ABBOTSHAM & THE BIG SHEEP

Driving between Northam and Clovelly on the A39 you will pass prominent signs to **The Big Sheep** (EX39 5AP ⌀ thebigsheep.co.uk). This large-scale family attraction began by being centred entirely on sheep; it still has some demonstrations of sheep management and sheep dog skills, and, entertainingly, sheep racing but you need to be with small children to enjoy the rides, which include Devon's biggest roller coaster, and other entertainments. Adults will find quieter pleasures in the award-winning **Thatched Inn pub** in **Abbotsham**, and the lovely St Helen's Church, described on page 57.

The award-winning Slow Travel series from Bradt Guides

Over 20 regional guides across Britain.
See the full list at bradtguides.com/slowtravel.

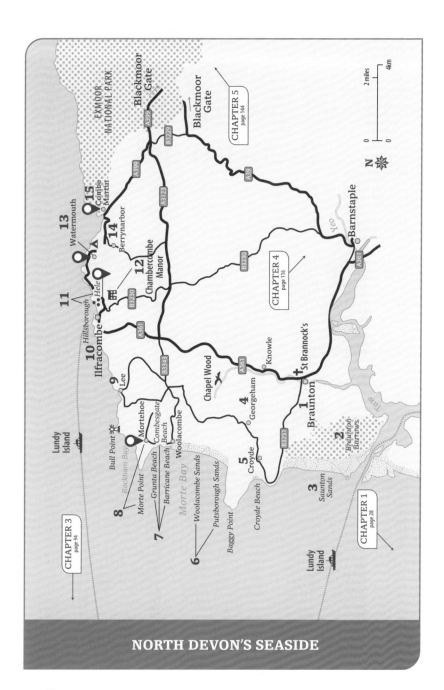

NORTH DEVON'S SEASIDE

2
NORTH DEVON'S SEASIDE

> The finest scenery in Devonshire is to be found in the north, between Lynton and Ilfracombe, where the offshoots of Exmoor abut upon the sea, or are based in woods and subalpine ravines.
> *A Handbook for Travellers in Devon and Cornwall*, 1872

North of the River Taw's broad estuary are Devon's most popular seaside resorts: the huge expanses of sand at Saunton and Woolacombe, with the smaller Croyde Bay tucked in between them, and the more intimate coves such as Barricane, Grunta and Lee, which take more effort to get to, so are relatively crowd-free even in the summer holidays. Here you'll find the best surfing beaches in north Devon and some of the most scenic stretches of the South West Coast Path, which hugs the shoreline for 35 miles from Combe Martin to Barnstaple.

The UNESCO Biosphere of Braunton Burrows lures nature lovers, with Braunton making an appealing base, and there's good birdwatching and marine wildlife viewing around the National Trust's Baggy Point and Morte Point.

Ilfracombe has its historic Tunnels Beach, Damien Hirst's *Verity*, great restaurants and the aquarium, while Combe Martin is a good centre for walking and watersports. In fact the latter is mostly in Exmoor National Park so should be in the next chapter, but it is near enough to Ilfracombe to fit better here.

 WET-WEATHER ACTIVITIES

Chambercombe Manor (page 82)
Combe Martin Museum (page 90)
Ilfracombe Museum (page 78)
Ilfracombe Aquarium (page 79)
Museum of British Surfing, Museum and Information Centre and
Countryside Centre, Braunton (page 64)

GETTING THERE & AROUND

Access from Exeter is via the A377 to Barnstaple, a reasonably fast road, or from Tiverton on the A361 North Devon Link Road. Thereafter progress will be slow in the holiday season when the smaller lanes in this pocket of North Devon get very crowded. Public transport is mainly limited to the 21A bus, which runs frequently from Barnstaple to Braunton, Saunton, Croyde and Georgeham, the 31 from Ilfracombe to Woolacombe and Mortehoe, and the 303, which runs from Woolacombe to Barnstaple via Braunton. Check an up-to-date bus timetable for changes in the schedule.

SELF-POWERED TRAVEL

Often a bike is the quickest way round the narrow lanes and their bottlenecks of cars, but cyclists need to be wary of fast-driving locals.

Most of the famous Tarka Trail is described in *Chapter 4* (page 118), but it continues north to Braunton. Further east the region is served by the Ilfracombe–Woolacombe cycle circuit, part of NCN27, which gives you a 15-mile circular route largely along roads but with a traffic-free section from outside Ilfracombe to Willingcott Cross along a disused railway, and the coast at Woolacombe Sands. Cycles can be hired in Braunton (page 67).

The area is terrific for walking, with the South West Coast Path and its offshoots providing the best routes.

BRAUNTON, THE BURROWS & SAUNTON SANDS

The rewarding town of Braunton, renowned as a surf centre, and the wide sands with a reliably rolling sea are the main attractions of this area, while the sand-dune system of the Braunton Burrows is a magnet for botanists and also played a major part in World War II (page 66).

Saunton (said to mean St Anne's Town) is justly proud of its two 18-hole championship golf courses, set in beautiful surroundings and listed as among the UK's best. Seventy-five years ago, a day's golfing

1 Braunton Burrows UNESCO Biosphere Reserve. 2 Saunton Sands – a great spot for less experienced surfers. ▶

there cost '5/- for gentlemen and 3/6d for ladies', but nowadays you'll need to pay a penny or two more. Back then the area was served by Saunton's 'aerodrome', which offered regular flights to and from Cardiff and Lundy Island.

1 BRAUNTON

🏠 **The Linhay** Butterhills (page 247)

Tourist information: Braunton Museum & Information Centre, Caen St carpark, EX33 1AA ✆ 01271 816688 ⌖ explorebraunton.org. An independently run, very helpful centre, with an excellent website.

This is one of North Devon's main surfing towns (actually, it's officially a village), as you would guess from the surf shops displaying boards and their trappings, and the nation's only surf museum. It is a compact, visitor-friendly place with all the main attractions clustered around the Caen Street carpark. Without having to open your umbrella you can find an exceptional small museum, the comprehensive Braunton Countryside Centre, and the Museum of British Surfing. Truly something for everyone.

When I visited the **Museum and Information Centre** they were having a derailment problem. The little model locomotive was soon back on its track and trundling around the perfect replica of the town in pre-Beeching days. That the museum and information centre is run by enthusiasts is obvious as soon as you step through the door, and the shifting exhibits show all aspects of rural and coastal life in times past, such as the Bulb Farm, which was one of the region's biggest employers. 'You might wonder why the big houses belonging to captains were built on West Hill, far away from the sea', a volunteer commented. 'It's said it was so the children could see their father's boat coming in and intercept dad and his money before he reached the Mariner's Arms.'

Across the carpark, the **Countryside Centre** (✆ 01271 817171 ⌖ brauntoncountrysidecentre.org ⌚ Apr–Oct, 10.00–16.00 Mon–Sat) gives detailed information on the Burrows, as well as the coast in general, and agriculture of the area. The museum has a microscope so that visitors can look at the details of their seashore finds. It hosts a talks programme and guided walks around the Burrows, and sells maps and guides.

The spacious **Museum of British Surfing** (⌖ museumofbritish surfing.org.uk ⌚ 10.00–15.30 daily) is next door to the centre. I was surprised to learn how old this sport is, although Hawaii, not Devon, is its natural home. Duke Kahanamoku of Hawaii took a primitive surfboard to Australia in 1920 and started the craze, which took off in the 1960s. Britain was not far behind in popularising this new sport, though the oldest surfboard dates back to the early 1900s. Agatha Christie used to go to Hawaii for the 'surf riding'.

Some way out of Braunton, on the road to Ilfracombe and set in a graveyard full of orderly rows of tombstones and equally orderly and splendid elm trees, is **St Brannock's Church**, topped by a spire. There is some speculation that the missionary, St Brannock, arrived from Ireland as part of an invading force. Nevertheless, he must have been accepted pretty quickly by the populace if only for his ability to perform miracles. He usefully persuaded two deer – harts – to accept the yoke and to 'draw timbers thence to build a church'. A cow, which was slaughtered and partially butchered, reassembled itself at his request and carried on grazing. His first church was built on a hill overlooking Braunton, but the Devil kept rolling the stones down to the bottom at night (in a reverse of the situation at Brentor on Dartmoor, where he moved the stones to the top of the hill; the Devil was particularly busy in Devon). Finally St Brannock had a dream that he should build the church where he came across a sow feeding a litter of piglets. The sow duly appeared and the church, built in the 13th century, is well worth visiting. The sow and her piglets are depicted on one of the roof bosses just above the font, but it is the carved bench ends that are special. The two stags, or harts, surely must be the ones that succumbed to the yoke, and on the third pew on the right from the altar is a hand grasping a severed head by the hair; presumably John the Baptist. Many of the bench ends are carved with the initials of the gentry who sat in those pews. Some are upside down; it is speculated that the carver, being illiterate, was unaware that it mattered.

Finally, if there's marmalade on sale (as there often is in Devon churches), don't miss this delicious homemade treat.

¶¶ FOOD & DRINK

Fine Foods of Braunton 25 Caen St ✆ 01271 267810 ⌖ finefoodsbraunton.co.uk ⏱ 09.00–17.00 Mon–Sat. A delicatessen and café selling local produce of all sorts: cheese, meat, preserves and baking, along with local gin and beers. They keep coming up with imaginative ideas such as little hampers as gifts for teachers at the end of term.

SQ Bar & Restaurant 3 Exeter Rd ✆ 01271 815900 ⌖ sqbarandrestaurant.com ⏱ 09.00–23.00 Sun–Thu, 09.00–midnight Fri & Sat. Run by the second and third generation of the Squire family who opened the fish and chip shop in 1969, this is a

COASTGUARDS, SMUGGLERS & WRECKERS

The clifftop cottages that formerly belonged to coastguards are now highly sought after for their views and their often quite isolated position. Few pause to wonder why they were built so far from the centre of the seaside villages that they were protecting. Equally, few speculate on the origin of the South West Coast Path. The answers lie in Devon and West Somerset's long history of smuggling and, more shamefully, wrecking. Originally the coastguards' duty was to prevent the smugglers and wreckers from going about their business, and these were local people – smuggling was an integral part of Devon's economy – so the coastguards were not welcome neighbours. Their cottages were in the best position for patrolling the cliffs, watching out for the activities of the miscreants and, coincidentally, beating out the path that, in 1978, became the final addition to the South West Coast Path.

Favourite haunts for smugglers were sheltered coves, preferably with caves, and with a lime kiln nearby so accessible by boat. What one might call benign smuggling was done to escape the high duty on luxury goods. Wreckers were another matter. By tying lanterns to the tails of donkeys, they imitated the bob of a ship's light at anchor and lured their victim to the rocks. As the sailors swam ashore they were killed; the law stated that if no-one was left alive after a wreck, the cargo could be claimed by local people.

bustling, reasonably priced restaurant and bar serving food throughout the day, along with a good range of beers and cocktails.

Squires Fish & Chips 1 Exeter Rd ✆ 01271 815533 ♺ squiresfishrestaurant.co.uk
⊙ 11.45–21.00 Mon–Sat, 11.45–19.45 Sun. The Squires family have been running their traditional fish and chip shop for more than 50 years and have a deserved reputation for being the best in the region. Take away or eat in.

Wild Thyme 5 Caen Field Shopping Centre, EX33 1EE ✆ 01271 815191 ♺ wildthymecafe. co.uk ⊙ 09.00–15.00 Mon–Sat. They call themselves a juice café – and quite rightly since there's a splendid choice of juices and smoothies on offer, as well as beer and wine. All-day breakfasts are a speciality, and the place has a lovely laid-back vibe.

2 BRAUNTON BURROWS

To a nature lover, the very word biosphere is alluring, conjuring up the image of rare species you wouldn't find elsewhere. And it's true of this UNESCO Biosphere Reserve (♺ northdevonbiosphere.org.uk), which recognises the uniqueness of this sand dune ecosystem. 'Sand' is misleading, since the dunes are clothed in vegetation, giving them a pleasing, green, blobby appearance. If you know your stuff, you could happily spend a few hours here, and if you don't know your stuff then go on one of the guided walks run by the Countryside Centre (page 64). The botanical secrets of the Burrows are revealed in *Wild Flowers of Braunton Burrows* by Mary Breeds, who worked at the Braunton Countryside Centre.

Braunton Burrows, along with nearby Saunton Sands, played its part in World War II, being given to the American army in 1943 to stand in for the Normandy beaches in rehearsals for D-Day (before the dress rehearsal of Exercise Tiger at Slapton in November of that year). Friends of the Assault Training Center ($\mathcal{O}$ assaulttrainingcenterfriends.co.uk) are active in preserving this history.

Perhaps the most rewarding way to see the area is by bike. The flat lanes are a godsend if coming from the hills of Exmoor, and cycling along the canal you'll see a good range of waterfowl. Braunton is also the start of the cycling section of the Tarka Trail, and bicycles can be hired in the town from **Otter Cycle Hire** (Station Rd, EX33, 2AQ $\mathcal{O}$ 01271 813339 $\odot$ Feb–Oct, 09.00–17.00 daily).

3 SAUNTON SANDS

This was one of the beaches used to rehearse the D-Day landings, its 3½ miles of sandy beach being similar to those of Normandy. Now it is one of the region's best surfing beaches, though with smaller waves than Croyde, so suitable for less experienced surfers. It's ideal for families, particularly those with dogs as they are permitted on most of the beach year-round. Those who don't like crowds have only to walk away from the carpark and facilities to find their own private place.

The splendid **Saunton Sands Hotel** ($\mathcal{O}$ sauntonsands.co.uk) has some of the best views in the area – go for a tea or cocktail.

GEORGEHAM & CROYDE

Most visitors drive straight through these two villages on their way to Croyde's popular beach resort. They're worth a stop, however, and between them have a particularly good range of pubs, restaurants and tea rooms.

4 GEORGEHAM

🏠 **Pickwell Manor** (page 247)

The village was just Ham in the *Domesday Book*, and gained its longer name through the church of St George, so the correct pronunciation is George-ham. Henry Williamson, author of *Tarka the Otter*, lived here and the little hut where he did his writing is now a listed building. He financed the building of the hut from the proceeds of *Tarka*. He is buried near the church tower, and it's worth pottering round the graveyard, which is as enjoyable to browse as a second-hand bookshop. Almost every stone from the 1830s to the 1890s has a four-line (or longer) commemorative poem, usually assuring the reader that the deceased is better off under God's care. For example, a sad little grave of an infant proclaims: 'Grieve not for me my parents dear/Nor be forever sad/The shorter time I lived here/The lesser sin I had'. It seems that no-one dared to die in Georgeham at that time without commissioning the local poet to write a verse. One stone has just a poem without any name or inscription – possibly a marketing ploy?

To balance the many children's graves, there's one to a woman who died aged 100.

¶¶ FOOD & DRINK

The Kings Arms Chapel St ✆ 01271 890240 ☞ kingsarmsgeorgeham.co.uk. This pub has a wide following for its excellent food. The menu focuses on meat (sourced locally) but there are plenty of other choices and daily specials. Excellent Sunday lunches.

The Rock Inn Rock Hill ✆ 01271 890322 ☞ therockinn.biz. A beautiful, flowery pub with a large, bright conservatory and some outdoor seating, serving a varied and imaginative menu, with pork from their own farm. No carpark and street parking can be difficult – use the village carpark and walk to the pub.

5 CROYDE

Croyde Bay is perfect; a real bay, this, not like Woolacombe or Saunton Sands, a mere ridge of sand. A real bay, to delight the eye, must curve out to a headland at either end ... and between the headlands the great green rollers should run across hundreds of yards of hard, yellow sand before they break.

L du Garde Peach, *Unknown Devon*, 1927

The village has 26 listed buildings, mostly old farmhouses and associated barns, and some good tea rooms and pubs. These include the **Sandleigh Tea Rooms** on Moor Lane (✆ 01271 890930), owned by the National Trust and handy for Baggy Point. The tea rooms have a lovely little walled garden. Look out also for the **Old Cream Shop and Tea Garden** on Hobbs Hill, which is famous for its ice cream but also has a good variety of pasties and **May Cottage Tea Rooms** on St Mary's Road (⊙ Wed–Sun in the summer), a delightful cottage with a garden full of flowers and a classic Devon cream tea served on elegant china. For serious eating and drinking there's the famous **Thatch** pub. Croyde is also the home of Mike Harrison, creator of the Croydecycle maps (see box, page 20); the full range of these maps is available in the well-stocked shop that is also the post office.

Croyde **beach**, still lovely, is renowned for surfing – the waves here are the biggest in the area. Croyde is the start of the World Surfing Reserve, which also includes Saunton, Woolacombe and Lynmouth. When I visited, on a blustery day, the sea was speckled with swimmers and surfers having a great time in the breakers. Parking is expensive here, but the Down End carpark (at the south end of the beach) has a popular snack shack called the **Drop In Café**, which sells a good range of snacks and drinks.

For cheaper parking, continue north, towards the headland Baggy Point, for the National Trust carpark that is free to members and cheaper than the beach ones for non-members. From here you have a choice: walk round Baggy Point to Putsborough Sands with a selection

GOLDCOAST OCEANFEST SURF & MUSIC FESTIVAL

Jennette Baxter

With new festivals popping up – and disappearing – all the time, sustaining a successful long-running music event takes some doing. Organisers and brothers Shaun and Warren Latham seem to have hit on a winning combination, placing equal emphasis on top-class music and outdoor sports at GoldCoast Oceanfest (⚓ goldcoastoceanfest.co.uk), a hugely popular family-friendly event in a beautiful beachside location in Croyde Bay. Starting as a grass-roots 'fun day' and now a fully-fledged, three-day festival over 20 years later, this celebration of outdoor life is held every year on the closest weekend to midsummer. Hosting big name performers as well as those 'on the up' (Ed Sheeran and Ben Howard among others played here before making it big), there is something for everyone. Keen surfers, Shaun and Warren also organise a festival football tournament and nationally recognised surfing, volleyball and surf life-saving competitions that make great spectator viewing. With a capacity of 10,000, this is a welcoming festival; big enough to create a great party atmosphere yet small enough not to be overwhelming for first-timer festival goers.

of footpaths to take you back to your car or, if it's low tide, investigate the tide pools at this end of the beach. There's a frequent bus service (21A) to Croyde Bay from Barnstaple and Braunton.

"There should have been a direct road between Georgeham and Woolacombe instead of the traffic-clogged inland route."

There should also have been a direct road between Georgeham and Woolacombe instead of the long, traffic-clogged inland route that is currently the way. Mike Harrison tells how Rosalie Chichester, of Arlington Court, left land and money to build this road. Mortehoe Parish responded with enthusiasm, and Marine Drive was constructed. Alas it goes nowhere (but provides ample parking for Woolacombe Sands). Georgeham, so Mike says, lacked the money – or enthusiasm – to finish the job.

FOOD & DRINK

The Blue Groove 2 Hobbs Hill ✆ 01271 890111 🖰 blue-groove.co.uk ◷ 09.00–21.00 daily. A lively place in Croyde village, serving local food (fish, Exmoor game, as well as international dishes). Popular with locals as well as visitors for its themed evenings (curry, quiz nights). Outside seating or a sunny conservatory for cooler days.

New Coast Kitchen 1 St Mary's Rd ✆ 01271 316026 🖰 newcoastkitchen.co.uk ◷ noon–14.00 & 18.00–23.00 Wed–Sun. Martin Baylis used to serve his customers in a converted double decker bus – his new restaurant is less eye-catching but the food is certainly not. The short menu features unusual combinations and a choice of small plates if you want to share a selection of dishes. Booking recommended for dinner.

The Thatch 14 Hobbs Hill ✆ 01271 890349 🖰 thethatchcroyde.co.uk. A beautiful old thatched pub, with plenty of seating and unusual food (the chef is Sri Lankan). Occasional live music.

CHAPEL WOOD RSPB RESERVE

Tucked away only a couple of miles east of Woolacombe Sands (page 71) is this haven of peace and birdsong. The reserve (♀ SS4817541060) is small but rewarding, with streams and the remains of a 13th-century chapel. The RSPB has fixed nest boxes on several of the trees, so in the spring and early summer you can sit quietly and watch the feathery comings and goings, take a stroll along the various paths and admire the display of bluebells. The bird list includes nuthatches, tawny owls and woodpeckers.

BEACHES & HEADLANDS: MORTE BAY

Between the two horns of Baggy Point and Morte Point is Morte Bay and the 2½-mile stretch of sandy beach that makes up Putsborough Sands and Woolacombe Sands (the two morph into each other). Woolacombe Sands has been voted one of Britain's best beaches, so it's not surprising that it is so popular with families. There's room for everyone along this expanse of golden sand and white surf, and in the several holiday parks for camping and caravans. But tucked into recesses on the southern face of Morte Point are smaller, less crowded beaches, as well as a gorgeous headland walk.

6 PUTSBOROUGH & WOOLACOMBE SANDS

Putsborough is the southern, more isolated, end of the beach, sheltered from west winds by Baggy Point, with rock pools and fewer amenities than Woolacombe Sands (and there is no lifeguard) so perhaps more appealing to adult Slow visitors. There's a dog-free area but otherwise it's dog-friendly, and the café serves good food. The carpark is expensive (as they all are in this region) but if you park at the NT place in Croyde and walk over Baggy Point you can get the best of all worlds.

Woolacombe Sands came into its own during the Victorian period when sea-bathing became all the rage and the large houses and hotels that we see today were built. The beach is privately owned and deserves its accolades. It has ample carparking close by, clean loos, plentiful refreshments including fish and chips, and is cleaned daily. Beach huts can be hired for the day. Lifeguards are on duty and there is a doggy stretch as well as a dog-free area in the summer. And there are tide pools. For families it really is ideal.

7 BARRICANE, COMBESGATE & GRUNTA BEACHES

If, like me, you prefer coves to huge expanses of sand, you may go for the smaller, less accessible Barricane, Combesgate and Grunta beaches (a steepish climb down rough steps and grass to Grunta, a shorter flight of steps to Barricane and Combesgate) with their rippled sand and satiny grey rocks. Murray's 1872 guide says that Barricane Beach 'almost entirely consists of shells.' You have to search hard to find any these days. **Barricane**, however, now has its own special attraction, the **Beach Café**.

1

2

Mortehoe Village Stores

Village   Stores

2

Grunta is my favourite, though; it has rocky alleys for children to explore, tide pools, plenty of sand at low tide – and good pickings for painstaking (or lucky) shell hunters, who may even spot a cowrie or blue-rayed limpet.

8 MORTEHOE & MORTE POINT

 The Smugglers Rest (page 247), **North Morte Farm Caravan & Camping Park** (page 248)

Mortehoe, up a dauntingly steep hill above the beaches, is a bustling little place with several gift shops, three pubs, tea shops, an all-purpose village store, an interesting **church** notable for its carved bench ends, mosaic and stained-glass windows, and a **museum** (⊙ Apr–Jun, Sep–Oct 11.00–15.00, closed Mon & Fri; Jul & Aug 10.00–16.00, closed Fri). This is in a lovely converted stone barn adjacent to a convenient carpark and well worth a visit. There are good displays of rural and maritime history, particularly shipwrecks; these are something of a speciality in this area, thanks to Morte Stone, the 'Rock of Death', a lethal projection beyond Morte Point. In one year alone, 1872, five vessels were lost. A local legend has it that 'No power on earth can remove [the rock] but that of a number of wives who have dominion over their husbands'; exactly how they are to achieve it remains a mystery.

Mortehoe **post office** and general stores sells everything, including hiking poles – handy if you left yours behind.

A network of paths straggles from Mortehoe across the headland to **Morte Point**. From here you might spot seals or even dolphins. The coastal path is particularly glorious here, bright with gorse, heather and bracken; you feel miles from anywhere, rather than a pebble-throw from one of the most popular beaches in the southwest. There is a stunning walk (page 74) from Mortehoe to Bull Point and back along a quiet lane, or you can walk south to Woolacombe Sands, buy an ice cream and toil up the hill back to Mortehoe. Or save your legs and catch a bus up.

In 2018 the National Trust created a new route for the SWCP around Mortehoe's Sharp Rock, then along Woolacombe Sands to Baggy Point. Mike Harrison reports: 'This has perhaps the finest views in North Devon, with gentle gradients.'

◀ **1** Morte Point is a good place for spotting marine wildlife. **2** Shopfront in Mortehoe. **3** Sheltered, quiet Putsborough Sands.

🍴 FOOD & DRINK

Barricane Beach Café Barricane Beach ☉ summer, 17.00–19.00 daily, weather dependent. This place is something else – literally: a fantastic Sri Lankan curry served from a shack on the beach in summer only, and only in fine weather. Get there at 17.00 to place your order. They do serve other meals at other times, but it's the curry that they're famous for. Bring a blanket (and a sweater – it can get chilly after sunset) your own booze and enjoy one of the region's best gastronomic surprises.

Miss Fea's Bistro North Morte Rd, Morthoe 🕾 01271 870891 ⬦ thesmugglersrest.co.uk/miss-feas-bistro ☉ 17.00–20.00 Tue–Sat, noon–16.00 Sun. Miss Fea's started life as a café but is now a really super bistro right in the middle of Mortehoe. The bistro serves award-winning food, including seafood and local steaks as well as a tasty vegan tortellini – and the dark chocolate terrine is not to be missed. Tables outside in the garden if it's fine.

✳ ✳ ✳

🚶 MORTEHOE TO BULL POINT OR ILFRACOMBE

※ OS Explorer map 139 or Croydecycle *Mortehoe & Woolacombe*; start: Mortehoe carpark, EX34 7DT 📍 SS45784524 ; 2.4 miles or 7 miles; moderate (some steepish hills)

1 Head up North Morte Road, by the post office, to a well-signed footpath on the left to Rockham Bay, opposite the North Morte Well. The footpath soon leaves the houses and takes you on a good path towards the intersection with the coast path; below you is beautiful **Rockham Beach**. There are many hidden beaches in this area, with grey sand, shingle and rock pools, but this one is sadly no longer accessible as the path and steps were washed away by the storms of 2014 and 2019.

2 Continue on the path, through bracken, gently up and down along the coast path.

3 At Bull Point and the lighthouse, you will meet the **Lighthouse Road**, which leads you back to Mortehoe. On a fine day it's easy to be seduced into keeping going to Ilfracombe –

there's a bus service back to Mortehoe and refreshments in Lee. Heading east along the coast path, your next place of interest is **Sandy Cove**, another lovely beach, accessed by steep steps, with shingle and sand at low tide. It's possible from this beach to scramble over the rocks at low tide to **Lee**, or you can continue on the coast path to this lovely little village. Here the SWCP runs along lanes for a while, so you might as well go into the village where there are two opportunities for good refreshments. To rejoin the coast path from the village, walk up Home Lane. It's a further three (hilly) miles to **Ilfracombe**, from where the number 31 bus runs on an hourly schedule (from St James Place Gardens) back to Mortehoe and Woolacombe.

✳ ✳ ✳

THE ILFRACOMBE AREA

The route from Woolacombe or Mortehoe to Ilfracombe is easier for walkers than drivers who must head inland and then back to the coast on narrow and often precipitous lanes. It takes some effort – and courage – to drive to Lee, to the east of Ilfracombe, but for lovers of charm and seclusion it should not be missed.

9 LEE

The writer L du Garde Peach described Lee in 1927 as 'making some pretence at being a fishing village, but the renown of Ilfracombe has made it rather the summer refuge of the more fastidious; the crowds which throng the Ilfracombe promenade, and bring fortune to its places of amusement, find little to their taste in Lee.' That sentiment holds true today: Lee is Devon as it used to be – at least for the time being: it is under threat of development.

The beach is inviting, with sand, seaweed and rock pools stretching back to the surf, guarded by giant slices of rock. The remains of a concrete slipway provide access over the seaweedy rocks to the sand. You could spend hours here investigating the pools, collecting pink quartz, and perhaps making your way around and over the rocks to Sandy Cove. At very low tide you may be able to walk round, but otherwise it's a bit of a scramble.

From the beach, a fuchsia-lined footpath leads to the village and its delightful pub, **The Grampus Inn** (✆ 01271 862906). 'Bill was a fiddle player,' Mike Harrison told me. 'He wanted to play in a pub so he bought one.' So the Grampus has live music from time to time and open mic on Friday nights. It also has real ales, cream teas and simple pub food. Next to the little church of St Matthew, with its Victorian wall paintings and Jacobean wood carvings, is the Old School Room (01271 864067), now a tea room and craft gallery selling local produce of all sorts.

It's only three miles via the coastal path from Lee to Ilfracombe – walk up Home Lane to get to the path – and the 35 bus connects the two places, but only on Tuesdays and Fridays.

10 ILFRACOMBE

Tourist information: The Landmark, Seafront 01271 863001 visitilfracombe.co.uk

> The situation of Ilfracombe is truly romantic. The port is a beautiful natural basin, sheltered by craggy heights that are overspread with foliage … The town consists chiefly of one street, full a mile long. It has a neat, healthy appearance, and is said to contain about two thousand inhabitants. The church stands on the upper part of the town and there is a chapel on a sort of knoll which may be called St Michael's Mount in miniature, being joined to the main land only by a narrow neck.
> W G Maton, travelling during 1794–96

As Maton noted, Ilfracombe's position is superb. The town fits where it can between giant crags and grassy mounds, with some imposing houses set high on the surrounding hillsides. It was a major seaside resort in Victorian times, when the arrival of the railway brought up to 10,000 visitors a day and encouraged the building of some grand hotels. One guest at the Ilfracombe Hotel in 1878 was the 19-year-old German grandson of Queen Victoria. Legend has it that the young prince was throwing stones at the ladies' changing huts on Rapparee Cove, and was asked to desist by 16-year-old Alfred Price, whose family had looked after the beach for generations. A fight ensued and, when his assailant became world famous some three decades later, Alfie was proud to boast that he had 'given the Kaiser a bloody nose'.

When the railway closed in 1970 the visitor numbers slumped, and the town has had to strive to reclaim them. If you arrive by car and park on the seafront, you may find the pervading smell of fast food, the jangle of amusement arcades and the blast of live music venues discouraging. Approach on foot, however, via the coastal path from

---

1 Ilfracombe harbour, the largest in North Devon. 2 Lee's rock pools. 3 Chambercombe Manor, complete with resident ghosts! 4 Beacon Point, known locally as the sleeping elephant. ▶

Hele (page 81), and your first view of the town and its harbour spread out below you is thrilling, even if the two conical towers known by some locals as Madonna's Bra (though the tourist office prefers Sand Castles) come as a bit of a surprise. They house the tourist information centre, museum and Landmark Theatre. As your eyes adjust to the scene, you will see Damien Hirst's extraordinary sculpture, *Verity*, standing, sword upraised, at the entrance to the harbour. Approached from the quay it is the sheer size that impresses (she is over 66ft high), but otherwise the statue appears to be of a beautiful, and pregnant, woman. But go round to the other side and you get the zombie shock; her skin has been peeled back to show the underlying muscles – and globules of fat – and her womb sliced open to show the developing foetus. A child I know had nightmares after seeing it. Hirst says that *Verity* stands for Truth and Justice, although the symbols of justice – the legal books and scales – are underfoot and held behind her back. Truth is clearly the dominant one. Perhaps justice is the last resort when the full disclosure of truth has failed. It's a controversial sculpture for such a traditional town, which is no bad thing.

From *Verity* you need to run the gamut of ice-cream licking, vinegar-dripping crowds on the Quay before escaping up Fore Street, where there are some good restaurants, leading into High Street, which is the main shopping centre. Keep closer to the shore and you will come to the Sand Castles – and the excellent **Ilfracombe Museum**. This merits an hour or so, being full of all sorts of unusual treasures. There are preserved freak animals such as a kitten with two heads and a chicken skeleton with four legs, a Lundy room, which will set you up information-wise before you visit the island, and the Mervyn Palmer room dedicated to one of those polymath naturalists in which the Victorian era specialised. This man collected everything: butterflies, an assortment of animals including an enormous python, and some pre-Columbian and Zulu art. Anything, really, that took his fancy. The museum also has a beautiful model of the *Bounty*, as in 'Mutiny on the'. The label explains that it was originally built to transport breadfruit trees to the West Indies to feed the African slaves. But they preferred plantains, so the whole endeavour was doomed.

The Landmark Theatre ($\mathcal{O}$ queenstheatre-barnstaple.com) has a wide variety of live performances and a very nice uncrowded café with a sea view.

Ilfracombe has an exceptional **Aquarium** ($\mathscr{O}$ 01271 864533 $\mathring{\mathscr{O}}$ ilfracombeaquarium.co.uk; $\odot$ from 10.00 daily, see website for closing times). Instead of gawping at tanks of tropical fish, here you can learn exactly what's in the waters of a typical local river, from its source high up in Exmoor, to its fast-flowing central stretch and down to the estuary and harbour. A typical rock pool is on show and finally the diverse and often surprising inhabitants of the Marine Conservation Zone around Lundy (the first such site in England). Handily near the parking area at the end of the Quay, this is perhaps Ilfracombe's main attraction.

Ilfracombe celebrates **Victorian Week** in June with much dressing up and festivities, and in early August the **Birdman Festival** sees the spectacle of young men (mostly) attempting to take to the air by throwing themselves off the pier. It's run by the local Round Table and all proceeds go to charity.

For a more sedate experience, the 100-passenger *Ilfracombe Princess* ($\mathscr{O}$ 01271 879727; $\mathring{\mathscr{O}}$ ilfracombeprincess.co.uk) runs daily cruises from the Quay lasting for one or two hours that take in the wildlife of the coast – seals and dolphins, or birds – during the summer months.

Ilfracombe's beaches

The town's public beaches are small and grey-sand, but they provide enough entertainment for children when the adults have finished looking at the town. Further east is the more secluded **Rapparee Cove** where the future Kaiser received his bloody nose. The number-one spot, however, goes to **Tunnels Beach**, which is as much a museum as a beach.

You'll find the entrance to the right of the large white Bath House building on Granville Road; pay a small fee at the kiosk and pass through a tunnel cut by miners to emerge, magically, on a beach surrounded by an amphitheatre of vertical black rocks topped with green. There is sand, tide pools galore and an artificial 'safe' bathing pool fed by the tides. This was the Ladies' Beach. The former Men's Beach is along to the left. On the approach walls are some delightful cuttings from the local newspaper of the time, *The North Devon Journal*, reporting various outrages. One (dated 1859) described the intrusion of two gentlemen on the ladies' bathing area. They swam round the point and 'not only mounted the rocks but plunged into the basin while the female bathers were engaged in their ablutions' (remember the female bathers would have been covered from neck to knees in their swimwear).

There are also stern rules governing the use of boats by gentlemen: 'Gentlemen unaccustomed to the management of a boat should never venture out with Ladies. To do so is foolhardy, if not criminal … Great care must be taken not to splash the Ladies … neither should anything be done to cause them fright.' Inevitably this lovely beach gets crowded in the holiday season.

¶ FOOD & DRINK

All good restaurants in Ilfracombe are heavily booked up during the holiday season. Don't risk turning up without a reservation in July and August, particularly on weekend evenings.

Giovanni & Luca Wilder Rd ✆ 01271 879394 ⌀ giovanniandluca.co.uk ◷ noon–14.00 & 17:30–21.00 daily. A proper Italian restaurant using old-fashioned family recipes for authentic Italian food. Vegan and gluten-free options.

Nelly May's Parlour 63 High St ✆ 01271 863877 ⌀ nellymays.co.uk ◷ 10.00–16.00 Tue–Sat. An award-winning traditional tea room oozing with olde-worlde character and charm. The extensive menu makes use of local suppliers and has many vegan and gluten-free options.

Relish Bar & Bistro 10–11 Fore St ✆ 01271 863837 ⌀ fishbistroilfracombe.co.uk ◷ 18.00–late Mon, Tues & Thu–Sat. A classy, popular place with a truly yummy menu focusing on locally sourced food such as Lundy crab and game casserole, with an emphasis on seafood, all beautifully presented. It only has a few tables so booking is essential.

Seventy One 71 Fore St ✆ 01271 863632 ⌀ seventyone.biz ◷ 18.30–22.00 Tue–Sat. A small, unpretentious and very popular place offering a limited, affordable menu focusing on locally sourced meat and fish.

Take Thyme 1 Fore St ✆ 01271 867622 ⌀ takethymefishrestaurant.co.uk ◷ Apr–Oct noon–16.00 Wed–Sat – check website for other months. A small, informal seafood restaurant handy for the quay and parking. An excellent menu featuring a large selection of fish and seafood dishes, plus one meat and one vegetarian.

Thomas Carr 1873 63 Fore St ✆ 01271 867831 ⌀ thomascarrdining.com. As befits a Michelin-starred restaurant, this is not cheap: for the six-course taster menu you need to set aside £95 and over three hours. But for a special treat, this is the place.

Ward's Bistro & Bar 6 St James Pl ✆ 01271 862112 ⌀ wardsilfracombe.co.uk ◷ 18.00–late Wed–Sat, noon–17.00 Sun. Different from most of the other recommendations here in that it's in an elegant Victorian mansion, rather than squeezed into Fore Street. Run by a husband and wife team and recommended for their lunch-time Sunday carvery, eaten inside or outside in the sunny courtyard.

11 HILLSBOROUGH EARTHWORK & HELE

To the east of Ilfracombe is the **Hillsborough earthwork**. This was probably once a fortress – it commands an impressive view of the harbour, and two ramparts are just visible – but it could equally well have been a ceremonial centre. In 1896 it was purchased by the Ilfracombe Urban District Council for 'public enjoyment'; it is now a nature reserve and affords the best views of Ilfracombe.

Hele (pronounced Heel) is little more than a small grey sand and shingle beach, most rewarding at low tide for its rock pools, and the exceptional Hele **Cornmill and Tearoom** (✆ 01271 863185 ⬧ helecornmill.com ☺ summer only, hours & days vary so check; cash only). This has been a working mill since 1525. In 1830 it was owned by John Hele, who managed to be a blacksmith, dentist, policeman and miller all at once, but over time the mill became derelict. It was bought in 1972 by Chris Lovell who restored it to working order. The current owners, Kathy and David Jones, bought it in 2011 although they had no previous experience of milling. 'We've learned on the job, so to speak,' David told me and then went on to describe the technicalities of using water power to grind wheat, and the catastrophe of being flooded in 2013 and, conversely, managing the mill during the 2018 drought. A guided, or self-guided, tour of the mill is well worth it; there's local history and legends, as well as the story of the mill itself. But it is the tea room that has won a batch of awards as the Best Tearoom from *Devon Life*: every year, in fact, except for 2016 when they were excluded for being too successful! You will see why when you indulge in the home-baked lunches or teas. It was here that I learned that cheese scones with cream cheese and onion chutney compete admirably with the traditional cream tea. If it's busy or you are here sheltering from the rain so have some time in hand, ask to try the nail puzzle or one of the other fiendish pastimes.

"Hillsborough earthwork was probably once a fortress, but it could equally well have been a ceremonial centre."

You can eat inside or out, or climb some steps to the shady Meryl's Garden or the enclosed Potting Shed, which can be booked in advance for small groups.

Note that there is no parking at the mill. You need to use the public (paying but inexpensive) carpark near the beach.

Hele is the start of a short bus-assisted walk (page 82).

✳ ✳ ✳

🚶 A SHORT BUS-ASSISTED WALK FROM HELE TO ILFRACOMBE

✽ Croydecycle *Ilfracombe & Berrynarbor*; start: Hele carpark, EX34 9QZ 📍 SS53584772; 1.6 miles; moderate (some steep bits)

By walking from Hele you can approach Ilfracombe from its most flattering side as well as taking in Hillsborough Fort on the way. It's a treat of a walk, short but with steep ups and downs, and some wonderful views.

From Hele Beach take the coastal path up to Beacon Point. This is a tough climb (made easier with steps) but the view of Ilfracombe from the top makes it all worthwhile. On a sunny day it's just gorgeous: the little squared-off harbour full of boats is backed by pink-, blue- and cream-coloured houses, behind which tower the incongruous cones of Madonna's Bra (page 78). The craggy green Lantern Hill provides a contrast on the right. After your descent to Ilfracombe, walk up Fore Street to Portland Street, from where regular buses run to Hele Bay.

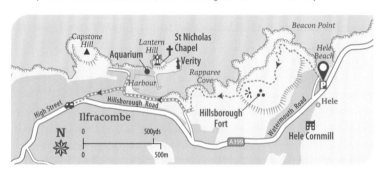

✳ ✳ ✳

12 CHAMBERCOMBE MANOR

Chambercombe Ln, EX34 9RJ 📞 01271 862202 🖥 chambercombemanor.org.uk
🕒 Easter–end Oct, guided tours 11.00–15.00 Mon–Fri, noon–15.00 Sun

Inland from Hele Beach, down a lane described by S P B Mais as one 'we shall be unwise to resist', is this manor house. It was built in the 12th century and was once the family seat of a branch of the Champernowne family – and is reputed to be one of the most haunted houses in Britain. How it gained its ghosts is the stuff of legend. There are many versions of the story but the one recounted by J L W Page is the most appealing:

> One summer evening the farmer, smoking his pipe in the garden, fell to studying the roof of his house, which needed repairs. While considering which of the windows would most readily give access to the roof, he was puzzled at noticing, for the first time, a window for which he could not account. Calling to his men to bring tools, he hurried upstairs and at once attacked the wall of the passage opposite the mysterious casement. In a few minutes the plaster gave way, and the farmer, creeping through the breach, found himself in a long, low room furnished with tables and chairs of ancient date, and hung with moth-eaten tapestry. But the object to which his attention was first attracted was a bed with close-drawn faded curtains. With trembling hand the farmer tore them aside and started back in horror, for before him lay a skeleton.

Page goes on to pour cold water on the story since, he claims, there is no room that fits this description and no window. This is backed up by Claire Barker (see box, page 84), who was shown a windowless, dark, forbidding room, almost like an attic, concealed between two other bedrooms. But the story of the skeleton persists; it is thought to be Kate Wallace, who was mortally wounded by wreckers in the 17th century – one of whom turned out to be her own father.

COMBE MARTIN & AREA

You are now approaching the western edge of Exmoor National Park, and the region's most strenuous but beautiful walking country. Before that, however, there's a more gentle landscape.

13 WATERMOUTH CASTLE

01271 867474 *watermouthcastle.com* Apr–end Oct, 10.30–17.30, last admission 15.30, daily; end-Oct–Mar Sat & Sun

Heading east by car or bus, you can hardly fail to be surprised at the neo-Gothic Watermouth Castle, a grey hulk which is not as old as it first appears. It is now a popular family attraction, part theme park and part museum, but its history is interesting. The castle was built during the early 1800s when grandeur was all the rage among the privileged classes, of whom the wealthy Bassett family was one. There is some mystery as to why it took 20 years to build when there was plenty of money available, but eventually it was inherited in 1880 by Walter Bassett who became obsessed with Ferris wheels, and built one in the grounds as well as in other parts of the world, including

THE GHOSTS OF CHAMBERCOMBE MANOR

Claire Barker

To my eyes, Chambercombe Manor (page 82) – a charming white manor house, set in pretty gardens and bathed in early autumn sunshine – didn't look very scary. In fact it looked more like a location for a magazine photo shoot. As a children's author researching locations for ghost stories, I reluctantly decided that it didn't look quite spooky enough for my purposes. But as I had already paid at the gate, I had little choice. I put away my notebook, deciding not to mention my reason for visiting and to enjoy the afternoon anyway.

Soon the tour guide appeared at the front door. As I trailed from room to room she was very knowledgeable and enthusiastic about the history of the house. She informed me that the place was positively heaving with ghosts and television's *Britain's Most Haunted* had even filmed there.

Rather thrillingly, every so often she would stop mid-sentence and say 'Can you hear that?' as if to suggest the presence of a wayward spirit, but all my sceptical ears could hear was the resolute cheerfulness of the blackbirds outside. However, I enjoyed looking at the suits of armour and the unusual furniture. After a while even the stubborn lack of ghostly activity became entertaining in itself.

Then as the end of the tour approached, I climbed the stairs to a narrow landing and took a small step down into an adjacent bedroom. To my great surprise, my whole body instantly began to tingle, from the top of my head to the tip of my toes. 'How peculiar,' I thought, and stepped back out again. The tingling promptly stopped, so I put my foot back into the room and it began again. I repeated this experiment several times with the same results. Throwing caution to the wind I stood in the middle of the room, tingling fiercely, only to become suddenly and inexplicably overwhelmed with tears. The tour guide nodded sagely as if she had seen all this before. 'Ah yes,' she said, 'this is the children's room. They like you. Do you work with children?'

I was shown several things after this but truthfully it's all a bit of a blur. All I wanted to do was get back in my car and drive home very, very quickly. My visit to Chambercombe Manor was the best piece of research I did all year, but I don't think I'm brave enough to return in a hurry!

the famous one in Vienna which featured in the film *The Third Man*. However, this was his eventual downfall. The patent was owned by George Washington Ferris, an engineer who created the world's first giant wheel for the World's Columbian Exposition in Chicago in 1893. This was a magnificent achievement, powered by a steam engine and 265ft high (still dwarfed by the London Eye, which is 443ft), and probably the first major engineering project to be built entirely for pleasure. It was an instant success, but Ferris gained little profit from his invention, and litigation to try to protect the patent not only reduced him to poverty but virtually bankrupted the Bassett family and they had to sell up.

Theme parks are not normally included in a Slow guide, but this is different. The castle is as much a collection of vintage games and curiosities as it is for small thrill-seekers. It seems the perfect place to bring the grandchildren provided you can cope with the steep hills and steps. Oldies will love the blast of nostalgia that comes with the optical illusions (remember them?), the one-armed bandits and so on. Many of the exhibits are educational as well as intriguing – such as the camera obscura, the gravity well and the Bernoulli Blower (I now understand, for the first time, what keeps a jet aeroplane in the air!). There's also a dollop of morality in Gnomeland; the little fellows lead impeccable lives of love, harmony and healthy eating. In cases of domestic strife 'the injured party sings until their spouse admits that he or she was wrong'. I wonder if that would work in international politics?

The gardens are spacious, with labelled trees, and there are enough good rides to keep the children entertained. All in all a worthwhile visit.

✳ ✳ ✳

𝕏 A BUS-ASSISTED COASTAL WALK FROM WATERMOUTH CASTLE TO COMBE MARTIN

Croydecycle *Ilfracombe & Berrynarbor*; start: Combe Martin west-end (beach) carpark , EX34 0DJ ♀ SS57774728; two miles; moderate (some steep bits)

The coastal path between Ilfracombe and Combe Martin has two sections following the A399 (although a huge amount of money has been spent creating a safe walkway beside the busy road). However, if you park in Combe Martin and take the number 301 bus, which runs hourly, to Watermouth Castle you can stroll back the two miles mainly on footpaths, and enjoy some of the best cliff views of this section.

From the castle the coastal path meanders along the cliff edge to bring you to one of the most heart-stoppingly lovely beach views in Devon. A curve of grey slate sand culminates in a tree-topped rock nodule, and is backed by high wooded cliffs. In true Slow form you must walk to **Broad Strand Beach** (also known as Broadsands) and the final descent involves 227 steps,

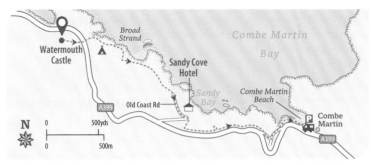

so it's worth checking a tide table since it is certainly more rewarding at low tide. The steps were washed away in the storms of 1990; they were mended by paratroopers, but whether this service would be repeated is debatable. Further sea and beach views bring you to Sandy Cove Hotel and the road, which you must follow, with periods of respite, to Berry Lane and Combe Martin.

* * *

14 BERRYNARBOR

Sitting above and to the west of Combe Martin, this lofty village is a frequent winner of Best Kept awards and you can see why: everywhere there are flowers and tranquillity. The post office and **community shop** sell everything including coffee to drink at the outside table, **Ye Old Globe** pub deals with other thirsts, and the carpark is free so it's a useful starting point for the region's walks. Beatrix Potter used to holiday here; no doubt she would have enjoyed the more modern addition of 'flowerpot men' who may be spotted in gardens, up drainpipes, or dangling from the roofs of some of the houses. The church is one of the most beautifully located in Devon, high on a hill with the billowing landscape behind it.

15 COMBE MARTIN

🏠 **Pack o' Cards** (page 247), 🏛 **Mary's Cottage** (page 247), **West Challacombe Manor** (page 248)

Combe Martin Museum & Tourist Information Point: Cross St ✆ 01271 889031
🖳 combemartinmuseum.co.uk. ◷ 11.00–14.00 Mon–Fri (but dependent on volunteers' availability)

◀ 1 Hunting the Earl of Rone. 2 Combe Martin's sheltered beach and rock pools. 3 An exhibit at the Combe Martin Museum. 4 Little Hangman on the South West Coast Path.

> We passed through Combe Martin, an old, and dirty, and poor place;
> one house, once a good one, bears the date of 1534; another is built in a
> most ridiculous castle style and is called The Pack of Cards
> Robert Southey, August 1799

Modern visitors will recognise the Pack of Cards but not the description of the town as a whole. Squeezed into the crease between two hillsides, within an AONB, this straggly but well-kept town once claimed to have the longest High Street in England. This has now been modified to the longest street party in England, and perhaps the largest number of name changes in one street: five. Once over 70 shops and 19 pubs lined this road; now there are only a handful. In the early 19th century Combe Martin was noted by writers, and not just the Poet Laureate Robert Southey, as being run down. Charles Kingsley called it a 'mile-long manstye'. There was a reason, however – landlords deliberately let houses deteriorate to avoid contributing to the Poor Law rates. Inhabitants were known as Shammickites, a shammick being a term for a slum.

Nowadays there's plenty to admire here. The town has a long and interesting history. The Martin part of the name comes from Sieur Martin de Turon, who was granted the lands by William the Conqueror. Legend has it that the last Martin failed to come back from a hunting trip so his

HUNTING THE EARL OF RONE

One of the most bizarre, colourful, historical and highly charged events to take place in the British calendar is Hunting the Earl of Rone in Combe Martin each Spring Bank Holiday (⬧ earl-of-rone.org.uk).

No-one knows how old this event is, but we do know that it was banned in 1837 because of the drunken and licentious behaviour that accompanied it. J L W Page, writing in 1895, describes a conversation with an old lady who remembered the festival with great affection. 'She told me with what an awful joy she would give her halfpenny to escape the jaws of the … hobby horse which laid hold of any non-paying delinquent.'

She is quoted as saying 'My dear soul, I should like to have 'un again!' It was revived, only a little more soberly, in 1973.

The hunt begins on Friday evening, when men dressed as Grenadiers, in scarlet jackets and beribboned conical hats, parade the length of the village, to the beat of drums and the firing of their muskets. Their quarry is a shipwrecked fugitive thought to be hiding out in the woods and subsisting on ship's biscuits. Perhaps he is Hugh O'Neill, the Earl of Tyrone, an Irish traitor who was indeed wanted by the government some 400 years ago. The Grenadiers are accompanied by a Fool carrying a besom, and a Hobby Horse,

father, assuming the lad was staying the night elsewhere, ordered that the drawbridge over the moat be raised. The unfortunate hunter returned in the dark, fell into the moat and was drowned, thus ending the Martin line. His father was so consumed with grief and guilt that he left Combe Martin forever. The family seat passed to the Leys, a descendant of whom built the town's most extraordinary building, the Pack o' Cards.

Once silver ore was discovered in the region, Combe Martin's fortunes blossomed. The first recorded extraction was in 1292, in Edward I's reign.

Miners had no choice of occupation: they were impressed from the Peak District and Wales to serve various kings and finance their wars in France. Both Edward III and Henry V paid for their claims on French territory through the wealth of Combe Martin. The harbour allowed the metal to be easily transported along with agricultural products, most notably hemp. One of the village industries was the spinning of this hemp into shoe-makers' thread and rope for the shipping industry (see box, page 52 for more on the rope-making business). More recently, but before refrigeration and polytunnels, the town became renowned for its strawberries, which ripened earlier in this sheltered valley than elsewhere in the country. The mines finally closed for good in 1880. A lively group of volunteers, the Combe Martin Silver Mines (CMSM) Society, keep the

a grotesque twirling figure in a huge, hooped beribboned skirt, a necklace of ship's biscuits and a teeth-clattering horse's head. This procession ends at the 'stable' at the Top George Inn. A miniature (in that it's enacted by children) procession takes place on the Saturday. The highlight of this day is the enormous strawberry cake, celebrating Combe Martin's fruit speciality. Sunday sees another procession, but on Monday things really hot up. After three days of noisy searching, they catch the man in Lady's Wood at the top of the village and, dressed in sackcloth, he is put backwards on a donkey and marched along with drums and music. Now and then he is shot and falls to the ground, only to be revived by the Fool or the Hobby Horse. He's then replaced, again backwards, on the donkey and continues his sad journey, accompanied by maidens carrying flower garlands. Eventually the procession reaches the church where, amid dancing and bells ringing, the Earl of Rone is shot once more. Then it is all the way down to the sea, where the dead Rone (now replaced by a sackcloth effigy), is thrown into the waves from the quay, and the women throw their garlands after him.

The TIC has a good display on this extraordinary festival.

history alive through open days and mine visits. Pick up a leaflet at the TIC or contact them (✆ 01271 882442 ✉ cmsmsoc@hotmail.com) for dates.

There are really only two buildings of interest, the **Pack o' Cards** pub and the church, but both are exceptional. The former is a piece of 18th-century eccentricity created by George Ley, a gambler, in homage to his success. All its numbers echo those in a pack of cards, hence its four floors (suits), 13 doors and 13 fireplaces (cards in a suit), and originally 52 windows (cards in a pack); also, the whole thing looks like a house of cards. Ley, who died in 1709, has a memorial in the **church** of St Peter ad Vincula (St Peter in Chains). Its 100ft-high tower has been dated at 1490, and was probably built by the same stonemason as neighbouring Berrynarbor and Hartland. A local jingle describes these towers: 'Hartland for length, Berrynarbor for strength, and Combe Martin for beauty'. It is indeed a decorative tower, with statues set in niches. Inside, the rood screen, which dates from the 16th century, has been expertly cleaned to bring out the colours and details of the painted saints in the panels. There are some carved bench ends and more recent poppyheads (three-dimensional wood carvings) in the choir including a Combe Martin fisherman and a whale. Carved on the capitals above the pillars are the usual vine leaves and grapes, but look out for the rare green woman. On the wall, but too high up to see the detail, is a highly regarded marble sculpture of Judith Ivatt, wearing an exquisitely carved lace collar.

There's a general store at the service station near the top end of town (if coming from Blackmoor Gate), a post office not far from the church and its carpark, and a small supermarket at the main carpark, with the TIC and museum, near the beach. This lower end of town is where the beachy shops are, the **Focsle Inn** and the **Outdoor Shop** (✆ oskcwatersports. co.uk) which hires out paddleboards and kayaks. The lovely little **beach** of sand and shingle has enough sand at low tide that you don't need beach shoes for swimming. It's contained within steep tree-hung cliffs making any on-water exploration of the bay particularly rewarding.

Near the beach and carpark is the excellent **Museum and Tourist Information Centre**. The museum is full of nuggets of information about the history of the town, its silver-mining industry, and the Hunting the Earl of Rone festival. Children can bring in their finds from the beach to study under a microscope or join an organised beach safari. There are ropes and pulleys to play around with to understand how heavy cargo such as limestone could be loaded on to a boat.

The town has more than its share of **festivals**. A lively carnival is held during the second week of August, when a giant 'grey mare', ridden by Old Uncle Tom Cobley and All, parades around the town on Wednesday evening, presumably looking for Widecombe Fair. There's also a Strawberry Fayre in June, celebrating the town's history as a major fruit-growing region, and the bizarre but hugely enjoyable Hunting the Earl of Rone (see box, page 88), which takes place on the Spring Bank Holiday. 'They like dressing up in Combe Martin,' the lady in the tourist office told me. Indeed!

FOOD & DRINK

Besshill Farm Shop 4 Borough Rd ✆ 01271 889350 ⌂ besshillfarmshop.co.uk ◷ 09.00–17.00 Tue–Sat. An excellent selection of free-range meat and fresh vegetables.
Black & White Fish & Chips Borough Rd ✆ 01271 883548 ⌂ blackandwhitefishandchips.co.uk ◷ 17.00–20.00 Mon & Tue, noon–14.00 & 17.00–20.00 Wed–Sat. A long-established, very popular chippie that sells seriously good take-away. Located at the beach end of town.
The Pack o' Cards High St ✆ 01271 882300 ⌂ packocards.co.uk. Straightforward food served indoors or in the spacious garden of this unique inn (see opposite).

BEYOND COMBE MARTIN

Next to Combe Martin are some of the highest cliffs in the country: **Hangman Cliffs**. Above them are Great Hangman and Little Hangman, and climbing them from sea level is quite a challenge, though the views make it worthwhile. When you stand on the top of Great Hangman, you are at the highest point of the South West Coast Path (1,046ft). The name comes not from a desperate walker nor from the rather appealing alternative, sometimes suggested, that a sheep-thief managed to strangle himself on the animal's rope as he made his getaway. Rather it's a corruption of 'An Maen', Celtic for The Stone or Stony Head. There are some good circular walks that include the peak, but the one described on page 92 cunningly avoids it and gives you some doses of history instead of exhaustion. If you decided to do the hard slog to the top of Great Hangman you may be tempted to continue east along the South West Coast Path. This is, after all, perhaps *the* most spectacular and varied stretch of the entire route. However, there is no bus link until you reach Lynmouth, 13 miles away; given the hilly terrain, this is a lot to do in one day. A good solution is to split the walk into two days, staying overnight at the welcoming The Hunter's Inn (page 159).

***

COMBE MARTIN LOOP: CLIFFS, BEACH & SILVER MINES

Croydecycle *Combe Martin & Hunter's Inn*; start: Combe Martin west-end (beach) carpark EX34 0DJ ♀ SS57774728; 2 or 5 miles; moderate (some steep climbs)

This walk is mainly along quiet lanes, though with very few level stretches. It gives you great views of the coast and down to the lovely cove of Wild Pear Beach. The walk also takes you near some reminders of the town's silver-mining past.

1 Park in the west-end carpark near the beach; from the upper end of the carpark follow the track signposted 'South West Coast Path'. It climbs steeply uphill to the cliff's edge; below is **Wild Pear Beach**, once busy with the traffic of limestone-carrying boats but now inaccessible and left to nature.

2 At the point where the path starts to climb steeply towards **Little Hangman**, look for a turning to the right where you'll join West Challacombe Lane, passing **West Challacombe Manor**, which is now owned by the National Trust and let as self-catering holiday accommodation. This is a beautiful 15th-century manor with a splendid Great Hall, which retains its medieval roof. No-one is certain what it was used for, but it could have housed the

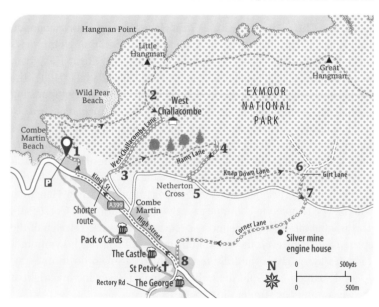

miners brought from Wales and the Peak District. The lane leads to Combe Martin's main street (King Street at this point) so if you want to cut your walk short here you are less than half a mile from the starting point.

3 To continue walking, turn a sharp left, signed to Great Hangman, to follow Hams Lane for a half mile or so.

4 When you meet a small lane, turn right and ascend steeply to Netherton Cross. You'll catch some lovely views of Combe Martin strung out along its valley.

5 At the junction, turn left and then left again, climbing steeply up Knap Down Lane.

6 At the junction with Girt Lane you've reached the highest point and it really is downhill all the way now; turn right here and then left at the bottom of the lane.

7 Soon after, turn right again to join Corner Lane. As you start down the lane, fork right; on your left are the tall remains of a double-cylindered engine house used in silver mining, a landmark for miles around.

8 At the bottom of the lane, turn right on to High Street/King Street back to your car. However, you emerge close to two pubs, the George and the Castle, so if it's that time of day ... Or for more spiritual refreshment you're also near the church.

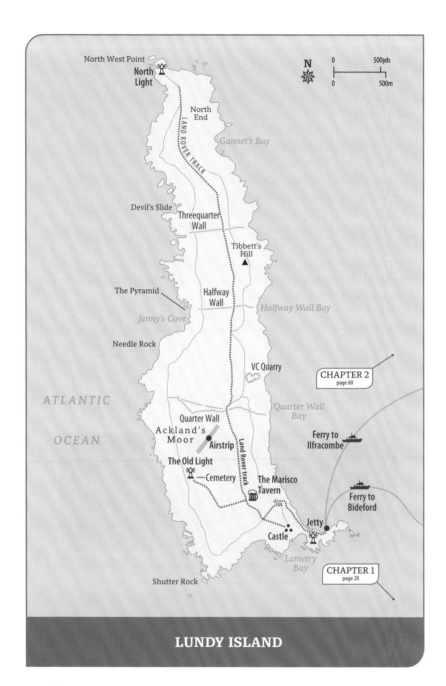

North West Point

North Light

North End

Gannet's Bay

LAND ROVER TRACK

N

0 500yds

0 500m

Devil's Slide

Threequarter Wall

Tibbett's Hill

The Pyramid

Halfway Wall

Halfway Wall Bay

Jenny's Cove

Needle Rock

VC Quarry

CHAPTER 2
page 60

ATLANTIC

Quarter Wall Bay

OCEAN

Quarter Wall

Ackland's Moor

Airstrip

Ferry to Ilfracombe

The Old Light

Cemetery

Land Rover track

The Marisco Tavern

Ferry to Bideford

Jetty

Castle

Lametry Bay

CHAPTER 1
page 28

Shutter Rock

LUNDY ISLAND

3
LUNDY ISLAND

With Simon Dell, Siân Scott & Rosie Ellis

I saw the Isle of Lundy which formerly belonged to my grandfather, William, Lord Viscount Say and Seale, which does abound with fish and rabbits and all sorts of fowls – one bird that lives partly in the water and partly out, and so may be called an amphibious creature; it is true that one foot is like a turkey, and the other a goose's foot; it lays its eggs in a place the sun shines on and sets it so exactly upright on the small end that there it remains until taken up, and all the art and skill of persons cannot set it up so again to abide.

Celia Fiennes, *Through England on a Side Saddle*, 1695

Although this description will not immediately strike a bell with modern ornithologists, one semi-amphibious bird that is indeed associated with Lundy is the puffin: the island was named after them. 'Lunde øy' is Norse for Puffin Island. The island was well known to the Scandinavian pirates who harried the shores of Wales and Devon, and is first mentioned by name in the *Orkney Ingasaga* (1139–48).

LUNDY'S HISTORY

Lundy lies about ten miles north of Hartland Point, where the Bristol Channel meets the Atlantic. It is a granite island three miles long and about half a mile wide, and with its wind and lack of trees feels, to the visitor, like a chunk of the Hebrides that lost its way.

Lundy's history is steeped in tales of piracy, plots, slavery, smuggling and general maritime skulduggery. Various owners, administrators and tenants are recorded from the mid 12th century onwards, among them Sir Richard Grenville of *Revenge* fame who acquired the fee simple of the island in 1577 from his wife's kinsman Sir John St Leger, as repayment of a debt. After Grenville's death in 1591 it passed to his son Bernard, who in 1595 was rebuked by the queen for not making greater efforts to prevent pirates from using it as a stronghold. Centuries

later came the long tenure of the Heaven family (1834–1917), when it was often referred to as 'The Kingdom of Heaven'. Then came the ownership of the Harman family, with Martin Coles Harman setting out to make the Lundy a 'haven of peace and natural beauty', when he bought the island in 1925. After his son Albion died in 1968 the future of the island looked bleak. In 1969, however, the National Trust acquired it after Sir Jack Hayward donated the asking price at auction. The Landmark Trust took on a 60-year lease and the responsibility to repair buildings, manage the land and employ the staff, and the island started to attract visitors. Today just over two dozen people live on Lundy – all employees of the Landmark Trust – and the island is established as a unique holiday destination.

LUNDY TODAY

Lundy inspires much interest, both nationally as well as further afield, enjoying, as it does, an unspoiled habitat (both terrestrial and marine) and a wealth of archaeology. It is now a Site of Special Scientific Interest as well as being made the UK's first Marine Nature Reserve in 1986 and the UK's first No Take Zone in 2003. It is rich in birdlife, with the iconic puffin making a comeback, thanks to ongoing conservation efforts, and supports rare lichens, including the golden hair lichen, which provides a splash of colour on the coastal rocks. It is also the only place that a primitive brassica, the Lundy cabbage, is found (see box, page 98), as well as being in the only area of sea around the UK where you can find all five British species of shallow-water cup coral.

Various domestic animals were introduced by the Harmans to keep the vegetation under control, including sika deer and Soay sheep. There are also some feral goats. The tough Lundy ponies are of mixed ancestry: mainly New Forest, Connemara and Welsh Mountain.

Since 1929 Lundy has had its own postage stamps ('puffinage'), introduced by Martin Coles Harman, and for a while it also had its own coinage sporting Mr Harman's head. You can still buy Lundy's stamps today, at the island's General Store, and use them to send a postcard home.

◀ 1 The MS *Oldenburg* docked at Lundy's jetty. 2 From March onwards, puffins return to the island. 3 St Helen's Church. 4 Grey seals are regular visitors.

THE LUNDY CABBAGE

The Lundy cabbage (*Coincya wrightii*) is a species of primitive brassica growing only on Lundy, with its nearest relative found in southern Spain and North Africa. It is likely that Lundy is sufficiently far from the mainland to have allowed the plant to evolve into a separate species. It is one of only about a dozen endemic plants in the British Isles but, even in this select company, it stands out, uniquely having its own endemic insects: the Lundy cabbage flea beetle and Lundy cabbage weevil rely on this unique plant for their survival. The Lundy Cabbage grows all along Beach Road and along the Eastern sidelands to a height of almost a metre, and its cross-patterned pale yellow petals (resembling oilseed rape) borne in showy heads can be seen flowering in May and June.

Archaeological interest ranges from Bronze Age huts and enclosures at the north end to ancient inscribed stones in the burial ground near to the Old Light. There are also the remains of the Victorian granite quarries on the east side (see boxes, pages 106 and 111). On and around Lundy there are no fewer than 14 Grade II-listed buildings and 41 scheduled sites and monuments, plus three protected wreck sites.

Lundy is divided by three walls: Quarter Wall, Halfway Wall and Threequarter Wall. Land in between these walls differs considerably; farmed fields at the south end, rough grazing in the middle, and bare granite encrusted with heather and lichens at the north end.

Overnight visitors are well provided for, with self-catering properties owned by the Landmark Trust as well as facilities for campers, and the availability of winter transport by helicopter from Hartland means that the year-round occupation rate is high. The island shop is fully stocked to meet all visitors' requirements, while the Marisco Tavern provides snacks and meals, and also functions as a social centre. There are no cars on the island, only farm tractors and a few Land Rovers.

Dogs are not allowed on Lundy.

Why do people come to Lundy? For the character of the island itself and the tranquillity that is found there. For birdwatching, rock climbing or diving; for interest in the plants, the fungi, the lichens, or the archaeology and history; for walking; or simply for a rest with a few good books.

One thing is for sure – after one visit most people are caught by the Lundy spirit and return time and again to this special corner of North Devon.

WILDLIFE

While the sea and its shore abound with life, there are almost no indigenous terrestrial mammals on Lundy. The pygmy shrew is the only one and can often be seen scurrying around properties and buildings in search of crumbs.

Until recent years there were no reptiles on Lundy, but slow worms are now being seen. There are generally plenty of rabbits, with a disproportionate number of black ones, which were much prized for their skins when Lundy was a Royal Warren. Rabbits were brought here by the Normans and, until the introduction of myxomatosis in the 1980s, were so plentiful that their burrows contributed to land erosion. But every seven years or so myxomatosis mutates to develop a new deadly strain, leaving the rabbit population greatly depleted until they gradually rebuild their resistance to the disease. So, depending on the time of

"The eerie and haunting calls of Manx shearwaters can often be heard reverberating around the island late at night."

your visit in this cycle, there may be plenty of rabbits or comparatively few. More damaging than the rabbits were the rats. Almost all historical reports of the island mention the depredation caused by the huge number of these rodents, introduced accidentally from ships and with no land predators to control their numbers. Whereas former residents of the island remarked on their pillage of food supplies, more recently it was the effect on the bird population that caused concern, with eggs and nestlings being choice meals in the rat diet.

In the late 1930s the population of puffins was thought to be around 3,500 breeding pairs; by 2000, there were just five individuals. Something had to be done – Puffin Island without any puffins was unthinkable. A programme of rat elimination was successfully initiated in 2002, and by 2006 the island was officially declared 'rat-free'. Since then the population of puffins has steadily increased, numbering 848 in 2021. Even more spectacular is the ten-fold increase in Manx shearwaters. The eerie and haunting calls of these seabirds can often be heard reverberating around the island late at night. In addition, storm petrels are making a comeback and guillemots and razorbills are also flourishing.

Despite the rats, seabirds were abundant in the 19th century. When the author J L W Page visited the island in the 1890s he wrote:

THE LUNDY ATLANTIC GREY SEALS

Lundy is home to a breeding colony of around 200 Atlantic grey seals, which are resident for much of the year, though it is thought that many travel across the Channel specifically to pup in this safe haven. They can be seen all around the island, particularly at their 'hauling-out' spots – favoured rocks and ledges for basking in the sun. Seals can often be seen in the Devil's Kitchen, bathing and hauling themselves on to rocks just offshore.

The same seals also come into the Landing Bay from time to time for an inquisitive look at visitors. Brazen Ward is also a good spot for seal watching.

In the 1890s, J L W Page reported that 'the natives, by the way, have the most exalted idea of the ferocity of these creatures. One youth actually told me that they had been seen to take up large stones in their flippers and hurl them at the head of an intruder'.

'In the breeding season they literally swarm – as one islander put it "You can scarcely see the sky, sir". The sea is covered with them, the land is covered with them; they sit in regiments and battalions on ledges of rock.' They were hunted for their feathers, with 379lb of feathers recorded as having been plucked by the women of Lundy in 1816 alone. Eggs from 'the Lundy parrot' were also collected and sold to visitors, causing more than one islander to fall to his death from the puffin nest sites on the cliffs.

Puffins start to come ashore in late March, returning to their former burrows above Jenny's Cove (page 105). After breeding they shed their brightly coloured beak casing and spend the winter at sea. If you fail to see puffins on the cliffs around Jenny's Cove you can sometimes spot their characteristic flight, with rapid wing beats, skimming close to the ocean's surface, or 'rafting' in groups on the sea. Although puffins feed on a variety of small fish, sand eels are much favoured, and the classic photo of a puffin holding a quantity of these fish in its specially adapted beak is the one all puffin enthusiasts long to capture.

GETTING THERE

Lundy is accessible year-round, by sea in summer and by helicopter during the winter months.

A word of warning: bad weather can cause the cancellation of both ship and helicopter, necessitating an additional day (or even more) on the island for 'stayers'. Factor this in when planning your trip, and be sure to bring enough of any regular medication you may need.

BY SEA

Between the end of March and the end of October the MS *Oldenburg* carries both day visitors and staying passengers from either Bideford or Ilfracombe. Sailing timetables can be found on the Landmark Trust Lundy website (∂ landmarktrust.org.uk/lundyisland). Departure ports depend on the tides, because Bideford requires high water whereas departures from Ilfracombe can take place at any tidal level. The sea trip takes about two hours from either port. Bideford sailings are infrequent, sometimes as few as two a month, but are well worth booking since not only do they allow you far more time on Lundy (seven to nine hours compared with a bit over four hours from Ilfracombe) but for the reward of sailing down the River Torridge, passing Appledore and other towns. Quite often at the end of a Bideford sailing day the *Oldenburg* will also do a 'round the island' trip for a small fee. It will be announced when you dock, lasts about an hour, and provides an excellent opportunity to see seals and, in the breeding season, puffins.

Parking in Bideford is available at the end of Bideford Quayside in the long-term carpark and in Ilfracombe on the opposite side of the harbour in the Marine Drive or Larkstone carparks. These are both some way from the quay, so allow plenty of time for parking.

SHORE OFFICES

The Lundy Booking Office The Pier, Ilfracombe EX34 9EQ ∂ 01271 863636 ⊙ Apr–Oct, 09.00–17.00 Mon–Fri & 09.00–13.00 Sat
The Lundy Shore Office The Quay, Bideford EX39 2EY ∂ 01271 470074 ⊙ 09.00–17.00 Mon–Fri

THE MS *OLDENBURG*

The MS *Oldenburg* takes 267 passengers and is a charming and comfortable vessel. She has upper and lower decks with a forward saloon, and a rear buffet and shop.

Built in 1958 in Germany, she operated ferry services between the German mainland and the Friesian Island of Wangerooge and to Heligoland until coming to Lundy in 1986, where she has given faithful service ever since. Her crew are friendly and helpful and are a mine of information. They really know Lundy and enjoy advising visitors.

An insider's tip is to use the toilets on board before you get off. There are no facilities on the island until you reach the village. And as the island's water supply is vulnerable, you will be doing Lundy a favour by flushing on the *Oldenburg* instead of the island.

BY HELICOPTER

Between the end of October and the end of March, when the *Oldenburg* is not running, seven-minute helicopter flights operate on Mondays and Fridays from Hartland Point, where parking is available (✆ 01271 863636 for bookings).

STAYING ON LUNDY

There are 23 self-catering properties available for short breaks and weekly holiday lets, a campsite near the village with room for 40 people, and a hostel (The Barn), with 14 beds (⌨ landmarktrust.org.uk/lundyisland).

As is normal for Landmark Trust accommodation, only essential electrical equipment is provided; this doesn't include radios, TVs, washing machines or dishwashers. There is no Wi-Fi for visitors and mobile phone signals are erratic.

Some of the properties have open fires, but many rely on electric storage heaters, so take as much warm clothing as your luggage allowance will permit. Even in summer it can be surprisingly cold. The island has

"Staying there is a peaceful delight that few will want to leave."

its own electricity supply, which is usually turned off between about midnight and six in the morning, so bring a torch, and also a simple first-aid kit. A radio, your favourite board games (although there are plenty available on the island), cards or books will help fill happy hours when it's too wet to walk. If this all sounds a bit austere, it isn't. Each property has its own mini library, often with a theme relating to its location, as well as scrapbooks and memorabilia. Staying there is a peaceful delight that few will want to leave. When we were forced to stay for an extra day because of bad weather, we were thrilled!

There is no need to bring any food supplies as the village shop stocks everything you might need, and when booking you can put in an advance order for specific food items.

There is even a *Lundy Cook Book* written by a frequent visitor using everything that is available in the shop.

---

1 From the top of the Old Lighthouse, the highest point on the island, you can see all of Lundy and as far as Wales. **2** Lundy cabbage – unique to the island. **3** The island's ruins hint at its history of piracy and skulduggery. ▶

GETTING AROUND LUNDY

Cars, apart from the Land Rovers used by staff, are not permitted on the island, nor can visitors bring bicycles. Canoes can be carried on the hold deck by prior arrangement. Visitors with mobility problems can hire one of the island's Trampers; do this in advance through the Shore Office (page 101). From the jetty in the sheltered easterly harbour it is a 350ft climb to the village, but you can ask for a lift in the Land Rover.

Basically Lundy is for walkers. The knowledge that the island is only three miles long should not deter keen hikers. With the rough up-and-down terrain you will feel well exercised at the end of the day, and can easily devise a walk of seven miles or so if you go to the north end.

WHAT TO TAKE

If you are on a day visit you need to make best use of the time available, so plan ahead.

Expect inclement weather and wear or carry a rain jacket and trousers; wear boots or stout shoes for walking across open ground that is often muddy; and bring a walking pole if you use one. Seasickness pills are useful for the sea journey.

You will need binoculars: some are available for hire in the shop.

A guidebook of Lundy, available in the shore offices and on board the *Oldenburg*, helps focus your attention on interesting aspects of the island, but below are some suggestions. A free map is also available at the shore office and on board, and there's a small informative display in a building near the jetty.

MAKING THE MOST OF A DAY TRIP

Some of Lundy's most important and interesting sights are on the lower southern half, so are easy to visit on a day trip – especially from Bideford, when you have longer on the island. Take a packed lunch and/or tuck in to *Oldenburg* snacks on the outward journey; the (Marisco) Tavern (page 115) can get quite busy on sailing days so it's better to postpone a visit there until after your walks, making sure you still allow yourself 30 minutes to get to the jetty in time for boarding.

Highlights include the cemetery, which contains four early Christian memorial stones dated between the 5th and 7th centuries, and the Old Lighthouse (Old Light), a disused lighthouse constructed at the highest point on the island in 1819. You can climb to the very top to enjoy wide panoramic views over the whole island and further. The castle overlooking the landing bay is also one of the island's most significant buildings, with its hidden Benson's Cave (page 110) underneath.

If you are visiting between April and July you will want to look for puffins at their nest site above Jenny's Cove. Other highlights are VC Quarry, just beyond Quarter Wall, and the North Light, which you'll have time to walk to if you're taking the later sailing to Bideford or staying overnight on the island.

Note that there is no signage for sights on Lundy; you must seek out the various places for yourself.

🚶 A FLOWER & WILDLIFE WALK

This walk allows you to enjoy the path along the sheltered east coast, where primroses, violets and foxgloves bloom in the spring and you are (mostly) out of the wind, and takes you to see puffins before heading to the Tavern for a final drink en route to boarding the *Oldenburg*. It will take roughly three hours, depending how long you spend puffin watching.

From the jetty, walk up the track, taking the right-hand path up past Milcombe House that is sign-posted 'Village'. Beyond the house a flight of stone steps takes you up to the village; about two-thirds of the way up these steps, look for a wooden seat and a grassy path leading off to the right. This brings you close to the cliffs, with lovely views and splashes of colour from the flowers. After 20 minutes or so you'll pass a towering rock face and the remains of one of the Victorian quarries, filled with water. This was stocked with golden orfe fish by Mr Harman and they still inhabit it today. Continue to VC Quarry and the memorial to John Harman VC (see box, page 111). The inscription is hard to read but there is a rubbing of it in the Tavern.

A LOOK AT LUNDY'S COLOURFUL HISTORY

Siân Scott, Assistant Warden and Education Officer

This walk encompasses some fascinating aspects of Lundy's colourful past.

Heading out of the village on the central path you soon come to Quarter Wall, and as you go through the gate take note of the foundations on the left of the Quarry cottages. Before tourism, the commercial possibilities of the island were few, but in the 1860s the Heaven family exploited the one resource that was readily available: granite. The Lundy Granite Company was active for only five years, between 1863 and 1868, because, like many things on this isolated island, the venture didn't exactly run smoothly. The remnants of their industry abound in this area.

From the foundations of the workers' cottages (the granite of which, when they were demolished, was used in the construction of St Helen's Church) you can see the large ruin of the Quarry Headquarters on your right, and a little further in the distance the remains of the Quarry Hospital. The Granite Company employed over 200 workers, compared with the current island population of just 28. The nature of their work was very challenging and dangerous, so it was necessary to have a medical centre. The company surgeon, Dr Linacre, admitted that he had come to Lundy 'to overcome a craving for drink – unsuccessfully', and many of the hard-working, rough-living labourers also turned to drink and caused much devastation to the farmland, finding their free time on this isolated rock weighing heavily on their hands. Accordingly, in 1864 the Bideford County Judge described Lundy as 'a refuge for the destitute... and the fag ends of society'. The company had reportedly been given the contract to supply the Thames Embankment with Lundy granite, but through their incompetence an inferior sample was sent, and the contract cancelled. The difficulty of getting the granite off the island, which resulted in several fully laden barges sinking, combined with the idle and destructive nature of the labourers, forced the company into liquidation by 1868. The four Victorian Quarries are now some of the best preserved in the UK thanks to the remote nature of the island. In summer, look out for the carnivorous sundew plant

Soon after VC Quarry there is a path, left, up to the main track where you turn right and walk north towards Halfway Wall. Just after a dip in the track and before the wall, keep your eyes peeled for a little path to the left that takes you to the remains of a German bomber (see box, below). Retrace your steps to the wall, through the gate, and follow the wall to the west side of the island. You are heading for Jenny's Cove and the puffins. On reaching the west coast path, cross the wall again via the stile and look for a jumble of rocks overlooking the sea.

that thrives in the boggy ground of the most northerly quarry.

Back on the central path, just before Halfway Wall there is a small grassy path on your left taking you up to another site of Lundy history, this time from World War II. In a small clearing are what remains of a German Heinkel III bomber, which crash-landed on the island in 1941. The plane was seen flying low and spewing out smoke, but the six German airmen managed to get out and set fire to their own fuselage, burning the secrets on board. They then surrendered to the first person that they encountered, who happened to be the North Lighthouse keeper, on his way back to his station after a heavy session at the Tavern. He fled from the soldiers in a drunken fluster, and radioed Admiral Franklin's HQ in Appledore in a panic, shouting over the radio that 'Hitler has arrived!' Meanwhile, the eight-year-old daughter of the legendary island agent Mr Felix Gade (to whom the Quarry Time-Keepers Hut is now dedicated) had witnessed the plane heading towards Halfway Wall, and raised the alarm with her father. They went to meet the airmen and,

with typical Lundy hospitality, escorted them to the Old Lighthouse for tea and cake before putting them on the next boat back to the mainland. On the walk to the lighthouse one of the airmen offered little Mary some chocolate but, aware of her parents' warning about accepting treats from the enemy, she refused. She remembers that he then threw it to the sheepdog and she was terrified that her pet would die. One of the airmen paid a return visit to Lundy 50 years later and made lifelong friends with some of the islanders. Mary passed away in 2018, just a few days before her 85th birthday, and she joins the list of Lundy legends, having come to the island at just 18 days old and spending most of her adult life living and working in the community.

Back on the main path, go through the Halfway Wall gate and then follow the old dry-stone wall west to the Atlantic Coast. Cross back over the wall and you are above Jenny's Cove, where the puffins nest on one cliff. Follow the meandering west coast path back towards the village, which will eventually take you to the Old Lighthouse (see box, page 108) and back to the village.

FOR THOSE IN PERIL ON THE SEA

Siân Scott, Assistant Warden and Education Officer

Built in 1819, the Old Lighthouse (or Old Light) stands proud on Beacon Hill, the highest point on the island. Normally you would think the highest point would be a good place to put a lighthouse, but unfortunately this was the downfall of the first one on Lundy. The island microclimate is dominated by fog that lies heavily on the plateau, but unusually the fog rarely seeps down the sidelands. Being at the highest point, the Old Lighthouse was always the first to disappear in the notorious fog, and so it was rendered useless for much of the time. The tower itself is a feat of engineering: a cavity construction with double granite walls three inches apart, and the entire structure magnificently built of Lundy granite. Trinity House (the authority in charge of shipping safety) was proud of the achievement and so was reluctant to give up on the lighthouse. It made several 'adjustments' but still received complaints from shipping, and in 1861 it went to a new extreme, building a fog signalling station (otherwise known as The Battery) to supplement the lighthouse in fog.

The Battery is a fascinating listed building, which you first glimpse clinging to the bottom of the western cliffs as you approach Quarter Wall on your way back from Jenny's Cove. At the end of the winding path you reach the remains of the building with the chimney still intact, and going further down you come to two 18lb cannons sitting on the edge, facing the endless Atlantic. The cannons were cast in 1810 and bear the cipher of King George IV. In thick fog, when the light from the lighthouse was obscured, the Battery keepers would fire the cannons to warn of danger; they fired every ten minutes as this is how long it took to reload the gunpowder – the longest they had to fire continuously for was 72 hours straight. They were replaced by signal rockets in 1878, and the Battery was abandoned in 1897.

It was a challenging and harsh life for the lighthouse and Battery keepers, who had to contend with isolation, hostile weather conditions and scarcity of food and water. The two couples that lived and worked at the Battery had been instructed by Trinity House not to have children, due to the difficult and dangerous conditions of the work. However, left to their own devices on the island, the Battery became home to nine children. Whenever inspectors from Trinity House visited the island (presumably by yacht) the lighthouse keepers would send up a flare, and Trinity House always believed it was because the islanders must be pleased to see them. The flare was actually to warn the Battery keepers of their employers' arrival, and the children would be sent to hide in crevices over the cliff edge. When it was time for their departure, another flare would be sent up, and while the folk from Trinity House would wave and feel sorry for the workers left on a lonely isle, the children could finally come running out of their hiding places and have the island to themselves again.

This is your puffin-viewing platform; the landmark is Needle Rock, which looks like a hand emerging from the sea with a finger pointing up to the sky. Settle down on the rocks with your binoculars and scan the lower part of the cliff ahead for those telltale orange feet. You won't get close to any puffins, but it's still a thrill to see Lundy's iconic bird, along with guillemots and razorbills, which from a distance look very similar to puffins.

Keep an eye on the time. You should allow an hour from here to the jetty, and will probably want to pause at the Tavern for some refreshment before you head for the boat.

A WALK THROUGH LUNDY'S PAST

Simon Dell

I devised this circular walk on the southern half of the island to keep within the limited time available for day trippers and to take in the most interesting historical sights. This three-mile walk is easy, but with some optional steep descents/climbs.

MS *Oldenburg* moors up to the jetty, which was constructed between 1998 and 1999. At the top of the jetty is the former Christie's Quay, which was built in the early 1920s as a small sheltered harbour tucked beneath the South Lighthouse.

The landing place is marked by the 'TH Landing Place' stone, which commemorates the construction of the original lighthouse on Lundy in 1819. This area of the landing beach has been renovated over the past few years with a new slipway constructed over the top of the old one.

At 'Windy Corner' the road bears left and inland under the oak trees where you have a fine view of the white Millcombe House, built by William Heaven after he purchased the island in 1836.

Most visitors head towards the village, taking the short cut past Millcombe House, but for this walk ignore this path and, at the gates to Milcombe House, bear left and under the trees up the vehicle track and around the low-walled battlements with fine views to be had over the landing place. Continue up the vehicle track passing Brambles bungalow on your right until you reach the track junction on the left that takes you south to the castle. Through the iron gate you can see the three Landmark Trust cottages that huddle within the castle walls.

The castle was built in 1244 by Henry III after the downfall of the piratical Mariscos who leased the island. You can go left around the castle on to the parade ground, with fine views of the South Lighthouse, and Hartland Point on the North Devon coast.

From the parade ground walk back up to the left of the castle, over the wall and find the footpath that leads down to Benson's Cave below. Walk down towards the South Lighthouse with the cliff on your right, descend a few steps, and you'll see the cave entrance. The cave goes under the parade ground and castle, and is named after the notorious Thomas Benson (see box, page 112) who brought convicts to Lundy to work for him on the island; some left their initials carved in the cave walls on the left.

After leaving the cave, go back up to the castle while looking out along the coastline to the west and left. You will see what looks like a wooden telegraph pole high on the cliff in the distance. Head for this along the grassy pathway, following the cliffs to a stile, which you cross; in a few yards look to your left and over the cliff to Benjamin's Chair, a ledge where the Heaven family used to enjoy picnics in the 19th century.

"After ten yards turn right into the long grass to find the deep pit of an ancient Bronze Age burial chamber."

Keep a stone wall on your right until it turns north towards the Old Lighthouse. Continue walking towards the wooden pole and after ten yards turn right into the long grass to find the deep pit of an ancient Bronze Age burial chamber.

Carry on to the Rocket Pole, which was used as a ship's mast for attaching breeches-buoy equipment when practising rescue techniques in the 19th century.

Walk uphill and slightly right to the large Rocket Pole Pond, which is a flooded quarry. The stone here was removed to build the new South Lighthouse in 1896. You can usually find ducks on the pond.

Continue to the southwest corner of the island to a rocky promontory with fine views over the coast and Shutter Rock, looking like a pyramid below, where seals are often spotted, along with a multitude of seabirds.

Just below you to the south is the Devil's Limekiln – a natural feature of a huge hole in the clifftop where the end of a sea cave collapsed. The Old Lighthouse can be seen ahead as you follow the coastal footpath with the sea on your left. After a small valley with an animal-drinking reservoir on the cliff edge, its sloped ramps allowing livestock access to the water, you'll continue to the lighthouse but just before entering the

JOHN PENNINGTON HARMAN VC

At the site called VC Quarry on Lundy is a memorial to John Pennington Harman who was posthumously awarded the Victoria Cross for outstanding bravery in Burma in 1944. During the siege of Kohima, about 500 men stopped the advance of 15,000 Japanese into India for 15 days until the British Second Division could fight their way through to relieve them.

There have been fewer than 1,400 recipients of the Victoria Cross since its inception in 1856 so John Harman has a special place in history.

The quarry was chosen for the memorial as it was John's favourite place to play as a boy.

Diana Keast, John's sister, recalls that he was a keen beekeeper, and kept bees on Lundy. There is a rural superstition that if the owner of a hive of bees dies and the bees are not told, they will pine away or desert the hive. The news of John's death was delayed by two weeks, but his father immediately sent word to the resident agent and asked him to tell the bees. Felix Gade went to the hive and found that all the bees had vanished.

enclosure turn right briefly and pay a visit through the five-bar gate to the cemetery. Here you will find graves from the 19th and 20th centuries as well as four standing stones erected beside the wall. These are early Christian, dated between the 5th and 7th century, but information about them is largely speculative.

From the cemetery continue to the lighthouse. You can go into the building; turn left and ascend the stairs to the very top for magnificent views across the whole island and, on a clear day, as far as Wales to the north. There are two deck-chairs here if you have time to relax.

The lighthouse was in use until 1896 when the new North and South Lighthouses were built to replace the Old Light, which never did its job effectively, being over 500ft above sea level so often obscured by fog (see box, page 108).

Once you have explored the lighthouse go around to the far side of the building and over a stile in the back wall. This leads you out on to Ackland's Moor, and to the east side of the island by cutting diagonally across over the airstrip. The runway is marked by white painted boulders. Head to the far end of the airstrip and to the main vehicle track at Quarter Wall gate.

If you want to return to the village, turn right and south along the track to the Tavern. To continue with the walk, pass through the gate where Lundy ponies often congregate. You will see the big boulders marking the way of the track for lighthouse keepers in the fog. Over to

THOMAS BENSON

This Bideford-born merchant trader's story is one of power and corruption. He inherited the family fortune in 1743 at the age of 37, and built up a fleet of ships that traded with the American colonies of Virginia and Maryland, as well as sending fishing vessels to the Newfoundland cod banks. Deciding that a place in parliament would be beneficial, he presented the Corporation of Barnstaple with a magnificent silver punch bowl and was duly elected as their MP in 1747.

In 1748 Benson became a tenant of Lundy, under lease from its owner at the time, Lord Gower. One of his contracts was for the transportation of convicts but, instead of shipping them to America, he brought them to Lundy where they worked as his unpaid servants, assisting in the smuggling of tobacco. At night they were shut up in the cave that now bears his name. To keep them docile he set them to work on building the dry-stone walls that now divide up the island.

Benson's smuggling activities were eventually discovered and he was heavily fined. J L W Page takes up the story: 'Benson went rapidly from bad to worse. Among other little villainies he insured a vessel's cargo and then caused her to be put back to Lundy where he stored the cargo – probably in the very cave that bears his name – and then had the ship scuttled and claimed the insurance money.' When his accomplices were caught he fled to Portugal and his connections with Lundy ended.

the right and eastwards towards the coast are the ruins of some cottages, once the homes of the quarry manager and doctor (see box, page 106). After visiting the ruins head north along the pathway to the quarries, and then uphill and north to the Time Keeper's Hut, which has a small round memorial to Felix Gade who lived on Lundy for over 50 years as agent.

Pass the hut and go downhill along the tramway past the willow trees to VC Quarry with its memorial to John Harman (see box, page 111). A visit to the next quarry will then lead you up around a left-hand bend in the track and on to the main track that runs the length of the island. Turn left, south, back to the village about 25 minutes away. The first building you come to on the right is the shop and on the left is a small detached hut that houses the island interpretation centre and museum.

Once in the village there is plenty to see, including the church, south of the village, built in 1896 and dedicated to St Helen. It has three fine high-relief alabaster carvings by the altar, depicting the Passover, the Last Supper, and the Scapegoat in the Wilderness.

It takes about 25 minutes to stroll down to the jetty from The Marisco Tavern; the quickest and most direct route is to come out of the Tavern and turn right down to the kissing gate by the toilets. Carry on downhill over the grass through another gate, and follow the path down past Millcombe House and out down the driveway to re-join the track that you came up on arrival.

🚶 EXPLORING THE NORTH

Simon Dell

This walk is for visitors staying on the island. Starting at the Old Light, it is a fairly easy six miles, but with some steep climbs and descents.

Head north from the Old Light, keeping to the coastal path. As you start to drop into a small valley, look out for a pile of stones beside the path in the bottom of the dip. This marks the point where you turn towards the sea and walk a few yards to find a path beside a wall, which takes you steeply down to the Battery (see box, page 108), a diversion of about an hour.

Once you have visited the Battery continue northwards over a stile to Halfway Wall, with the big granite formations known as the Cheeses on your left. Before you cross the wall look back at the coast and south to the cliffs where Needle Rock sticks out of the sea (page 109). Here, during the breeding season, you can look for puffins on the cliffs to the south above Jenny's Cove, which is named after an African trading ship, bound for Bristol, that went aground in the 18th century with a cargo of ivory and gold dust.

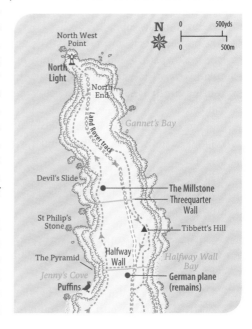

When you have finished your puffin watching, cross Halfway Wall and continue to Threequarter Wall and over the stile. Continue towards the sea, find

GIANTS' GRAVES

In 1851, some farm workers discovered two huge granite coffins, one of them 10ft long and the other eight. When these were opened they were found to contain two skeletons. The larger one had its head resting on a 'pillow' of granite, and both graves were covered with limpet shells. In or beside the coffins were some blue stone beads and fragments of pottery.

J L W Page takes up the story: 'Mr Heaven was sent for, and the skeletons carefully measured. The larger had a stature of 8ft 2in. Mr Heaven was present the whole time, and not only saw the measurement taken, but, as he himself told me, saw one of the men place the shin bone of the skeleton against his own, when it reached from his foot half way up his thigh, while the giant's jawbone covered not only his chin but beard as well ... Mr Heaven exclaimed, when he saw the larger skeleton, "The bones of Hubba the Dane!"'

The bones were reburied and have never been found again, so the age of the skeletons – and indeed their size (the second, probably female, was of normal height) – has never been ascertained. Medieval seems to be the favoured period.

somewhere to sit and look south towards the cliffs by St Philip's Stone, the triangular rock that you can see in the distance. It's cut off by the sea at high tide. There are, unsurprisingly, more puffin nests in this area in the breeding season.

Continue north for about 200yds and you'll pass the millstone in the grassy path. A number of granite millstones were produced on the island's west side; this one is actually incomplete and was abandoned during construction. You get a better view of it once you have passed it and are looking back over your shoulder southwards.

Look out for the Devil's Slide ahead of you. It is the longest single slab of granite in the country and popular with climbers.

From here it is not far to the north end of the island: you can see the Land Rover track winding its way there. Depending upon how tired you feel, you can either stay on the west coast path or simply head towards the main track.

At the far end of the Land Rover track there is a turnabout for vehicles. From here the footpath continues north to the metal bridge and steps which lead down to the North Light, built in 1896 to replace the Old Light.

When you get down to the lighthouse you will find a tramway, constructed to transport heavy equipment and goods from the loading crane to the lighthouse. Turn right along this tramway and, just before you reach a concrete platform at the end, look to your left: you will find the steps that lead down to the water's edge where the lighthouse keepers used to be landed by boat. There are usually seals around this landing place but be warned: it is quite a steep climb down and up again.

When you rejoin the Land Rover track you'll follow it south, all the way back to the village: a walk of about 1½ hours.

FOOD & DRINK

The Marisco Tavern 01237 431831. More than just a pub, the Tavern provides a restaurant and social centre for island staff and staying guests, as well as catering to the large numbers of day-trippers arriving on the *Oldenburg* or visiting ships. It also doubles as the island library; evening talks take place here in the Wheel House room (look out for talks by Siân Scott whose contributions have enlivened this chapter) and there are plenty of games available. The Tavern offers a comprehensive range of quality food at prices that even on the mainland would be considered competitive. The chef uses mostly the island's own produce: their own selectively bred lamb and rare-breed pigs, plus the wild sika deer, Soay sheep, goats and rabbits.

Breakfast (which includes their own pork sausages), lunch and dinner are served every day. Lundy lamb is always on the menu, as are homemade burgers and pasties. Evening meal options include a separate blackboard of vegetarian specialities and a few vegan options, as well as a selection of desserts.

Tables cannot be booked in advance; they operate on a first come, first served basis.

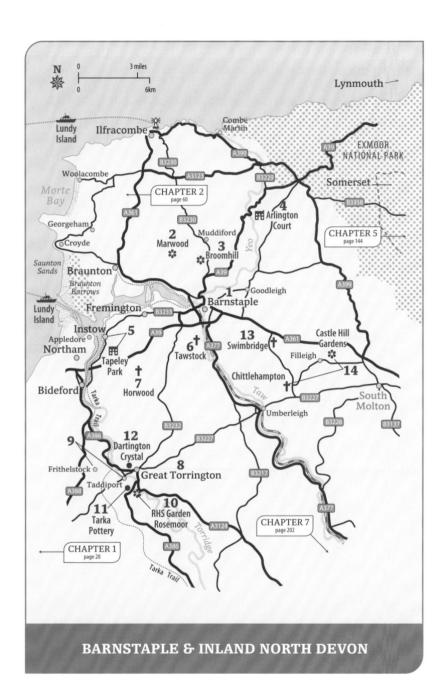

N

0 ____ 3 miles

0 ____ 6km

Lynmouth →

Lundy Island

Ilfracombe

Combe Martin

B3230

A399

EXMOOR NATIONAL PARK

Woolacombe

A3123

B3229

Somerset

Morte Bay

CHAPTER 2
page 60

B3230

A361

B3358

Georgeham

B3230

Muddiford

4
Arlington Court

CHAPTER 5
page 144

2
Marwood

3
Broomhill

Croyde

Yeo

Saunton Sands

Braunton

A39

A399

Braunton Burrows

1
Goodleigh

Lundy Island

Barnstaple

Fremington

B3233

Appledore

5

A39

13
Swimbridge

A361

Castle Hill Gardens

Instow

Northam

6
Tawstock

A377

Filleigh

14

Tapeley Park

Chittlehampton

Bideford

7
Horwood

Taw

B3227

South Molton

Umberleigh

B3226

B3137

9

A386

12
Dartington Crystal

B3232

B3227

Frithelstock

8
Great Torrington

B3217

A388

Taddiport

A377

11
Tarka Pottery

10
RHS Garden Rosemoor

A3124

CHAPTER 7
page 202

A386

Torridge

CHAPTER 1
page 28

Tarka Trail

BARNSTAPLE & INLAND NORTH DEVON

4

BARNSTAPLE &
INLAND NORTH DEVON

> I crossed the river Tau and found another sort of face of the country,
> the red soil with the red sandstone, and all of the country full of rising
> ground, and small hills beautifully improved.
>
> Richard Pococke, *Travels through England*, 1750

This region shows the marketing power of a popular book. Henry Williamson was one of the finest nature writers ever. His love for North Devon stemmed from a childhood holiday and shines through his subsequent writing. Utterly out of his environment as a soldier in World War I he wrote vividly of life in the trenches (*A Chronicle of Ancient Sunlight*). In the latter part of his life he became embittered and succumbed to extreme right-wing views, but that doesn't diminish the importance of his most famous work, *Tarka the Otter* (1927), written in Georgeham (page 67) where he lived for eight years and is buried. His otter ranged widely over the rivers of North Devon, hence the Tarka label attached to the oblong of countryside stretching from the north coast's sandy shores to the edge of Dartmoor.

The selected attractions here are scattered over a wide region: some of the loveliest gardens in the county and a handful of exceptional churches. More peaceful than the busy seaside resorts, it's a good area to base yourself during the crowded holiday season.

 WET-WEATHER ACTIVITIES

Arlington Court Nr Barnstaple (page 125)
Barnstaple Museum (page 120)
Dartington Crystal Great Torrington (page 138)
Plough Arts Centre Great Torrington (page 135)
Queen's Theatre Barnstaple (page 120)
Tawstock church (page 131)
Torrington Museum (page 135)

GETTING THERE & AROUND

Barnstaple, as the main town in North Devon, has excellent road links with Tiverton, Exeter and Plymouth, as well as Cornwall. However, the rail link between Exeter and Barnstaple, the **Tarka Line**, is so scenic, and the bicycle hire shop in the station so conveniently placed, that a combination of train and bike is an obvious alternative to the car for exploring the region. The local bus service isn't bad either, with routes fanning out from Barnstaple and covering almost all the areas in the North Devon chapters. All transport information, including self-powered travel, can be found on the very useful website ∅ traveldevon.info.

THE TARKA LINE

This branch railway from Exeter to Barnstaple is one of the most scenic in the county. It runs for 39 miles from the River Exe to the Taw estuary, following much of the river and countryside that featured in *Tarka the Otter*. The leisurely journey takes an hour. Bicycles are carried free, but are normally limited to two. For more about the Tarka Line, see *Chapter 7* (pages 205 and 211).

SELF-POWERED TRAVEL

The area hosts the West Country's most famous cycle path, the **Tarka Trail**, but there are also quiet, fairly level country lanes to explore so the bicycle remains an effective way of getting around.

The Tarka Trail

A scenic 32-mile, traffic-free section of this 180-mile recreational trail runs along a disused railway line from Braunton to Meeth. Families who pedal happily in the sunshine have reason to bless Dr Beeching who closed this unprofitable branch line in 1965. Freight trains continued to use it until 1982 and the line was purchased in 1985 by Devon County Council. It must carry far more cycles on this nearly level route than ever it did rail passengers, and deserves its popularity.

Probably the most popular section for cyclists is Barnstaple to Instow and back or, for the more energetic, to Great Torrington (14 miles), but some bike hire companies may collect you and your bike from your end point, thus allowing you to ride a longer distance. While walkers may feel overwhelmed by the number of cyclists on this section of the Tarka Trail, you are likely to be alone on the loop north of Barnstaple.

The South West Coast Path and the Tarka Trail hug the coast all the way to Lynmouth. From here, the South West Coast Path heads east towards Somerset while the Tarka Trail turns south across Exmoor before turning west to complete the loop back to Barnstaple. There is also the option of the 310 bus from Lynmouth back to Barnstaple.

OS Explorer maps 139 and OL9 cover the whole of the Tarka Trail's northern loop and there is more information on the Tarka Trail website ($\mathscr{\oslash}$ tarkatrail.org.uk/the-tarka-trail).

CYCLE HIRE

The following companies are organised geographically, north to south.

Otter Cycle Hire Braunton (page 67).

Bideford Bicycle & Kayak Hire Torrington St, East-the-Water EX39 4DR $\mathscr{\mathcal{O}}$ 01237 424123 $\mathscr{\oslash}$ bidefordbicyclehire.co.uk $\odot$ 09.00–17.00 Mon–Fri. Has a wide variety of bicycles, also trailers for small children.

Tarka Trail Cycle Hire Railway station, Barnstaple EX34 8DL $\mathscr{\mathcal{O}}$ 01271 324202 $\mathscr{\oslash}$ tarkabikes.co.uk $\odot$ Mar–Nov 09.15–17.00 daily; check website for winter months. As well as a wide range of bicycles, including e-bikes, they have a trikidoo, a tricycle incorporating a child seat (takes two small children).

Biketrail The Stone Barn, Fremington Quay, nr Barnstaple EX31 2NH $\mathscr{\mathcal{O}}$ 01271 372586 $\mathscr{\oslash}$ biketrail.co.uk $\odot$ 10.00–16.00 daily; check website for peak months and out of season. Huge selection. Will pick up bikes by arrangement if you want to do a linear route.

Torrington Cycle Hire Station Yard, Torrington (behind the Puffing Billy pub) EX38 8JD $\mathscr{\mathcal{O}}$ 01805 622633 $\mathscr{\oslash}$ torringtoncyclehire.com $\odot$ 09.30–17.00 daily; check website for peak months and out of season.

1 BARNSTAPLE

Anderton House Goodleigh (page 248)

Tourist information: North Devon Museum, The Square, EX32 8LN (unmanned) $\mathscr{\mathcal{O}}$ 01271 346747

Historically, Barnstaple has always been compared with Bideford, the fortunes of one rising as the other waned. It, too, has a bridge over the Taw, which has had an even more exciting history than its rival since it was begun, so they say, by two spinster sisters who spun the first two piers with the help of local children. John Leland called it a 'right great and sumptuous Bridge of Stone having 16 high Arches'.

The river silted up in the 19th century and maritime trade switched to Bideford. However, Barnstaple prospered as a market town; it's now the largest town in North Devon and the only one to have a railway connection with the rest of the county. And it is that railway that brings visitors to Barnstaple, and allows them to escape, for the megastored area around the station initially discourages further exploration.

Once you've crossed the bridge the town centre turns out to be agreeably compact with a pedestrianised town square, a daily market and a very good **museum**, which also houses the (unmanned) TIC. The museum has the usual collections of local history and Devon life in addition to some boldly decorated Barum Ware from the Brannam pottery, and Arts and Crafts furniture made by Shapland & Petter in Barnstaple. There is also an exceptionally interesting natural history section. I was particularly intrigued by the fossilised fragments of a straight-tusked elephant, found in 1844. It stood 12ft high and lived around 150,000 years ago when Devon, Britain and its whole vast continent lay close to the equator. The museum has a lovely old tea room (☉ 10.30–16.00 Tue–Sat) and is easy to find, near the Albert Clock.

Not far from the museum, off The Strand, is the little pedestrianised **Maiden Street**, so named, ironically, because it used to be lined with brothels. On Bear Street, accessed from the large carpark, is the impressive **North Devon Home Brews** (✆ 01271 374123 ⌨ brewingathome.co.uk), with a huge range of brewing supplies for home beer- and wine-makers.

At the indoor **pannier market**, off the High Street (☉ Tue–Sat), you can buy everything, including a good variety of local produce. A Real Food Market is held here, too, on the second Sunday of each month. It's changed a bit since being described fondly by S P B Mais: 'Here sit old wives from the country behind stalls covered with trussed chicken, bowls of cream, fruit and vegetables, while their husbands sell calves and pigs in the open market across the way'. Local crafts are sold on Mondays and Thursdays and antiques on Wednesdays. The pannier market also stages a one-day North Devon **FOODfest** in October.

The **Queen's Theatre** (100 Boutport St ✆ 01271 324242) hosts touring companies year-round.

1 Barnstaple's waterfront on the River Taw. 2 The pannier market, Barnstaple. ▶

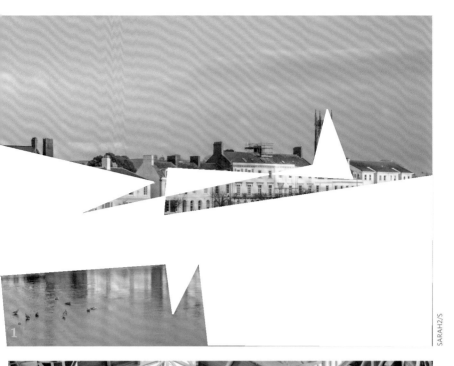

THE PRIOR'S RING

Claire Barker

Imagine for a moment that it's 1535 and the Reformation is in full swing. Henry VIII is on the throne and Thomas Cromwell has arranged for inspections of all the smaller religious houses around the kingdom. Much plundering and punishment lies ahead.

Now, imagine you are the Pilton Prior who has received word that Cromwell's cronies are coming to find you and your hoard of treasure. This is very bad news – but then you have a bright idea: maybe you could hide something quickly? What about the gold ring that's your mark of office? You slip it from your plump finger and roll it in a ball of clay, then bury it in the priory garden, planting a sapling over the top to be pulled up when everything settles down. You have outwitted the dastardly Thomas Cromwell. You are cleverer than a box of foxes.

But the prior never did return for his treasure. Instead the sapling steadily grew, guarding its secret beneath the earth for 334 years until, in 1867, it finally crashed to the ground. On inspection, the new owner of the garden – Doctor Forrester – discovered a mysterious clay ball in its root system. Forrester cracked it open and thus the light of day shone on the ring once more.

He took it to the British Museum and they declared his find to be a medieval ecclesiastical gold ring dating back to the 1100s. Set with a cabochon sapphire, it was surrounded with a bezel, engraved with a Hebrew inscription translated as 'May Jesu Emmanuel Jehova be with us', and on the reverse, in Latin 'Lord Jesus be with us'.

Perhaps unsurprisingly, Dr Forrester held on to his tree booty. Eventually, however, in 1979, his descendants handed the ring over to Barnstaple Athaeneum for safe keeping. This act of civic grace means that today the ring is on display in the Barnstaple Guildhall. You will find it in a dark corner of the very dark Dodderidge room; check ⬧ barnstapletowncouncil.gov.uk/heritage-and-culture/the-guildhall-barnstaple or call 01271 373311 for when the room is open. But perhaps it's only fitting that it should tuck itself away from the light, even after all these centuries.

🍴 FOOD & DRINK

Claytons & The Glasshouse 2 Cross St 🕿 01271 323311 ⬧ claytonsbarnstaple.co.uk ⊙ noon–22.00 or later Mon–Sat, 10.00–18.00 Sun. A classy, modern place offering exceptional food for that special night out. Upstairs there's seating under the sun or stars (and under glass) while there is also an open-air terrace for warm evenings.

Everest Gurkha Chef 3 Maiden St 🕿 01271 376863 ⬧ everestgurkhachef.co.uk ⊙ Mon–Sat 17.30–22.00. And now for something completely different. This tiny, unlicensed, eat-in or take-away restaurant is just what it says: run by Som, a Nepalese Gurkha who learned to cook in his home country and brought his family and his skills to Barnstaple.

The New Inn Goodleigh EX32 7LX ☏ 01271 342488 ⌖ newinngoodleigh.co.uk. The village is a few miles east of Barnstaple and the inn is in a typically rural setting, near the church and with a beer garden. The menu is traditional, the portions large, and the welcome warm. Very popular so book ahead.

NORTH OF BARNSTAPLE

The small pocket of countryside between Barnstaple and Ilfracombe has two exceptional gardens, close to each other, and a trout farm, as well as Arlington Court, run by the National Trust, and home to a famous carriage collection.

2 MARWOOD HILL GARDENS & CHURCH

Marwood, nr Barnstaple EX31 4EB ☏ 01271 342528 ⌖ marwoodhillgarden.co.uk
☉ Mar–Sep 10.00–16.30 Wed–Sun

On a hillside, stretching down to the valley below, is this delightful garden, with a fresh surprise around every corner. It was the loving creation of a retired GP, Jimmy Smart, who wanted somewhere hidden where his former patients wouldn't find him. He succeeded. Although only four miles from Barnstaple this little hamlet feels untouched by time. Dr Smart started with nothing but 20 acres of overgrown Devon and three lakes, but his enthusiasm and vision created perhaps my favourite North Devon garden which, with its adjacent church, is not to be missed. Late spring is the best time to see the 600 camellias, as well as azaleas and rhododendrons in every conceivable colour, but any time of year is rewarding. I was last there in August, when the hydrangeas were a mass of deep blues. Winding paths meander through flowering shrubs to emerge on sunlit lawns dotted with sculptures including Dr Smart, in rumpled gardening clothes, gazing proudly over his creation. A bog garden provides added interest and variety as do the lakes. Dr Smart died in 2002; the gardens are now owned and maintained by his nephew, Dr John Snowdon. Outside the excellent **tea room** is a bird list – over 40 species have been recorded here.

It's quite a walk from the carpark so don't get discouraged – and there's a disabled drop-off place near the gate.

The **church of St Michael and All Angels** is only a short walk from the gardens and also rewarding. You are immediately struck by the carved bench ends depicting a variety of subjects, including the initials of pew owners. There are all sorts of grotesque faces and figures doing goodness knows what, as well as an easily recognisable bird and possibly a fox. The intricately carved screen also shows extraordinary detail, as does the equally detailed one in front of the organ. A wall plaque from 1828 records that the Reverend Richard Harding gave £100 – a significant amount of money in those days – 'to such poor labourers of this parish as have been exemplary in their good behaviour in life, and have been constant partakers of the blessed sacraments'. In the graveyard is the simple tombstone of James Smart, 'creator of Marwood Hill Gardens'.

3 BROOMHILL SCULPTURE GARDEN

♠ Broomhill Art Hotel Muddiford (page 248)
A few miles north of Barnstaple, off the B3230, EX31 4EX ✆ 01271 850262 ⬡ broomhill-estate.com ◷ 09.00–17.00 daily

The sculptures here would be impressive in a gallery setting, but here, chancing upon them as you wander down meandering paths in the woods or alongside the tree-shaded river, you feel that such a garden is the only setting in which to exhibit large sculptures. Not that they are all large. Sometimes you are alerted to their presence by the sign before you see the piece almost hidden in the shrubbery.

Broomhill happened because Rinus and Aniet van de Sande, from the Netherlands, started a gallery to encourage young artists in their home country, but they wanted an outdoor venue. Holland was not an option 'because so many galleries and sculpture gardens already existed', so when they found a run-down hotel with a large, overgrown garden on the outskirts of Barnstaple, they knew it was the right place. Broomhill's ten acres are now a mixture of formal garden and natural woodland, and even without the sculptures the steeply terraced and wooded grounds would be a pleasure to stroll in. The combination of the two is stunning and a must-see for anyone with an interest in art. Or in Slow Food, for its award-winning restaurant is exceptional, focusing mainly on Mediterranean cooking (page 126).

BLAKEWELL TROUT FARM

EX31 4ET, just south of Broomhill ✆ 01271 344533 ⬡ blakewell.co.uk ◷ 09.00–17.00

There's everything trouty here. You can do some fly fishing and children can catch their own fish, or they can feed the fish. Or buy fish to feed yourselves. A café serves good cream teas and you can buy fresh or smoked trout to take home.

4 ARLINGTON COURT

EX31 4LP ✆ 01271 850296 ⊙ Mar–Nov, 10.00–16.00; National Trust

The Chichester family owned the estate from 1384 until 1949 when Miss Rosalie Chichester bequeathed it to the National Trust. She was the only child of Sir Bruce Chichester, who used to take her on long voyages around the Mediterranean on his schooner, *Erminia*. And, yes, Sir Francis Chichester, the round-the-world yachtsman, was a relative: Rosalie's nephew. Her interest in ships is evident throughout the house in the many exquisite models made from bone and spun glass. Some were made by French POWs (see box, page 126). On her foreign travels she collected shells and took an interest in tropical birds from South America – stuffed ones are on show in a glass case.

Completed in 1822, the house is described as neo-Greek, and was added to, rather clumsily, in 1865.

It is the collection of **carriages** in the old stables that is the focus of most visits. It's a bit of a walk there, but a buggy is available to transport those with mobility problems. This collection is the most comprehensive in the country, and is spread through several buildings. There's enough variety to retain interest, from the governess cart, which can be compared, in its utility design, to the Morris Minor of later years, to the state coaches. The 17th-century Speaker's Coach is a gorgeous extravaganza in gold, with paintings inset on its sides, looking to the uninformed eye just like the famed Coronation Coach. The museum acquired it in 2005 when it was the oldest working state coach in the world. It was made for William III, and its last outing was for the wedding of Prince Charles and Diana.

The display boards are informative, with some nice human stories such as the footmen who had to stand at the back of the state coach, bolt upright and immobile, even though they only had two straps to hold on to, and the stable boy who lived in a loft above the stables and had to be available at all times. And it wasn't only horses that pulled these vehicles: ponies, donkeys, goats and even a Newfoundland dog also did their bit to keep the population on the move.

Upstairs in one of the buildings is an exhibition commemorating the brief flirtation with steam-powered vehicles, which were expected to

'LET'S VISIT THOSE HANDSOME FRENCH PRISONERS!'

Beautifully crafted models of ships made by French prisoners of war (Napoleonic Wars) are a feature of many great houses and museums in Devon, including Arlington Court. One of the volunteers at Arlington told me that a popular outing during the early 19th century was a visit to see prisoners. Although Dartmoor is the place best known for housing French POWs, some were detained at Bideford.

It sounds as though security was fairly relaxed (they weren't convicts, after all) and the ladies of the time were intrigued to see if Frenchmen were indeed better looking than their English counterparts. And they could return home with a souvenir – a ship made with whatever materials the prisoners could find: mutton bones, human hair or threads drawn from their garments, straw and wooden shavings.

With the money from the sale of their model ships, they could buy some luxuries and also better tools and materials to make finer ships to sell for a higher price. The ships they made were based on actual British ones, but subtly 'Frenchified'.

replace the horse. They only lasted 50 years, however, having faced fierce opposition in the late 1700s from those who depended on horse-drawn vehicles, and finally lost out to the arrival of the railway in the mid 1800s.

Finally, don't miss the Tom Thumb exhibit, including his custom-made carriage and a life-sized model of this tiny man (40in high) who certainly made a good living by being a Barnum 'freak'.

Behind the house in a dripping cellar you'll find a batcam. Devon's largest population of lesser horseshoe bats spends its summers here in the roof space, and they hibernate in the cellar.

🍴 FOOD & DRINK

Besshill Farm Shop Arlington EX31 4SW ✆ 01271 850311 🖮 besshillfarmshop.co.uk ◷ 09.30–17.00 Mon–Sat. The Maher family sell their own free-range meat and a wide variety of fresh local vegetables, fruit and other produce.

Broomhill Dining EX31 4EX ✆ 01271 850262 🖮 broomhill-estate.com ◷ noon–15.00 & 18.00–21.00 Wed–Sat, noon–15.00 Sun. Broomhill was one of the earliest proponents of Slow Food, sourcing almost all their ingredients locally (a noticeboard tells you where) and from their own garden. The combination of top-quality food (which has won many awards) and wonderful art is hard to beat. See page 124.

The Pyne Arms East Down EX31 4LX ✆ 01271 850055 🖮 pynearms.co.uk. An award-winning pub close to Arlington Court. Very popular with locals who'll drive some distance to enjoy the warm atmosphere and excellent food. A map on the wall shows where the ingredients come from and the dishes are well presented and very tasty, with a menu varying from traditional pub fare to some more exotic recipes. Child and dog friendly.

SOUTH OF BARNSTAPLE

Between the rivers Taw and Torridge is Williamson country, with the Tarka Trail (page 118) and Tarka Line running close to each river respectively. The Tarka Trail and adjacent attractions dominate the region, but there are some delightful and isolated little churches, and the town of Great Torrington, with the famous Royal Horticultural Society (RHS) Garden Rosemoor, marks the southern boundary.

5 INSTOW & TAPELEY PARK
Instow

This agreeable village lies at the junction of the Taw and Torridge; it has a little harbour, a broad sandy beach (at low tide) a pub – the **Quay Inn** – and the excellent upmarket deli and café, **Johns** (there's another one in Appledore). There is also a **Johns Beach Hut** serving snacks.

Across the water, Appledore (page 51) is accessible by ferry in the summer, a couple of hours each side of high tide (the timings for the week ahead are displayed by the quay). They will carry bicycles, if there's room, for a small additional charge.

The village failed to impress J L W Page, who hailed a ferry to take him across the river in the late 1800s. 'It is some time before the fluttering handkerchief is noticed. [Instow] is bracing, it is fairly cheap, it has a pretty view and a long stretch of beach, and it is on a railway – that is all that can be said for Instow. Though only six miles from Barnstaple and three more from Bideford, it is neither lively nor picturesque.' Not fair, as you will see if you visit it.

Instow 'station', on the Tarka Trail, comes as a surprise. The platform is still there, as is the signal box. There are even some milk churns waiting until eternity to be loaded on the absent train.

Tapeley Park

Westleigh EX39 4NT ☏ 01271 860897 ⊙ Mar–end Oct, 10.00–17.00 Sun–Fri

Tapeley Park has a long, colourful history and an even more colourful current owner. There has been some sort of house here since before the

127

Norman Conquest, but its most notable inhabitants were the Clevland family who, for 150 years, were in service to the government. Archibald Clevland was one of only three officers to survive the Charge of the Light Brigade – only to be killed a month later. One of his letters describing the campaign is on display in the History Room and on the website.

Archibald's sister married William Langham Christie in 1855, and his daughter-in-law, Lady Rosamund, created the house and gardens that we see today, after removing her husband, Augustus, to Saunton due to his 'childish behaviour', expressed by kicking the furniture with hobnailed boots. Alas, he turned the tables by dying and leaving the house to a distant cousin, and Lady Rosamund spent the last six years of her life in the law courts proving her rightful ownership. She was successful, but died soon after. John Christie, her son, took over, spending part of the year at Tapeley and part at Glyndebourne where he had founded the opera house.

Eccentricity arrived in the form of another Rosamund who, until her death in 1988, ran the house as a visitor attraction, with haphazard cream teas and house tours, which she often conducted with a parrot on her head. Hector Christie, the current owner, has also left his personality quite gloriously on Tapeley Park. The gardens are run so sustainably that the whole pile could safely be put on the compost heap. Solar panels light and heat the History Room and Hector writes: 'It is my dream that now we could survive off the land … we become off-grid with a mixture of wind, solar, biomass, hydro, anaerobic digesters, and any other new inventions. The idea is to demonstrate to visitors the newest, cheapest, most efficient forms of renewable carbon-neutral energy on the market.'

The garden is a delight, with the view up to the house from the **Italian Garden** one of the best of its kind in Devon. Garden experts Mary Keen and Carol Klein left their mark on the formal gardens and everywhere there is colour and originality. The teas, taken at tables set out on the lawn (or inside) are excellent, with some mouth-watering home baking. Finally, don't miss the **Permaculture Garden**, which Hector describes as 'companion planting using predominantly perennial herbs and vegetables, and working with nature as opposed to constantly fighting against it [as in the modern monoculture approach to farming]'. Then

1 Instow's old signal box is now on the Tarka Trail. **2** Broomhill Sculpture Garden delights at every turn. **3** There are some 20 acres of private gardens at Marwood Hill. ▶

there's the attractive straw bale house and an extraordinary, low, long green building that, on closer inspection, turns out to be entirely composed of a type of holly. By the 18th-century ice house is a notice: 'The entrance to this ice house is blocked off because the temptation for parents to drop their screaming children into the 8ft pit could prove too much for some…'

Refreshingly different from the National Trust!

Some distance from the house and main gardens, along a grassy path, is **The Monument**. This was once an obelisk, standing on the highest point of the grounds with splendid views over the River Torridge and beyond, and commemorating Archibald Clevland (the Light Brigade fellow). Then it was struck by lightning: chunks of concrete were thrown high into the air, to the astonishment of a farmhand who witnessed it. These chunks now lie on the ground, some inscribed with lettering, and form a labyrinth that can be walked around.

The **house**, which has one of the country's finest collections of William Morris furniture, is only open to prebooked groups.

Cyclists can access Tapeley Park from the Tarka Trail; motorists follow the signs from the A39, on the east side of the bridge.

SOUTHWEST OF BARNSTAPLE

If you're heading for Great Torrington along the B3232 you'll pass close by two churches of exceptional interest. Even if you're not normally a church visitor, these deserve a detour.

6 TAWSTOCK

⌂ **Hollamoor Farm** (page 248)

> The Erle of Bathe hath a right goodly Maner and Place at Tawstoke on the West side of the Haven.
> John Leland, travelling during 1534–43

This extraordinary place illustrates the historical position of the local aristocracy in its community better than anywhere I know. The entrance is intimidating enough for a modern visitor, so must have been awe-inspiring for a 17th-century labourer. As you drive or cycle down a narrow lane, you pass between stone pillars topped by faithful hounds. To the left are the huge remains of the manor gatehouse with its vast oak door that would admit a carriage and team of horses. Above it is a coat of arms and the date: 1574. A catastrophic fire in 1787 destroyed the rest of the manor, which was rebuilt in 'Gothick' style by Sir Bourchier Wrey.

The original lords of the manor were the Bourchiers, created Earls of Bath in 1536; it passed, through marriage, to the Wreys in the 17th century.

"The inside of the church is so crammed with Wrey memorials that they compete for holy space."

Through the centuries the earls could look down on **St Peter's Church** in its lowly position with a sweep of green hills behind it, and feel they had God just where they wanted Him. The inside of the church is so crammed with Wrey memorials that they compete for holy space; uplifting inscriptions, monuments and memorial stones take over the chancel and much of the side aisle. Nor is it just the memorials that make the church so impressive – and different. Its organ is massive, with pipes almost framing a modern stained-glass window. The additional south aisle was formed by knocking holes into the existing side of the church, and creating arches. The pillars that support them are topped with rather smug carved faces and wreaths of foliage. The eagle lectern is ornithologically worrying: this bird would have been unable to close its splendid beak. The chancel is completely paved with inscribed stones commemorating people who died in the 17th and 18th centuries. You can spend a happy half hour reading these, before moving on to the memorials. The most impressive is to Henry Bourchier, the fifth Earl of Bath, who died in 1654. His giant sarcophagus is guarded by 'dogs' that spring from the pages of Harry Potter, with curly manes, menacing claws and oversized canines – another animal that could not have closed its mouth. Only the cropped ears suggest domesticity. Then there are the painted memorials to the third Earl of Bath, William Bourchier, and his wife Elizabeth.

Moving on from the Wreys, there are panels listing the charitable actions of the wealthy towards the poor – and the church. In 1677 the Dowager Countess of Bath 'laid out in Land to the benefit of the Poor of this parish for ever' and 'Shee hath also gave the parish a rich embroidered crimson velvet pulpit cloath and cushion and yearly bound out several poor children apprenticed and done many other excellent acts of charity.' Such was the path to the Kingdom of Heaven. Others were less generous – but also certainly less rich; there are several

donations of ten shillings. In the side aisle they've also found room for two secular items of rural history: a coffin cart and a plough. Note, too, above the side aisles, the more recent but beautiful plaster ceiling decoration of delicate flowers and tendrils.

If you only see one church in North Devon make it this one. No other is as rich in visual history inside and rural beauty in its setting. It's as English as you can get, a vivid reminder of the power of the aristocracy, and is only about two miles from Barnstaple station down a quiet lane so you can walk or cycle here with relative ease.

7 HORWOOD

Horwood village seems to be little more than a thatched cottage or two, a sprinkle of modern houses and a church – but what a church! Everywhere you look there is something old, intriguing or beautiful. When you enter, your attention is immediately caught by the bench ends. These are carved in high relief with a mixture of coats of arms, including a very sweet little horse rearing out of the water – the symbol of the Trevelyan family – saints and the initials of the pew owners. Soon you will realise that you are walking on words; almost every inch of the floor is occupied by old memorial slates, finely carved with skulls, angels and inscriptions. Those 17th-century carvers knew how to produce beautiful lettering. Where there is any space between the slates, there are equally old glazed tiles (the informative church leaflet recommends 'careful inspection on one's hands and knees'). Once you've finished looking down, look up. The wagon roof is exceptional, particularly above the north aisle, where there are some fine carved bosses. Then take a look at the carvings on the capitals (above the columns). Among the foliage are faces, some portraits of distinguished-looking men with beards, but others are grotesque death heads. Another has a curious selection of angels and creatures that are part-human, part-beast. Three of them are clasping stones – possibly the 'tablets' presented to Moses. The exception is a rather voluptuous female angel. Then comes a winged figure with a lion's body and human head and hands, and finally there's a mermaid, impractically clad in baggy robes.

◀ **1** St Peter's Church, Tawstock, is crammed with memorials. **2** A glass-blowing demonstration at Dartington Crystal. **3** Rosemoor is the RHS's showpiece garden, with over 200 varieties of rose in its 65 acres.

In the lady chapel is the effigy of Elizabeth Pollard, who died in 1439. She is wearing a horned headdress, with her four children tucked into the folds of her robe. The stained glass in the lady chapel's east window is very old – 15th century – but the other windows are Victorian. Finally the piscina, near the altar, is unusual: it has a horn-shaped drain. It is nearly a thousand years old.

GREAT TORRINGTON & AREA

ⴷ **Woodland Retreat** Langtree (page 248)

Praised by residents for its friendliness, Great Torrington (usually just called Torrington) is a market town in a magnificent setting on a cliff high about the river with some lovely surrounding countryside and the famous RHS Garden Rosemoor nearby, as well as the popular Dartington Crystal.

8 GREAT TORRINGTON

Tourist information: South St, EX38 8AA ☏ 01805 626140 ⬩ onegreattorrington.uk
⏲ 10.30–16.00 Mon–Fri, 10.30–13.00 Sat

> Arriving in the main carpark, the valley view across the Leper Fields is glorious, announcing straight away that Great Torrington is something special. Although it is a small town in the middle of a farming community, it also has a thriving arts scene that has been going strong for years.
> Claire Barker, author

The town played a prominent part in the English Civil War (see box, page 143), 'blown into history by the explosion of eighty barrels of gunpowder' (Arthur Mee). The West Country had been a Royalist stronghold, but in a fierce battle in 1646 the town was captured by the Parliamentarians, and the prisoners were held in the tower of the church, which was also being used to store the Royalists' arsenal. What could possibly go wrong? Somehow the gunpowder ignited and the resulting explosion partially destroyed the church and killed 200 men, as well as nearly killing Fairfax on his horse. This marked the end of the Royalist efforts in the region and the battle of 1646 is re-enacted in Torrington each year in February by the energetic Torrington Cavaliers. Every five years a much more spectacular reminder of the explosion is enacted in the **Great Bonfire** (see box, opposite).

THE TORRINGTON GREAT BONFIRE

Unique to Torrington is the extraordinary spectacle of a meticulously built replica of a famous structure being burned to the ground. Organised by the Torrington Cavaliers to raise money for charity, the event takes place every five years. In the past, the Houses of Parliament, Torrington Church and HMS *Victory* have all been burned. In 2021 a life-sized replica of the *Mayflower* was burnt to coincide with the 400th-anniversary celebrations of its sailing from Plymouth. More information from ⟢ torrington-cavaliers.co.uk.

Like many Devon towns, Torrington has a thriving **pannier market**, open daily and under cover, with an assortment of craft and antique shops as well as a range of produce.

Next to the pannier market is a good **museum** (14 South St ✆ 01805 938008 ☉ 10.30–16.00 Mon, Tue & Thu, 10.30–13.00 Wed, Fri & Sat), enthusiastically run by volunteers, with all sorts of displays: gloving, Civil War costumes, rope-making and country crafts. And you can learn about Thomas Fowler, who invented a unique calculating machine in 1844; a replica of his machine, based on contemporary descriptions, has been donated to the museum. There's also a first edition of the *Concise British Flora in Colour* by that industrious churchman, the Reverend William Keble Martin who was vicar of Great Torrington in the 1930s. He had formerly been archpriest of the little church of Haccombe, near Newton Abbot, where I first came across the story that he was urged to find something else to do by his exasperated parishioners after he had visited them all twice in one week. Hence the meticulous botanical illustrations in his celebrated work.

"There's an entrance to the secluded Secret Memorial Garden, a little haven of tranquillity, open to all."

Finally, at the **Plough Arts Centre** (9–11 Fore St ✆ 01805 624624) you can watch films or plays, have a snack, look round an exhibition or do a spot of arty stuff yourself at one of the workshops.

From the carpark on Castle Hill, near the helpful tourist information centre, there's an entrance to the secluded **Secret Memorial Garden**, a little haven of tranquillity, open to all. Also from the carpark you can look down on the river and some narrow strips of land. These are **Leper Fields**, which were once tilled by lepers who lived in the old leper village of Taddiport, which you can see on the right of the two preserved fields by Little Torrington.

9 TADDIPORT & FRITHELSTOCK

Both these little villages lie close to the Tarka Trail and make a worthwhile diversion for cyclists – and for drivers. Visit **Taddiport**, with its tiny chapel, to get the feel of what it was like to be a leper in the Middle Ages. Through no fault of their own, they lost their liberty and the right to inherit or bequeath property. However, they seem to have been well looked after at Taddiport, which had a hospital, the little chapel where they could pray for a cure, and the leper fields where they could grow food. Quite a bit of this history is retained: the church, the fields, and even a (privately owned) Leper Cottage.

WITCHY WATERS

Claire Barker

Tales of witchcraft are plentiful in Devon. I once met a man who unearthed a leather bag when renovating the wall of a very old house in Combe Martin. It was full of odd and unusual objects so he showed it to an elderly resident, wondering what they might be. On hearing it was a witch's bag he wisely put it back, for fear it might bring him bad luck. A Barnstaple pizza restaurant once displayed a tiny, blackened shoe discovered in their chimney, a tried and tested method of keeping curses at bay and presumably ensuring your garlic bread won't turn you into a toad.

However, some locations are said to be more densely witch-populated than others, and rumours of the witches of Great Torrington will be familiar to many local ears. Torrington is just nine miles away from Bideford, home to the last people in England to be executed for witchcraft in the 1600s. As someone who has spent the last two years writing about an anarchic little witch, my curiosity was piqued and I decided to investigate further. No luck. I probably shouldn't have been surprised to discover that gossip did not equate to fact.

With the help of an old book and a helpful librarian, however, I discovered a little-publicised piece of magical information about the town. Torrington, like Glastonbury, has its own sacred spring – something that came as a surprise to every local I asked about it.

Tucked away in the undergrowth behind a carpark, on the slope behind the old bowling green, is the ancient Covety Well. Named after the Roman water goddess Coventina, the water from this well, which has been found to be high in zinc, was believed to cure eye complaints.

The bowling green is on the edge of town and very easy to get to. I parked next to the ice-cream van, walked past the public conveniences, down a little path forking to the left and there it was: a small pool of water with coloured devotional ribbons tied in the tree beside it.

I may not have found witches wandering the streets of Great Torrington, but I did find a quietly pagan place, so that's not bad. Maybe the coven I was looking for was to be found in Coventina after all.

The tower of the **church** of St Mary Magdalene is only 5ft high and 5ft square, yet it doesn't look disproportionately small on this little medieval building. The floor space is L-shaped, with an organ taking up much of one side. A touching stained-glass window dedicated to the lepers is the work of a 19-year-old lad in 1972. Here, as in many Devon churches, the Ten Commandments are painted on one of the walls, but what is one to make of the biblical text on the adjacent wall that evidently points an accusing finger? 'Woe to them that devise iniquity and work Evil upon theyr beds … And they covet feilds and take them by violence, And howses and take them away: Soe they oppress A man and his howse.' It is assumed that this refers to some ancient misappropriation of land, but no-one knows for sure. Intriguing!

Frithelstock lies a few miles to the northwest, and is a quintessentially English village. A stately line of lime trees lead to the church door, still bearing its sanctuary ring which granted protection to all miscreants who could grab it while being pursued by the Law. Abutting the church are the ruined walls of a medieval priory; the west wall is the best preserved, 40ft high with a fine door and lancet windows remaining.

"More intriguing, however, are secular carvings of two heads, facing each other, with their tongues protruding."

Inside the church, it is the carved bench ends that catch your attention. They date from the 15th century and depict a variety of religious symbols from the crucifixion, such as the crown of thorns, a whip, and a reed. More intriguing, however, are secular carvings of two heads, facing each other, with their tongues protruding. It seems that these may represent the Bishop of Exeter and the Prior of Frithelstock, who fell out with one another in the Middle Ages and now insult each other through eternity.

10 RHS GARDEN ROSEMOOR

 Rosemoor House (page 248)

Great Torrington EX38 8PH ✆ 01805 624067 ⬦ rhs.org.uk/rosemoor ◷ 10.00–17.00 daily

The RHS's showpiece garden, Rosemoor, has 65 acres with 200 varieties of rose. And that's just the beginning – there's every plant imaginable and every colour in the spectrum. There are vegetables galore, soft fruit, orchards and woodland walks. It takes a while to see it properly; the highlights are all accessible within an hour or so, but if you can spend the day here, do. Come here on a sunny day, any time of the year, and take your time to breathe in the scents and sights. The knowledge of your fellow visitors can be intimidating: on my last visit a voice boomed out: 'Did you tell Daddy about the pelargonium?'. The child looked about five.

The RHS runs daily events and exhibitions, as well as courses, and the **Reading Room** is open to non-members who can browse the 1,300 reference books. The award-winning **Garden Kitchen** serves hot meals (see opposite) while the **Wisteria Tea Room**, part of Lady Anne's House, is open in the summer.

11 TARKA POTTERY

Little Torrington EX38 8PS ✆ 07931 306414 ⌂ tarkapottery.co.uk ⊙ booking essential

Just two miles southwest of RHS Rosemoor is a very special place where a talented young team can turn you into a potter. Jax led us, step-by-step, through the process of 'throwing a pot' on the potter's wheel, decorating that pot and then glazing it ready for firing. It was incredible – we had no prior experience but with her skilled guidance we created our own pots!

We were at Tarka Pottery for an afternoon on one of their short classes but you can come for longer – a day or maybe a few. They even have accommodation on-site for those who wish to stay longer. Groups are encouraged – next to us were a grandfather, daughter and granddaughter, all working together and offering each other encouragement.

Jax learnt to pot while at school and then came back to it when she discovered that the house they were buying had a potter's wheel and kiln in the barn. Built up over years, her small team are all local, enthusiastic and able to explain each step of the process. Book early to avoid disappointment.

12 DARTINGTON CRYSTAL

Linden Close, Great Torrington EX38 7AN ✆ 01805 626262 ⌂ visitdartington.co.uk
⊙ 10.00–17.00 daily

There's plenty to see and do here as well as buy high-quality glassware. It's not cheap so allow enough time to go to the AV Theatre and round the factory to see glass-blowing and engraving in action. You can try glass-blowing yourself if you book ahead. The website is exceptionally good, so watch the video of how they create complicated one-off pieces as well as standard hand- and footprints.

🍴 FOOD & DRINK

The Globe Inn Exeter Rd, Beaford EX19 8LR 🕿 01805 603920 🖉 globeinnpub.co.uk
🕒 closed Mon. CAMRA North Devon Pub of the Year 2020, this traditional country pub
has excellent ale and beer, and locally sourced food (a map on the menu shows you where
everything comes from). The friendly staff will even match your beer to your food. Open fire
in winter.

Rosemoor Garden Kitchen Rosemoor Gardens 🕿 01805 626822 (page 137). Excellent hot
meals served 10.00–15.00 using ingredients from the garden and locally sourced high-quality
meat. In the afternoon, cream tea is served (🕒 15.00–17.00), with optional prosecco.

Torridge Inn 136 Mill St, Great Torrington EX38 8AW 🕿 01805 625042. This may look
like a typical Tudor Devon pub, but it serves great Thai food like stir fries, pad Thai and, our
favourite, the jungle curry. Vegan and gluten-free options.

SOUTHEAST OF BARNSTAPLE: BETWEEN THE A377 & A361

Easily accessible from either main road, this green corridor has a scattering
of notable churches, a spacious garden and an unusual museum.

13 SWIMBRIDGE

'No dogs please – even Jack Russells!' says a sign on the gate. This church
is famous because its long-term vicar was the **Reverend John Russell**,
who bred the first Jack Russell terrier (see box, page 140). His plain but
conspicuous grave is round the corner in the graveyard – follow the
arrows – and the original Jack Russell terrier, Trump, has her portrait
on the inn sign for the **Jack Russell pub** opposite the church. The pub
is full of Jack Russell memorabilia and less strict than the church about
canine visitors.

The church of St James is unusual in several ways. It has a lead-coated
spire rather than the more familiar tower, and a mass of exceptional
carvings, in both wood and stone. The most notable is the extraordinary
Jacobean font cover, enclosing the font in a sort of cupboard, with
a canopy above, all beautifully carved. Indeed, the portrait heads
and fantastical creatures would normally be found on bench ends.
The 15th-century stone pulpit is very fine, carved with saints and angels,
as is the long and intricately carved wooden screen dating from the 16th
century, and don't forget to look up at the impressive roof. All in all, a
church worth visiting, even if you don't own a Jack Russell.

THE REVEREND JOHN (JACK) RUSSELL

By all accounts the Reverend John Russell most perfectly combined his hobby with making a living. He was a popular minister at St James's church for 46 years, having arrived, with his pack of hounds, in 1833, and indulged his passion for hunting until two years before his death at the age of 87. An estimated 1,000 people attended his funeral. Despite hunting almost daily – he was rumoured to wear his hunting clothes beneath his surplice for a quick getaway – he managed to increase the services at Swimbridge from one each Sunday to four, restored the dilapidated church and its school, and was conscientious in visiting his most needy parishioners. He was also remembered for his charity towards gypsies, who were much persecuted in those days. In return they protected the Rectory from thieves.

Not everyone was happy about his obsession with hunting, however, and eventually he yielded to the pressure to give up his pack of hounds, partly instigated by that scourge of licentious clergymen, Bishop Philpotts of Exeter. For two years Russell was without his own pack, which cast him into such depths of depression that when he was offered the gift of 13 foxhounds his resolve faltered. 'There they stood,' he said, 'the greatest beauties my eye had ever rested on, looking up in my face so winningly, that I mentally determined to keep the lot and go to work again.' His wife told him that he had as much right to enjoy life as other men, and so he kept them.

These days Jack Russell is famous for the terriers that bear his name. The story goes that while he was at Oxford – doing precious little work but a lot of hunting – he was strolling in Magdalen Meadow trying to memorise some Latin, when he met a milkman with a little terrier bitch and bought it on the spot. The terrier's name was Trump, and she became the first of a distinct breed of dog now called the Jack Russell terrier. Russell was a founder member of the Kennel Club and a respected judge of fox terriers so he knew a thing or two about dog breeding.

In his lifetime this larger-than-life character was better known for his hunting than for his sermons, although he managed to combine both in a visit to Sandringham. At the invitation of the Prince of Wales who asked him to 'put a sermon in his pocket' he danced in the New Year with the Princess of Wales and preached his sermon in Sandringham's church the following Sunday.

The village itself is most attractive, with a skein of white and cream houses climbing up a lane, and some well-tended allotments.

UMBERLEIGH

⋏ Fisherton Farm's Vintage Vardos Nr Atherington (page 248)

Umberleigh is a place you might whizz past on the main road, half registering the name but little more. Set by the River Taw and its arched bridge, it has a quiet sense of community – and pride in dealing with the region's flood problem by dredging the river and clearing the arches so rainwater could safely run away. There's an excellent pub, **the Rising Sun**, a post office and a railway station. It has ancient royal connections, too. The Georgian Umberleigh House was once the site of one of those preconquest English monarchs no-one has heard of: King Athelstan.

14 CASTLE HILL GARDENS & CHITTLEHAMPTON

Close to Filleigh, with its splendid thatched pub (page 143), is **Castle Hill Gardens** (EX32 0RQ ✆ 01598 760336 castlehilldevon.co.uk ⏲ 11.00–16.00 Mon–Fri). The formal gardens with colourful herbaceous borders are enjoyable, but really it is the parkland with its extensive views and huge mature trees that is the attraction here. It's an ideal place to exercise lively children and dogs.

Nearby at **Chittlehampton** is the church of St Hieritha, which has some intriguing features, not least its saint who was buried here. St Hieritha, or St Urith, is Devon's very own saint. Converted to Christianity by Glastonbury monks, she was accused of causing a severe drought, and scythed to pieces by the local farmers. A spring gushed forth where her severed head landed and Chittlehampton had not only a reliable source of water but subsequent centuries of wealth from the pilgrims who visited her shrine. A satisfactory outcome for (almost) all concerned.

"The formal gardens are enjoyable, but it is the parkland with its extensive views and mature trees that is the attraction."

Donations by pilgrims helped create the imposing **church** with its high and frilly tower. This is considered to be one of the loveliest in Devon, a view endorsed by a 17th-century writer: 'I observed the tower of the Church to be a work more curious and fair than any in that County.'

Inside, the carvings on the stone pulpit are unusual and interesting; four glum-faced men wear what appear to be log rolls round their heads; they have been described as Latin doctors or leaders from church history. The fifth figure is St Hieritha herself, carrying a palm, which symbolised martyrdom. Above the choir the roof is supported by angels, and there's a charming plaque commemorating St Hieritha by her tomb or shrine. The craftsman has made no attempt at fitting the words into

DEVON & THE ENGLISH CIVIL WAR

The English Civil War was in fact three armed conflicts that ravaged the land and divided families between 1642 and 1651, but it is the first war, 1642–46, that features in Devon's history. Wars can never be simplified in a few words, but this book contains enough references to the conflict to make a little background information useful. Broadly speaking the dispute was between the Royalists, also known as Cavaliers, who supported King Charles I despite his despotism and enthusiasm for ruling England without the help of parliament, and the Parliamentarians or Roundheads (a reference to the shaven heads of the rabble-rousing London apprentice boys) who backed the Republican, Puritan ideals of Oliver Cromwell and Sir Thomas Fairfax, his superior (Cromwell was a better politician than a soldier).

A prominent name in Devon's Civil War was Sir Ralph Hopton, who led a small force of Royalist cavalry from Minehead into Cornwall, joining forces with Sir Bevil Grenville. Devon's most significant battle was in Great Torrington (page 134) in 1646 between General Thomas Fairfax's Parliamentarians and Lord Hopton's Royalist forces. This marked the end of Royalist resistance in Devon, Hopton surrendered to Fairfax in Truro, the Parliamentarians triumphed and King Charles I was executed in 1649.

the space or even hyphenation, so that 'foundress' becomes 'fo' (next line) 'undress' which is certainly eye-catching.

When you've finished in the church you can make for the very good pub, the **Bell Inn**. Or maybe go straight to the pub.

¶¶ FOOD & DRINK

The Masons Arms Knowstone EX36 4RY ✆ 01398 341231 ⌂ masonsarmsdevon.co.uk ⊙ noon–14.00 & 19.00–21.00 Tue–Sat. From the outside this looks like a typical Devon pub in a small Mid-Devon village (Knowstone is just north of the A361 between Tiverton and Barnstaple), and indeed it has its bar called the Village Local, which serves light meals. But this is a Michelin-starred restaurant owned and operated by Mark Dodson, formerly head chef at Michel Roux's Waterside Inn, Bray. That's all you need to know, really. Exquisite food, and lunches are surprisingly affordable.

The Stag's Head Filleigh EX32 0RN ✆ 01598 760250 ⌂ stagshead.co.uk. A long-established favourite with visitors and locals alike, this thatched pub is within the Castle Hill estate, and is not only a beautiful building but offers excellent local food including pheasant from the estate and proper desserts such as fruit crumble and bread-and-butter pudding.

◀ Castle Hill Gardens.

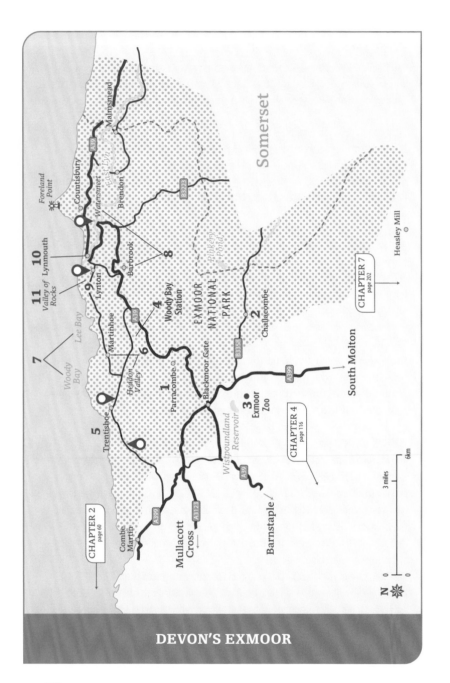

DEVON'S EXMOOR

5

DEVON'S EXMOOR

We came to the great River Exe ... which rises in the hills on this north side of the county ... The country it rises in is called Exmoor. Camden calls it a filthy barren ground, and indeed, so it is; but as soon as the Exe comes off from the moors and hilly country and descends into the lower grounds, we found the alteration; for then we saw Devonshire in its other countenance, cultivated, populous and fruitful.
Daniel Defoe, 1724

This is still an accurate picture of Exmoor if you change 'filthy barren ground' for something more complimentary, for it is the heather-covered moorland as much as the cultivated, populous and fruitful lower ground that draws visitors. This is one of England's smallest national parks, a soft landscape of rounded hills, splashed yellow from gorse and purple in the late summer when the heather blooms, and of deep, wooded valleys. And Exmoor has the coast, adding pebble coves and sea views to its attractions, along with the many rivers that race to the sea from the high ground, slicing into the soft sandstone. With so much of Exmoor managed by the National Trust, clear signposting makes walking or cycling a real pleasure. Astonishingly, for such an utterly delightful region, it's one of England's least visited national parks. You may not believe this on a sunny weekend in Lynmouth or at The Hunter's Inn when they're buzzing with visitors, but solitude is not hard to find.

The publication of *Lorna Doone* in 1869 gave Exmoor tourism a marketing high that persists to this day. Blackmore's novel is more identifiably set in a genuine English landscape than most other literary classics, and the number of visitors to Exmoor testifies that fiction is as powerful as fact.

Other Exmoor enthusiasts were the Romantic Poets descended on Exmoor a couple of hundred years ago when Samuel Taylor Coleridge and his pal William Wordsworth tirelessly walked the hills and coast.

Coleridge lived in Nether Stowey in the Quantocks, with William and Dorothy lodging nearby. In the autumn of 1797 they walked the coastal path to Lynton, and are said to have planned Coleridge's most famous poem, *The Rime of the Ancient Mariner*, during that walk.

In 1812 Shelley burst in on the tranquillity of Lynmouth, scattering pamphlets and scandal. All in all, anyone who had anything to do with poetry at the turn of the 18th century seems to have ended up on the Exmoor coast.

WET-WEATHER ACTIVITIES

Exmoor Zoo (page 152)
Lynmouth Pavilion (page 171)
Lyn Valley Arts & Crafts Centre (page 167)
Woody Bay Station (page 155)

FESTIVALS

Two Moors Festival ⊘ twomoorsfestival.co.uk. Every October a most unusual music festival takes place in Exmoor and Dartmoor. Firstly, the music is classical, rather than popular or folk, and secondly it's performed in churches – often quite remote ones that are described in this book. What could be better?

GETTING THERE & AROUND

There is no fast way of getting to Exmoor, only slow. The A39 hugs the coast from Somerset to Lynton before heading inland to Barnstaple. It's not a fast road but has wonderful views and a high chance of meeting ponies or even red deer.

Public transport around Exmoor is very limited and there is almost none in the heart of the national park. However, there is a great bus service from Lynmouth that heads east along the coast to Porlock and then Minehead. The Exmoor Explorer (⊘ firstbus.co.uk/adventures-bus/services/exmoor-coaster) runs up to six times a day, often with an open-top bus; this must be one of the most spectacular bus rides in Britain – hold on tight for the descent down Porlock Hill!

Exmoor is poorly served by railways, a fact that has contributed to its lack of development. The nearest regular service is the **Tarka Line** (pages 205 and 211) from Exeter to Barnstaple, from where you can pick up a 310 bus to Lynmouth (page 170).

CYCLING

The **West Country Way** (NCN3) traverses the southern part of Exmoor, going through high moorland, and the many quiet lanes on the moor are ideal for cyclists who don't mind hills (of which there are many) – most of the lanes are wide or across open moor so there's less danger from traffic.

Exmoor is ideal for **mountain biking**. Bikes are allowed on bridleways and RUPPs (Roads Used as Public Paths) but not on public footpaths or open moorland.

WALKING

Despite its small scale, there are hundreds of miles of footpaths on Exmoor, including several long-distance paths. This is recognised with

THE RED DEER OF EXMOOR

The red deer (*Cervus elaphus*) is the largest native British mammal, with stags nearly 4ft high at the shoulder and hinds slightly smaller. Red deer have lived on Exmoor since prehistoric times, and the current population – estimated at around 3,000 animals – is thought to be one of the last truly indigenous populations in the British Isles. For most of the year hinds tend to herd together with their calves in certain areas while stags form bachelor groups, but it's common to find young 'prickets' with hinds and not unusual to find older stags in small groups or even by themselves.

Only the stag has antlers (or horns, as they are called locally), which it sheds in the spring every year. As the animal matures so the annual growth of its antlers increases, adding new points each year until 14 or even 16 points are attained, after which he is usually past his prime and starts to 'go back'. Finding horns that have been shed is a local tradition, and they are highly prized. There are often stags' horn competitions at shows during the summer – Exford Show in August, for instance.

All the energy put into growing these antlers is important to achieve supremacy over rival stags during the annual rut from late September until November. The dominant stags round up a harem of hinds, strut around showing off their size, and bellow their challenge to intruders. Fights often ensue. The calves are generally born in June, and to begin with spend much of their time lying concealed in undergrowth while their mothers graze nearby, returning regularly to let their young suckle. It's very important not to get too close to a calf if you see it, nor touch it, as the hind may abandon it if you do.

You may come upon deer at any time. They are most visible on farmland, where they sometimes congregate in large numbers, but can also be found in woodland and on open moorland (where they are particularly well camouflaged).

the new statue of *The Walker* in Lynmouth. The 102-mile **Two Moors Way** runs from Lynmouth to Ivybridge on the far edge of Dartmoor, or can be extended to the south Devon coast to form a coast-to-coast path; the **Macmillan Way West** (also 102 miles) begins in Castle Cary, enters Exmoor at Withycombe and goes to Barnstaple; the 52-mile **Coleridge Way** runs from Nether Stowey in the Quantocks to Porlock and then to Lynmouth. Finally there's the superlative 35-mile Exmoor section of the **South West Coast Path** (SWCP).

If you are planning to do some extensive walking, then it's worth making the most of the best seasons: spring or autumn for woodland or the coast, when the landscape is at its loveliest and the crowds are fewer, but August or early September for the heather. At this time of year the moorland areas are particularly gorgeous, with a mixture of bell heather and ling so that the landscape glows with different shades of purple.

If you prefer a **guided walk**, these can be organised with the national park (✆ 01598 751065 🖥 exmoor-nationalpark.gov.uk); the Exmoor Society (🖥 exmoorsociety.com) also runs regular Exmoor walks.

With so many hotels and B&Bs near the main walking routes, few people will choose to carry a tent out of necessity, but there are some wild spots where camping is permitted. You should be aware, however, that no wild camping is allowed anywhere on Exmoor, although there are organised campsites varying from the comfortable to the very rustic.

Walking maps & guides

The Croydecycle walking maps at a scale of 1:12,500 cover a good proportion of Exmoor, including all of the coastal area, while *Coast Path Map 1*, at a scale of 1:15,000, comprises the entire Exmoor stretch of the South West Coast Path from Minehead to Watermouth.

The OS double-sided Explorer map OL9 covers all of Exmoor at a scale of 1:25,000 but its size makes it unwieldy to use and the area you want always seems to be on the other side.

A variety of walking guides are available from TICs and Exmoor National Park outlets, but should always be used in conjunction with an OS or (better) a Croydecycle map.

HORSERIDING

One of my fondest teenage memories is of pony trekking for a week in the 'Lorna Doone country' of Exmoor with my younger sister. I can remember so vividly the woodland rides and the huge sweep of purple moor, and the exhilaration of being able to gallop without worrying about roads or traffic. We started off gently with a couple of hours of morning and afternoon rides, and culminated in a full day trek with lunch at a pub (so grown up!). I can even remember the name of my cob: Satan.

Not much has changed. You can still go for short or long treks across the heather, you can still have lunch in a pub on the long days, and no doubt there are still bolshy cobs called Satan. If you can ride, there's no better way of seeing the moor, and no better way of getting up those steep hills and across the streams.

If you have your own horse, there are several farms that offer accommodation for your horse as well as yourself – indeed, with over 400 miles of bridleway, Exmoor is probably the best place in the country for this sort of holiday. A leaflet available from some TICs lists all the B&Bs that can provide this type of accommodation.

RIDING & TREKKING STABLES

Brendon Manor Riding Stables Between Lynton & Simonsbath EX35 6LQ ✆ 01598 741246 ⬧ brendonmanor.com. Also offer horse B&B.

Dean Riding Stables Trentishoe EX31 4PJ ✆ 01598 763565 ⬧ deanridingstables.co.uk

FURTHER INFORMATION

WEBSITES

Visit Exmoor ⬧ visit-exmoor.co.uk. The first-stop website for all things Exmoor.

Edible Exmoor ⬧ edibleexmoor.co.uk. A really useful website for foodies, showing a wide range of food producers in Exmoor.

Everything Exmoor ⬧ everythingexmoor.org.uk. An information site that is extraordinarily comprehensive, with contributions from members of the public.

Exmoor National Park Authority Dulverton ✆ 01398 323665 ⬧ exmoor-nationalpark. gov.uk

Exmoor Society 34 High St, Dulverton ✆ 01398 232335 ⬧ exmoorsociety.com. Founded 60 years ago, the society organises walks, talks and other events.

PUBLICATIONS

Exmoor Magazine ⬧ exmoormagazine.co.uk. In-depth articles of Exmoor interest.

Exmoor Visitor Published by the national park, this free newspaper repeats the information found on their website. Widely available in shops and tourist information centres.

EXMOOR PONIES

Victoria Eveleigh

The most obvious thing about Exmoor ponies is that they all look remarkably similar – short and hairy, with brown bodies that are dark on top and lighter underneath, dark legs and hooves and a characteristic 'mealy muzzle' (an oatmeal colour over their muzzles and round their eyes). White markings are not permitted on registered Exmoor ponies.

The distinctive colour of the Exmoor pony has led people to believe that it is a direct descendant of prehistoric wild horses, but neither recent genetic research nor studies of documentary evidence support this view. However, it is still a valuable and rare native pony breed.

During the early 20th century it became fashionable to 'improve' native ponies with Arab and Thoroughbred bloodlines, so in 1921 several local breeders got together and formed the Exmoor Pony Society with the purpose of keeping the breed true to type by working with the Rare Breed Survival Trust.

The ponies nearly died out during World War II; most of them were killed for food, leaving only about 46 mares and four stallions, but the local farmers soon re-established their herds with the help of a remarkable lady called Mary Etherington.

Today there are about 300 free-living Exmoor ponies on the moor and about 1,300 worldwide, but only a fraction of these are

WESTERN EXMOOR: TO LYNTON VIA BLACKMOOR GATE

⋏ **Westland Farm** Bratton Fleming (page 248)

When you're approaching Exmoor, all roads seem to lead to Blackmoor Gate, and from there most drivers heading east towards Lynton take the relatively uninteresting A39 where they know they will make reasonably good progress. From this route, however, the church at Parracombe really shouldn't be missed by anyone who loves old churches. Those approaching (or leaving) Blackmoor Gate via the A399 have two worthwhile diversions: **Challacombe** for its famous pub and walks (including to a longstone and some wild swimming); and **Exmoor Zoo**.

Blackmoor Gate itself has its place in history. It was once an important railway station on the narrow-gauge Barnstaple-to-Lynton railway, and a livestock market (mainly sheep) is still regularly held there (⊘ exmoorfarmers.co.uk). The preserved two-mile stretch of this railway, down which shiny little steam locomotives currently puff their way from Woody Bay Station to Killington Halt (page 155), is scheduled

used for breeding. There are 20 moorland herds on Exmoor, including two owned by the Exmoor National Park Authority. All the Exmoor pony herds that graze the different areas of moorland are free-living (not truly wild, like red deer) because they are owned by farmers with grazing rights on the moorland. For most of the year the ponies fend for themselves, but in the autumn they are rounded up and the foals are weaned and inspected. Until recently all foals that passed inspection had to be branded, but microchipping is now allowed as an alternative to branding.

Exmoors are well camouflaged in their natural moorland habitat. However, you will have a good chance of spotting them, even from the road. Please don't try to feed the ponies as it encourages them to associate cars with food, which means they are more likely to be victims of a traffic accident. Also, ponies can be dangerous if they start fighting over food.

The Heritage Exmoor Pony Festival (♂ mepbg.co.uk) is held from August to the end of September, with events ranging from photography workshops to guided walks to see the ponies.

For more information about the ponies, or if you are interested in buying one, the Exmoor Pony Society website (♂ exmoorponysociety. org.uk) is a useful starting point.

to be extended, which will (if it takes place) bring trains and their passengers to Blackmoor Gate once again.

1 PARRACOMBE

Cupped within a bulge of the A39, and almost lost in a maze of steep, narrow lanes, is this lovely little village with two churches and an excellent pub (page 155). The old church, St Petrock's, is rightly the one that draws visitors. It was scheduled for demolition in 1878 when a more conveniently located church had been built, but was saved after a protest led by John Ruskin and is now cared for by the Churches' Conservation Trust.

It stands high above the village, overlooking its usurper church and the scatter of white houses, with the fields of North Devon stretching to the horizon. The squat tower is a landmark from the main road, the pinnacles looking as though they were added as an afterthought by a farmer. They're more like slightly wobbly cairns than stone-mason's art, and all the more charming for it. Inside, the church is plain and unadorned. No-one has 'improved' it, but it is clearly cared for and cared about. The first thing you notice on entering is the wooden 'tympanum', boldly painted with a royal coat of arms and improving texts: the Ten Commandments and the Creed. The only carving is the screen and even this is less intricate than usually found in Devon churches. The plain box pews are rough with old woodworm, and at the back there's a musicians' area where a hole has been cut in the pew in front to allow free movement for the bow of the double bass. Note, too, the hat pegs by the door.

2 CHALLACOMBE & PINKERY POND

⌂ **Shoulsbarrow Farmhouse** Challacombe (page 248)

Apart from the famous Black Venus Inn (page 155) and its well-stocked village store, **Challacombe** is best known for the nearby **longstone**, the most spectacular prehistoric monument on Exmoor, standing 9ft high and remarkably slender. It's marked on the OS Explorer map OL9 (⦿ SS70514307), which you'll need to find it. It's a mile or two from the road (the B3358), northeast of Challacombe, near the source of the River Bray. It used to stand in a hollow that filled with water after rain, and a nearby spring made it even wetter; archaeologists levelled it off with gravel in 2003, but the area around it is still very marshy, so be prepared with the right footwear if you decide to look for it.

To the east of the longstone, just into Somerset, is **Pinkery Pond**, a lovely place for a wild swim (see box, page 154) and the source of the River Barle. Pinkery used to be Pinkworthy (though always pronounced Pinkery), but that spelling is now lost. Nearby is the **Pinkery Centre for Outdoor Learning**, run by the national park, which introduces youngsters to every aspect of Exmoor's wild side.

3 EXMOOR ZOO

South Stowford, Bratton Fleming EX31 4SG ✆ 01598 763352 ⬦ exmoorzoo.co.uk
◷ 09.00–17.00 (summer) or until dusk (winter) daily, except 3 days at Christmas

Off the A399 is this well-managed zoo. A black leopard, thought to be the Exmoor Beast of local legend, is the most promoted exhibit (though melanistic big cats such as this are not that unusual), but there

---

1 The longstone near Challacombe. 2 The Lynton & Barnstaple Railway is a popular ride with families and nostalgic oldies. 3 Wistlandpound Reservoir, great for walking and wildlife. ▶

VISIT DEVON

ANTONY CHRISTIE/LYNTON & BARNSTAPLE RAILWAY

SJOFX/S

WILD SWIMMING IN PINKERY POND

Joanna Griffin

Pinkery Pond, situated just into Somerset on the bleak northwestern plateau of Exmoor known as The Chains, really is a remote spot for a dip. Formed in 1830 by the damming of the River Barle near its source and occupying around 1.2ha, it is large and deep enough (reportedly 30ft-deep in parts) for a long swim. In the southeast corner is a tiny gravelly beach that gently shelves down into the water, providing easy access to the red, peaty depths. Just beside this entry is a narrow moss- and fern-clad tunnel cut into the rock, through which the shallow stream flows into the river.

It is a bit of a trek across boggy moorland to reach the pond, but well worth the effort. It's clearly marked on the OS map at ♀ SS72364230.

From Goat Hill Bridge on the road between Challacombe and Simonsbath, pass through the gate and follow the road to the right of the River Barle towards the Pinkery Exploration Centre. Take a track to the left just before the centre, and pass through a copse of trees on the other side of the field, before reaching open moorland. From here, continue along the stone track that winds alongside the infant Barle, watching the river becoming increasingly narrow as you climb. The pond will suddenly come into view as you reach the bridleway between Wood Barrow Gate to the west and Exe Head to the east.

You could combine your swim with a visit to the prehistoric longstone, which can be reached by returning to Wood Barrow Gate and heading due west.

are 175 species in total, some of which are rarely seen in zoos, with intriguing names such as Chacoan mara, New Guinea singing dog, and dusky padamelon. Animal welfare and breeding of endangered species have high priority, so animals are given the chance to hide within their enclosures. To counteract any visitor disappointment at not seeing their favourite, there are animal encounters with easy-going creatures such as tapirs and wallabies, and the opportunity to be a keeper for a day.

This is an exceptionally child-friendly zoo, even to the extent of having a lost-child trail so small children can find their way back to the entrance. A great idea!

WISTLANDPOUND RESERVOIR

North of the zoo is this pleasant lake surrounded by conifers and encircled by trails. It's popular with dog-walkers and runners, and accessible to buggies and wheelchairs since the paths are tarmacked.

The carpark furthest from the reservoir is free; there is a charge for the one by the lake.

¶¶ FOOD & DRINK

The Black Venus Challacombe EX31 4TT ✆ 01598 763251 🖰 blackvenusinn.co.uk.
This lovely 16th-century pub is a good reason to visit Challacombe. Hearty meals of nicely presented, traditional pub food, with a few unexpected treats and a great atmosphere. Dog friendly.

Fox and Goose Parracombe EX31 4PE ✆ 01598 763239 🖰 foxandgooseinnexmoor.co.uk. Recommended for its exceptional food and wide range of beers. The décor is genuine Exmoor, with foxes' masks and deer antlers, as well as antiques; the food is locally sourced where possible and traditional as well as imaginative. As popular with locals for conversation as for food. Dog friendly.

4 WOODY BAY STATION

EX31 4RA ✆ 01598 763487 🖰 lynton-rail.co.uk

Although currently only two miles long, this narrow-gauge railway is the highest in England and its trains puff their way through some of Exmoor's best scenery, making it a rewarding family excursion or a nostalgic trip for oldies. The enthusiasm of the volunteers who run this stretch of the original Lynton & Barnstaple Railway, which operated from 1898 to 1935, is evident in every detail, from the loving maintenance of the steam locomotives to the tea room. The station was originally planned to serve the actual Woody Bay (or Woodabay, as it was then called), nearly two miles away, with a branch line, as part of the scheme to make Woody Bay a major tourist attraction (page 162).

In 2018 the park authorities gave permission to extend the line west to Blackmoor Gate and eventually on to Barnstaple, recreating its orginal route, but there is fierce opposition from some landowners so whether this will actually be achieved is uncertain.

THE COASTAL TRIANGLE

Between Combe Martin and Lynton the A399 and A39 roads form the southern edges of a triangular slice of Exmoor of quite extraordinary beauty. No serious road builder was going to give priority to this chaos of moorland, hills and valleys when a more level highway to the south had served its purpose for centuries. As you approach the deep Heddon

Valley, with its popular The Hunter's Inn, driving becomes increasingly challenging, as does walking: the hills are *very* steep. But the scenery, in all its Exmoor variety, is sublime: high moor, ancient meadows and hanging woods of sessile oaks, accessible by lanes so steep and narrow that even devoted drivers will feel challenged. The coast, tracked by one of the most scenic stretches of the South West Coast Path, is indented with shingle beaches hidden by high cliffs. Altogether an area not to be missed.

5 TRENTISHOE

Trentishoe is one of those isolated communities that make Exmoor so special. It is best accessed from the west to avoid a near-vertical hill from Heddon Valley (now marked 'unfit for motors'). The drive there along the narrow lane from Combe Martin is in the lead for the most dramatically beautiful in Exmoor – particularly if the heather is in bloom, when bursts of purple plus yellow from the gorse alternate with sea views.

Shortly before the scatter of houses and a church that make up this hamlet you pass between Holdstone Down and Trentishoe Down, both of which have some good walking possibilities (page 158).

Chiselled into the hillside is St Peter's Church: tiny and, at first glance, pretty ordinary. But at first sniff it's not ordinary: it smells. Bats have taken over the interior, and as protected species it is compulsory for churches to make them welcome. The human congregation who attend the occasional service co-exist with them as best they can. Visitors, however, love the bats and the negative comments I used to see in the visitors' book have been replaced by warmly positive ones. This tiny village has supported its church since 1260 (though most of the present-day church is a Victorian restoration) and bats are expensive guests so perhaps you can spare a bit more than usual for the upkeep box.

Apart from the bats the church has a unique feature. In its musicians' gallery is a hole cut in the woodwork to allow for the bow of the double bass. There's a similar one at Parracombe, but I believe this is the only one in a gallery – so many such galleries were removed by Victorian 'restorers'. The little organ came from the ocean liner the RMS *Mauretania*, which was scrapped in 1965.

---

1 It's a steep walk down to Woody Bay. 2 St Peter's Church, Trentishoe is home to bats.
3 Heddon Valley with riverside, woodland and coastal walks. ▶

SS

MARTIN FOWLER/S

VISIT DEVON

✳ ✳ ✳

⚐ TRENTISHOE DOWN: COAST, WOODS & MOOR

❀ Croydecycle *Combe Martin & Hunter's Inn*; start: The Glass Box carpark, Trentishoe Down
⚲ SS62614767, postcode EX34 0PF or, for the shorter walk, the next carpark to the east
⚲ SS6348748017; 2½ miles or 2 miles; moderate to strenuous

This delightful walk encompasses a short section of the South West Coast Path (SWCP), a lovely level stroll through woodland and a climb up to heather and gorse moorland. Don't be fooled by the apparent short distance, however. It took me nearly two hours because of the steep descent and ascent. The walk can be shortened by omitting the coast path section.

The house aptly named 'the Glass Box' makes a convenient landmark for finding the carpark on the north side of Trentishoe Down. Before starting your walk, if the weather is clear, you might want to climb up to Trentishoe Barrow, a Bronze-Age burial mound, though there is nothing to see here these days except a fine view. A faint path leads up beside the fence of the Glass House, bearing left after a few yards (so don't follow the clearer path along the fence), and continuing up to the cairn, which marks both the barrow and the highest point on Trentishoe Down.

1 The walk proper starts from the carpark, where a path runs north to meet the SWCP – here you turn right towards The Hunter's Inn (signposted) and follow the stony trail, with lovely sea and cliff views.

2 Take the path signed County Road to the next carpark (park here if you're doing the shorter walk). At the Holdstone Down signpost turn right, following the National Trust sign along the road.

3 When you, soon after, come to the footpath to Trentishoe Manor on the right, follow this steeply downhill, first through

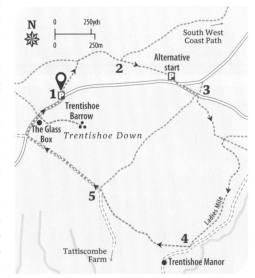

bracken and then past some magnificent old beech trees that were once part of a wall. The level stretch of Ladies Mile comes as a relief as it contours the side of the hill, passing through lovely groves of silver birch and oak. The path was cut into the side of the hill in Victorian times, supposedly so the ladies of Trentishoe Manor could walk to church.

4 Just before reaching the road and manor, look out for an unsigned path forking right through the trees. Follow this steeply uphill, a hard slog of 20 minutes or so, first through woodland, then bracken, and finally heather and gorse. Don't forget to look back at the super view.

5 You'll reach a broad farm track that links Tattiscombe Farm with the coastal road. If you left your car at the first carpark you need to follow this track to the road where you turn right, past the Glass House. If doing the shorter walk, however, take the fainter track to the right. This climbs up over Trentishoe Down and comes out on the road by the path down to the Ladies Mile, a short distance from the second carpark.

❃ ❃ ❃

6 THE HUNTER'S INN, HEDDON VALLEY & MARTINHOE

🏠 **The Hunter's Inn** Heddon Valley (page 248), **The Old Rectory Hotel** Martinhoe (page 248)

The Hunter's Inn, in the deep fold of **Heddon Valley**, was originally a thatched cottage that served ale to thirsty workers in this isolated place, but when it burned down in 1896 Colonel Lake (page 162) funded a new design based on a Swiss chalet. It has now morphed into something more in keeping with the scenery and is deservedly the most popular and best-known inn on Exmoor. Its future was secured in 2018 when it was bought by the National Trust, who will now manage the whole valley. The food has always been good here and promises to be even better when the Trust achieve their plans to use produce from their farm.

A spacious picnic area surrounded by woodland completes the scene.

The Hunter's Inn is the start or finish of several outstanding walks, all taking in sections of the South West Coast Path, and all involving strenuous hill climbing. The mile-long walk to Heddon's Mouth, down the gorge-like Heddon's Cleave, is the exception, being blissfully level and ending with the opportunity for a swim. Leading off from The Hunter's Inn is the Old Carriage Way, a broad track taking you up and along the cliffs for some of the best views on Exmoor. The path passes The Beacon, which was a Roman fortlet or lookout post.

On the opposite side of Heddon Valley, up another alarming hill, is **Martinhoe**. This hamlet consists of a few houses, the Old Rectory Hotel, and a peaceful church. There is little else to it apart from height and scenery, and it's none the worse for that.

* * *

THE HUNTER'S INN & TRENTISHOE CIRCUIT

Croydecycle *Combe Martin & Hunter's Inn*; start: The Hunter's Inn EX31 4PY

SS65504813; 3½ miles; strenuous

This tough walk brings you through some of the most sublime and varied scenery in Exmoor. Perhaps *the* most sublime, so you won't mind your bursting lungs as you climb the hills or your knees aching as you slither down them. It takes you through wooded valleys and along a superb stretch of coast path, purple with heather in the summer, close to the cliff edge (so if you're afraid of heights, this might not be for you). There's also the opportunity to visit little Trentishoe church and its resident bats. The description below has the long descent down a rough and stony path, though often with steps; many people find it easier to go uphill on rough terrain, in which case just reverse the route; it's very easy to follow.

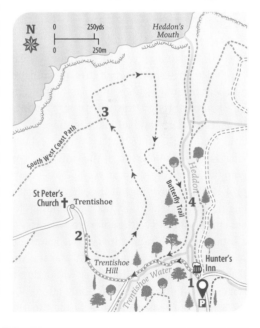

1 Park at The Hunter's Inn carpark. Walk past the inn on your right along Joses Lane, crossing first the River Heddon and then Trentishoe Water. Take the right turning up the lane towards Trentishoe church. As you gasp your way upwards you'll realise why it's been declared unfit for motors: it's very steep.

◄1 Trentishoe Down. 2 Red deer are a common sight on Exmoor.

2 Towards the top of the hill, before the few houses and farms that comprise Trentishoe, you'll see the route to the South West Coast Path on your right. (Trentishoe's church deserves a visit, however, and is only five minutes or so further on up the hill.) The footpath is grassy underfoot and takes you through bracken, with grand views of the wooded Heddon Valley to the right. It's close on a mile of easy walking before you meet the coast path.

3 Turn right, following a stony trail along the cliff edge where the view of sea, headland and heather (in the summer) is absolutely gorgeous. Being the SWCP it's carefully made, mostly following contours and with steps down the steepest part, but you still need to take care on the pebbles. The last part of the descent to the valley, still following the SWCP, is along the NT's 'butterfly trail' through woodland.

4 When you meet the Heddon Valley trail, turn right to follow the river to Joses Lane and The Hunter's Inn for some well-deserved refreshment.

To reverse the route, take Joses Lane towards Trentishoe Hill, turning right just after the second river crossing. The SWCP, up the Butterfly Trail, is signposted to the left, first through woodland, then steeply up to the cliff top.

✱ ✱ ✱

7 WOODY BAY & LEE BAY

🏠 **Treetops** Woody Bay (page 248)

Beyond Martinhoe the road continues east towards **Woody Bay**, a secluded horseshoe-shaped cove overhung with woods, through which a waterfall plunges. Its name has become inappropriately prominent in Exmoor through the efforts of a 19th-century solicitor, Colonel Benjamin Lake, who had plans to make it a major tourist attraction to rival Lynmouth. In 1895, J L W Page explained that the new road to what is now Hunter's Inn 'is the work of a syndicate, who are, it is said, going to do great things at Woodabay – towards the opening up (and probably cockneyfying) of this shady retreat. When I was last there an engineer was already busy taking soundings for a landing stage. As there are only six houses … the enterprise seems, as the Americans would say, a little previous.' Indeed it was, but it was storms that put paid to the plan, not the small population. A pier was indeed built in 1895. Lake's plans were for a 100yd-long pier with a dog-leg extension and landing stage, but eventually he could only afford 80yds. It was completed for the arrival of the first pleasure steamer in 1897, but the steamers were unable to dock at low tide and the service was sporadic. Three years later, storms had all but destroyed the pier and it was finally pulled down in

1902. Colonel Lake also funded a replacement for the original Hunter's Inn (page 159). He ended in bankruptcy and, having used some of his clients' money for his project, prison.

These days, Woody Bay has its attractions but is really only worth visiting at mid-to-low tide when there is some sand. The 800ft descent from the little carpark on the road above is enough to deter most people, though SWCP walkers will find it worth the relatively short diversion. A swim here is the reward for your efforts, with the surrounding rocks and overhanging woodland making an appealing view from the sea. Beware of trying to rinse off under the waterfall: the rocks are *very* slippery.

"A swim here is the reward for your efforts, with the surrounding rocks and overhanging woodland an appealing view."

The lazy option is to drive or walk west to **Lee Bay**. This private shingle cove is the most accessible in the region, with parking nearby and the lovely **Tea Cottage** providing snacks and cream teas. A toll road beyond the bay takes you to the Valley of Rocks (page 174) and on to Lynton and Lynmouth.

LYNTON, LYNMOUTH & AREA

Without doubt this is the most popular part of Exmoor – and deservedly so. It really does have everything, and all within walking distance: a pretty seaside village, a cliff railway, a tumbling river cutting through forested slopes, the heather-clad moor and a dollop of recent history. Painters and poets have rhapsodised about its beauty: Gainsborough thought it the perfect place to paint, and Shelley (see box, page 171) lived in Lynmouth for nine weeks with his first wife. Writing in 1928, S P B Mais felt that: 'Ordinary standards simply won't do to describe this corner of Devon. One realises dimly and dumbly that no other combe of one's acquaintance comes quite so obligingly near to the hotel door to show its beauty of wood or majesty of cliff.'

Lynmouth was 'discovered' in the early part of the 19th century when the Napoleonic Wars had closed the continent to English visitors, and the English gentry had to be satisfied with holidaying nearer to home. The Rising Sun Inn was already there to cope with this influx and other inns were hastily built, but it seems that, once the war was over, there was fierce competition between the three lodging houses for potential customers.

Murray's travel guide of 1856 warns that: 'telescopes are employed at the rival houses for the prompt discovery of the approaching traveller. He had better determine beforehand on his inn, or he may become a bone of contention to a triad of postboys, who wait with additional horses at the bottom of the hill to drag the carriage to its destination.' When you look at the hills they had to climb you can see why additional horses were required. Stage coaches continued to be used here well into the 1900s; the hills were too steep and too rough for the new-fangled charabancs.

The popularity of the village was noted, somewhat sourly, by J L W Page in 1895: 'Lynmouth consists of a single street facing the river. Every other house is a hotel or a lodging house [not much change there, then], but the general appearance of the place is not unpicturesque, and some regard has evidently been had for the romantic surroundings.' He points out that Lynmouth was once the centre of herring fishing until, in 1797, 'they suddenly departed. So Lynmouth had to fish for other fry, and does it pretty successfully. Every year does the shoal of visitors increase, and probably they pay better than herrings.'

The publisher Sir George Newnes lived in Lynton, at Hollerday House, and gave the town its cliff railway in 1890, as well as its town hall. Newnes founded the racy magazine *Tit-Bits* and followed it up with the altogether more serious *Strand Magazine*, which was the first to publish Sherlock Holmes stories.

In addition to its other attractions, this area is superb for walking, comprising not only cliffs and moorland but a selection of walks, both circular and linear, along the beautiful East Lyn River and its accompanying woodland. Indeed, Croydecycle's Mike Harrison believes 'There's no better place to walk in Britain than this area.' Just two sample walks are described here; buy Mike's *Lynton, Lynmouth & Doone Valley* map and devise your own.

8 BARBROOK & WATERSMEET HOUSE

🏠 **New Mill Farm** Barbrook (page 248)

Lynmouth is almost encircled by the A39 and accessed down dramatically steep hills, bearing the brunt of through traffic to Porlock, while Lynton, to the west of the main road, is quieter. All traffic passes

1 Lynmouth harbour, the endpoint to the Two Moors Way and the Coleridge Way. **2** The cliff railway rises 500ft using just the gravitational power of water. ▶

through **Barbrook**, with its handy service station, and farms nearby that are rearing some of Exmoor's very best meat (see box, page 168).

The less precipitous road to Lynmouth and beyond is Watersmeet Road, which takes you past one of the area's most popular tea rooms, the National Trust-operated **Watersmeet House** (☉ Easter–Oct daily, Nov–Easter Sat & Sun). Most people walk here from Lynmouth (page 172) but there is a (paying)

"The less precipitous road to Lynmouth takes you past one of the area's most popular tea rooms: Watersmeet House."

parking area on the road above with a steep path down. Everything about this former fishing lodge is perfect: the choice of snacks and cakes, and especially the location.

9 LYNTON

🏠 **Highcliffe House** (page 248)

Tourist information: Post Office, Lee Rd ☎ 01598 753313 ⬙ visitlyntonandlynmouth. com; ☉ days/hours vary seasonally

Lynton's sturdy Victorian houses and extraordinary town hall are surprising in a place that otherwise feels like a modern, upmarket holiday centre. The **town hall** is described in *The Shell Guide* of 1975 as 'a jolly edifice, "15th century" stonework, "Tudor" half timbering, and "Flemish" barge boarding'. The former Methodist Church has been put to good use: the church itself houses the rewarding Lyn Valley Arts and Crafts Centre and the hall is now a cosy 70-seat **cinema**, a charming place run by volunteers.

Lynton has a particularly good selection of accommodation, most with superb views, and some excellent shops and restaurants (page 169). Even with such a range of craft shops the **Arts and Crafts Centre** (☉ 10.00–17.00 ⬙ lynvalleyartandcrafts.co.uk), next to the town hall, stands out for its range of high-quality but affordable crafts, which includes preserves, honey and soap.

Notable shops include **Lyn Candles** on Lee Road, selling a huge range of the eponymous things with great enthusiasm, the **Lynton Sheepskin Shop**, also on Lee Road, with a comprehensive range, and **John Arbon textiles** down Queen Street with lots and lots of pure wool socks.

◀ **1** North Walk, part of the South West Coast Path, near Lynmouth. **2** Watersmeet House, an idyllic spot for lunch or a cream tea in the summer months.

MARVELLOUS MEAT

Two farmers near **Barbrook** raise animals that lead as natural lives as possible, providing the highest quality meat that can be bought direct from the farms. Other meat producers are listed in the box on page 182.

Hidden Valley Pigs (Hidden Valley Farm, Barbrook, EX35 6PH ✆ 07870 724042 ⊘ hiddenvalleypigs.co.uk) is the enterprise of Simon and Debbie Dawson, who swapped their London lives as estate agent and solicitor for rural Devon. Their smallholding focuses on rare-breed Berkshire pigs, and the Dawsons offer a variety of courses including a pig butchery and processing weekend. They also offer 'Rear a Pig'. Sadly this doesn't mean you take your piglet home with you – it remains at the farm, growing slowly and naturally, foraging in the woodland, and more or less writing progress reports to its mum. (Debbie ensures that you are kept properly informed of its wellbeing; you even have visiting and naming rights if you want.) When the time comes, the slaughterhouse is only a few miles away and the pigs get a special treat the night before.

Simon is the author of several books, including *The Sty's the Limit* and *Pigs in Clover*. The couple are currently building an off-grid ecohouse on their land – which will no doubt provide plenty of material for another book.

Victoria and Chris Eveleigh live about a mile away from Simon and Debbie, farming 'red ruby' Devon cattle and Exmoor horn sheep at **West Ilkerton Farm** (✆ 01598 752310 ⊘ westilkerton.co.uk). Their animals are born and raised on the farm, grass-fed, allowed to mature slowly and given a life that is as happy, healthy and natural as possible. The Eveleighs use the local abattoir at Combe Martin and transport their animals there themselves to ensure minimal stress at all times. The result is wonderfully succulent meat that can be ordered fresh in advance or bought frozen at any time, subject to availability. The Eveleighs sell their meat in a variety of selection boxes, and sometimes also have individual cuts available. Their gluten-free beef sausages and burgers are especially popular. During the summer months tours are available around the farm.

Linking Lynton and Lynmouth is the **cliff railway**, a masterpiece of simple engineering and a model of 'green' energy. The two carriages are counter-balanced by water. Fill the tank at the top, and it's heavy enough to pull the other carriage up as it descends. We watched the 'driver' at the bottom judge the amount of water to let out to counterbalance not only the weight of the carriage but the passengers as well. Really neat, and a great way to get to the top of a 500ft cliff. The year 2015 marked 150 years of continuous operation. Dogs and bicycles are allowed. Before the road was built in 1828, tourists were transported to Lynton on donkeys or Exmoor ponies, as were all the goods arriving in the harbour.

FOOD & DRINK

Nartnapa at The Cottage Inn Lynbridge EX35 6NR ✆ 01598 753496. ⌂ nartnapa.co.uk. This is a restaurant with a difference. First of all, it's in Lynbridge, a ten-minute walk up Lyn Way from Lynton; and it's Thai. But this is superior Thai food that has gained a host of enthusiasts. It's also well known for its Sunday roasts — and the owner brews his own beer, FatBelly Ale. Each year they host a FatBelly Festival, which spans three evenings of music and merriment.

The Oak Room Lee Rd (opposite the town hall) ✆ 01598 753838 ⌂ theoakroomlynton. co.uk. Renowned for its tapas, though the regular menu of unusual Spanish dishes and a splendid seafood platter is good too. Popular with both locals and visitors.

The Picnic Box 1 Castle Hill ✆ 01598 753721. The best place in Lynton for a morning snack, lunch or tea. Or a take-away picnic, which you can phone ahead to order. Excellent sandwiches and cream teas, with a great selection of gluten-free and vegetarian choices.

The Vanilla Pod 10 Queen St, Lynton ✆ 01598 753706. The café is average but the meals — lunch or dinner — are beautifully cooked and very popular. The menu is varied and imaginative, with a Mediterranean bias.

✳ ✳ ✳

🚶 HOLLERDAY HILL & THE VALLEY OF ROCKS

❀ Croydecycle *Lynton & Lynmouth* map; start: Lynton town hall EX35 6BT; 2.4 miles (or via Lee Abbey, 6 miles); ♀ SS71894950 easy (mostly level but some ups & downs); steep ascent from Lee Abbey.

A track goes from beside the town hall and winds up to the site of Hollerday House, over the top of Hollerday Hill and on to the Valley of Rocks. Although it is a steep climb, Hollerday Hill and the scarcely visible remains of the house are a wonderfully peaceful place with great views along the coast to Foreland Point.

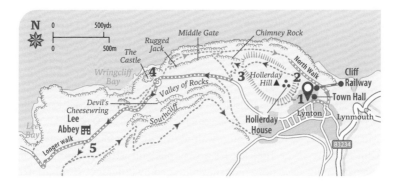

1 Follow the track as it winds left up the hill. After about 500yds, turn right – signed to the house – and you will soon reach the the terrace, originally at the front of Hollerday House, and and its splendid sea view.

2 From the terrace, bear left and follow the level path, parallel to the sea; you will soon see the first sign of the rocks, a monolith aptly known as The Castle. Other rocks, strewn around, have been given names: Rugged Jack, Devil's Cheesewring (see page 174 for an explanation for this strange name), Middle Gate and Chimney Rock.

3 The path zigzags down to the flat valley bottom, where feral goats and Exmoor ponies graze. Head towards the roundabout opposite The Castle. If you are feeling particularly energetic, and have a head for heights, The Castle can be climbed by a steadily rising path, with superb views to the west and the sheer cliffs to the north bringing home the scale of this striking landscape.

4 For the shorter walk, turn right at the roundabout to take the well-maintained path along North Walk. This is a most beautiful path, cut into the side of the cliff, with benches where you can sit and admire the view. And what a view! Behind you are the rocks, in all shapes and sizes, and ahead is Lynmouth and the Bristol Channel.

The Castle (Castle Rock) can be climbed by a steadily rising path with superb views to the west and the sheer cliffs to the north bringing home the scale of this striking landscape. It's considered by a Lynton resident to be the area's best kept secret: 'Swimming is a challenge at low tide, but great at high tide for confident swimmers. And it gets the sun for most of the day.'

For the a longer walk, with the goal of a swim in Lee Bay or a light lunch or cream tea in a delightful garden, continue heading west until you see the impressive **Lee Abbey,** a Christian community centre and retreat. Beyond it, just before Lee Bay, is **Lee Abbey Tea Cottage** (🕾 01598 752621 ⊙ May–Sep 10.00–17.00 Fri & Sat), with tables set out in sun or shade in a tranquil garden.

5 Return to Lynton on the track that zigzags up Southcliff on the south side of the road – a very steep climb, but you're rewarded with some splendid views.

10 LYNMOUTH

🏠 **Orchard House** (page 248)

Tourist information: Exmoor National Park Centre, The Pavilion, The Esplanade, Lynmouth EX35 6EQ 🕾 01598 752509 🖉 exmoor-nationalpark.gov.uk ⊙ 10.00–17.00 daily

Most people staying in Lynton walk down to Lynmouth and take the Cliff Railway (page 168) up. It's a very pleasant, steepish stroll down, the path lit by solar-powered lamps donated by different organisations.

Lynmouth is clearly very much older than its partner and very pretty with its harbour, cliffs and wooded hillsides.

Close to the Cliff Railway on The Esplanade in the western part of Lynmouth is **The Pavilion** and the **Exmoor National Park Centre**. It has a café, a well-stocked shop with maps and guides, displays of wildlife, webcams, an audiovisual presentation giving an overview of Exmoor and a microscope with which you can study marine creatures collected on a guided tide-pooling excursion.

Continuing to the harbour, you can take a boat trip to Valley of Rocks and Lee Bay (Lynmouth Boat Trips ✆ 01598 753207 or book at Glen Lyn Gorge, just by the water spout) or continue

PERCY BYSSHE SHELLEY & LYNMOUTH

The poet Shelley was born in 1792. His father, a Whig MP and baronet, had high hopes that his son would follow him into parliament, sending him to Eton and Oxford. He was bullied at the former and expelled from the latter because of his rather too-free distribution of a pamphlet he had written, *The Necessity of Atheism*. His next act of rebellion was to marry 16-year-old Harriet Westbrook, not so much because he loved her but because his father had told him that he would support any number of illegitimate children, but would not countenance an unsuitable marriage. He was 19. His father immediately stopped his allowance.

In 1812 the couple came to live in Lynmouth. Shelley described their approach to the village, down Countisbury Hill, as 'a fairy scene – little Lynmouth, then some thirty cottages, rose-clad and myrtle-clad, nestling at the foot of the hills. It was enough.' There is some debate as to where he lived, but most agree that it was at the cottage now named Shelley's Hotel.

Though he explored the area widely, he seems to have written little poetry in his new home, being more interested in disseminating information on radical politics. To this end he would row out from Lynmouth with leaflets sealed into bottles and even suspended from fire balloons. In this endeavour he was joined by a schoolmistress, Elizabeth Hitchener, and also co-opted his manservant Dan Hill to post extracts of Tom Paine's *Rights of Man* in Barnstaple, for which the poor man was arrested and imprisoned.

Life then became a little too hot in Lynmouth and the couple fled to Wales by boat, leaving a mass of unpaid debts and precious little poetry.

Subsequently Shelley fell in love with another 16-year-old, Mary, who went on to write *Frankenstein*. Harriet drowned herself in the Serpentine, and Mary and Percy married and moved to Italy where he was safe from prosecution, and where he started to write his best poetry. He died at sea aged 29 in 1822.

strolling and buy an ice cream from one of the dozen or so outlets. **The Lynmouth Flood Memorial Hall**, on pedestrianised Lynmouth Street, houses two exhibitions. On the ground floor is the story of the famous lifeboat rescue of 1899, while the upper floor is given over to the great Lynmouth flood of 1952 when, after torrential rain on Exmoor, a wall of water carrying broken trees and boulders washed down the East and West Lyn rivers. It happened in the dead of night, with the electricity supply one of the first casualties, so all the terrified villagers could do was listen to the roar of the approaching torrent. Many houses were destroyed and 34 people lost their lives. As with all major disasters, this has its own conspiracy theory – that at that time the government was experimenting with cloud seeding.

Some visitors only get as far as the main street, Riverside Road, and the pedestrianised Lynmouth Street. This is a pity since beyond this, on Watersmeet Road, is a working pottery, **Lynmouth Pottery** (✆ 07821 817105 russellkingstonceramics.co.uk ☉ generally 10.00–17.00 Mon–Sat), with a range of ceramics and some charming sculptures.

⅄ FOOD & DRINK

The Esplanade Fish Bar 2 The Esplanade ✆ 01598 753798 ☉ noon–20.00 daily. A deservedly popular fish and chip shop facing the bay. Huge portions. Eat in or take away: beware seagulls if you eat outside!

Pavilion Dining Room First floor, Lynmouth Pavilion, The Esplanade (next to the Cliff Railway) ✆ 01598 751064 ☉ 10.00–17.00 daily. Just the place for a light lunch or tea; uncrowded and with wonderful views over the harbour.

* * *

⅄ WATERSMEET & THE COASTAL PATH OR VIA THE LYN TO ROCKFORD & BEYOND

✤ Croydecycle *Lynton & Lynmouth* map; start: Lynmouth, Tors Rd , EX35 6EP
♀ SS72404942; 5 miles (or more); moderate with some steep climbs

This half-day walk takes in the full spectrum of Exmoor: village, river, tea room, moor, pub and coast. And it can be extended deep into Lorna Doone country. The 1½ mile-path from Lynmouth to Watersmeet is both dramatic, up a deep, wooded gorge, and very easy, following the Lyn gently upstream. The path is often surfaced, so you can admire the woods and river, and look out for birds, without having to watch where you're going.

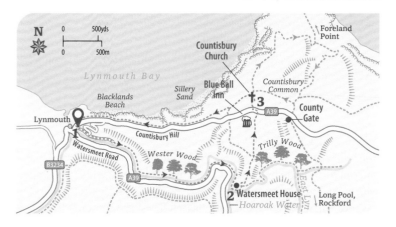

1 Start walking on the left side of the river; you'll cross to the right for a stretch, and then back again to Watersmeet, where the East Lyn River and Hoar Oak Water come together at the National Trust tea room at **Watersmeet House** (page 167).

2 From the lodge continue upstream, and you'll soon see the sign to Countisbury. Zigzag up the hill through a fairy-tale grove of stunted sessile oaks, all bent and twisted, and emerge on to the moor brightened by clumps of bell heather. Walk over the hill to the A39.

3 Here, enjoy a pint or meal in the welcoming **Blue Ball Inn** or resist the temptation and cross the road to visit Countisbury Church, its pinnacled tower peeping above the horizon. Ahead is **Foreland Point**, which adds another couple of miles to the walk if you want to stand on Devon's most northerly point, or you can take the coast path to the left and walk west back to the town. For Foreland Point, set your sights on the radio mast, accessed by a grassy path, and admire the view before dropping down the other side. A path runs round the side of Foreland Point to the lighthouse, but it's precariously narrow, so not very inviting; best to take the lighthouse road there.

If you want to keep to the river and enjoy the best wild swimming on Exmoor, you have a choice from Watersmeet: take the path that follows the northern bank of the river or follow the stony track on the opposite side that leads through oak and beech woods. Either way, it's 1½ miles to the hamlet of **Rockford** and The Rockford Inn, with **Long Pool**, which is marked on the Croydecycle map, roughly a mile from Watersmeet. Joanna Griffin describes this as 'the absolute pinnacle of wild swimming'. Follow the river along the south bank upstream from the National Trust tea room: a short steep path to the left, shortly after Ash Bridge, leads to the pool. 'Long Pool is easy to miss, being below the main footpath, but this, along with the moss-covered banks, gives it a special secluded feel,' says Joanna. 'It's a bit of scramble over rather slippery rocks to get in but once you're in there is a lovely deep stretch, long enough for a good swim upstream towards the waterfall. The current can be strong here, providing an endless-pool effect for stronger swimmers, or you can let it sweep you back downstream to shallower water.'

From Rockford you can take the quiet lanes back to Hillford Bridge and down the River Hoar Oak Water to Watersmeet.

* * *

11 THE VALLEY OF ROCKS

The Valley of Rocks is accessible by car, but it's such a lovely walk that if you can it's well worth doing on foot from Lynton (page 169). The valley, which would be unexceptional on Dartmoor, is quite extraordinary on Exmoor where the soft sandstone has left few sharp contours. The most likely explanation for these heaps and castles of rock is that this was once a river valley, the boulders being deposited during the ice age, before the river changed its course. Glaciation and weather erosion did the rest.

The place was already well known when R D Blackmore wrote *Lorna Doone* in the 1860s. The hero John Ridd goes there to consult a wise woman, noting that 'foreigners, who come and go without seeing much of Exmoor, have called [it] the "Valley of Rocks".' The rocks already had their names: 'On the right hand is an upward crag, called by some "The Castle", easy enough to scale... Facing this, from the inland side and the elbow of the valley, a queer old pile of rock arises, bold behind one another, and quite enough to affright a man, if it only were ten times larger. This is called the "Devil's Cheese-ring" or the "Devil's Cheese-knife" which mean the same thing, as our fathers were used to eat their cheese from a scoop; and perhaps in old time the upmost rock... was like to such an implement if Satan ate cheese untoasted.'

The Valley of Rocks. ▶

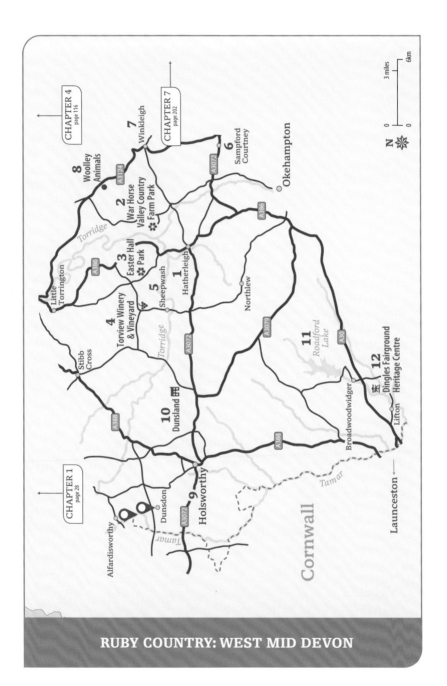

RUBY COUNTRY: WEST MID DEVON

8 Woolley Animals

7 Winkleigh

2 War Horse Valley Country Farm Park

6 Sampford Courtney

Okehampton

Torridge

A3124

A386

A3072

3 Easter Hall Park

1 Hatherleigh

Little Torrington

5 Sheepwash

Northlew

A386

4 Torview Winery & Vineyard

Torridge

A3072

Roadford Lake

A3079

11

A30

Stibb Cross

12 Dingles Fairground Heritage Centre

A388

10 Dunsland

Broadwoodwidger

Lifton

Alfardisworthy

Dunsdon

A3072

9 Holsworthy

A388

Tamar

Launceston

Tamar

Cornwall

N

0   3 miles
0   6km

6
RUBY COUNTRY: WEST MID DEVON

Ruby Country is quiet and unspoilt – a tranquil, pastoral land far removed from the hurly-burly of the coast. Hidden in this rolling countryside is a Devon of villages and hamlets and just two small market towns, Hatherleigh and Holsworthy. Bounded by the coast to the north, Dartmoor to the south and the Cornish border to the west, this region has always been cattle country. In 2001 the whole area was heavily affected by Foot and Mouth Disease: markets closed, movement was limited and businesses collapsed. Challenged by this devastation, the region's councils, businesses, Wildlife Trust and, most of all, its people came together under the Ruby Country banner to reinvent themselves – the name Ruby Country coming from the Ruby Red Devon cattle that are raised here.

"Many small farms have diversified, so you'll now find vineyards, farm parks and even a gin distillery here."

Farming is still important but many small farms have diversified, so you'll now find vineyards, farm parks and even a gin distillery here. New cycleways, footpaths and horse trails have opened and traditionally farmed Culm grasslands have been adopted by the Devon Wildlife Trust and are now unspoilt reserves full of wildflowers, insects and birds. With plenty of opportunities to fish, sail, walk or ride, it is easy to reconnect with the natural world here. Ruby Country's history is all around you, whether you are staying in a thatched cottage or spending the evening in a traditional pub, drinking local beer and eating beef raised by the farmer at the next table.

 WET-WEATHER ACTIVITIES

Dingles Fairground Heritage Centre (page 199)
Holsworthy Museum (page 195)
Torview Vineyard (page 186)

GETTING THERE & AROUND

Travelling around Ruby Country by public transport requires planning. There is no rail service in the area; the nearest station is at Okehampton, served by the new Dartmoor Line from Exeter, which was reinstated as a normal passenger service in 2021 having been closed in 1972.

Buses cover a surprisingly good, if infrequent, network across Ruby Country; you're likely to find buses are timed to be convenient for school children or market shopping rather than visitors, however. Buses 5A and 6 link Okehampton with Hatherleigh (20 mins) and Holsworthy (about an hour), respectively; both run about every two hours. Devon Council provide a lot of information about trains and buses on their website (⌀ traveldevon.info).

The A30, running along the southern border of Ruby Country, is the only dual-carriageway in the region and you'll find the other A-roads much slower. Off these main routes, expect to be on a single-lane track with blind bends and, sometimes, grass growing between your wheels.

SELF-POWERED TRAVEL

For cyclists, the region's network of narrow lanes offers a choice of routes, although you will have to dodge the odd pot-hole. Sustrans Route 3, from Lands End to Bristol, passes through Holsworthy and Sheepwash before joining the Tarka Trail near Hatherleigh, while Sustrans Route 27 runs south from Hatherleigh to form the Devon Coast to Coast route and attracts both cyclists and walkers.

This is good walking country, with river valleys, tiny villages and country pubs providing countless focal points for walks. The many wildlife reserves managed by the Devon Wildlife Trust (⌀ devonwildlifetrust.org) are great places for a short walk that gets close to nature. OS Explorer maps 111 and 112 cover the area.

Ride The Ruby Country (⌀ ridetherubycountry.co.uk) has produced a number of walking, riding and cycling guides. All are available from the tourist information offices in Holsworthy and Hatherleigh or you can download them from their website.

---

1 Bridge Street, Hatherleigh. **2** Harvest time at Torview Winery. **3** Roger Dean's sculpture in Hatherleigh. **4** Sampford Courtenay. **5** Obelisk to Lt Colonel William Morris, Hatherleigh. **6** Ruby Red Devon cattle, near Black Dog village. ▶

HATHERLEIGH & AREA

This eastern half of Ruby Country is in the catchment of the River Torridge. Villages of cob cottages, pretty churches and unusual customs are to be found among a landscape of green hills and tiny lanes. At its heart is Hatherleigh, set above the River Lew, with two good pubs. It makes a good place to base yourself.

1 HATHERLEIGH

🏠 **The George** (page 249) 🗼 **Belvedere Tower** (page 249), **Lemon Cottage** (page 249)
Tourist Information: 15 Market St, EX20 3JN ✉ charlesdumpleton@yahoo.co.uk

> 'It is perhaps fortunate that Hatherleigh is discovered only by the lucky or discerning tourist since it has been able to retain its character as a close-knit, real, working community.'
> *The Story of Hatherleigh* by Hatherleigh Parish Council (1981)

Six miles north of Okehampton and with a population of just 1,300, Hatherleigh is the smallest town in Devon – don't be caught calling it a village. Henry III declared it a town with its own market over 800 years ago and wandering the narrow streets that snake up the hill from

PANNIER MARKETS

Pannier markets could once be found all over Devon; the Tiverton market has been open since AD740. Their name comes from the pannier baskets carried by the horses and ponies to the market; farmers, or more often their wives, left their farms and smallholdings early on market day with all their fruit and vegetables, pies and preserves loaded into their pony's panniers for the long walk to market. Once there, goods were sold directly from the pannier baskets and, with any luck, the baskets would be empty by late morning. With a pocket full of money, they might then shop for tools, seed, foods they could not grow and, perhaps, for a pint or two of local ale.

In the 19th century, some pannier markets moved to an indoor hall and this often led to more permanent market stalls being established. Other markets fell into disuse, unable to compete with shops and supermarkets. In recent years, the pannier markets have enjoyed a renaissance as 'farmer's markets' where consumers can, once again, buy directly from the farmer.

So-called pannier markets are still popular, although the ponies are long gone. They can be found in Bideford (Mon–Sat), Holsworthy (Wed), Hatherleigh (Tue), South Molton (Thu, Sat), Barnstaple (Tue–Sat), Tiverton (Mon–Sat) and Great Torrington (Mon–Sat). They are all best visited in the morning.

the River Lew really does feel like living history. Many houses date back to the 15th century and they come in all shapes and sizes: tiled and thatched, cob and stone. But this is also a town where history and tradition blend comfortably with modern life – the community centre, for example, boasts a flood-lit Astro Turf pitch and a popular skate park. Staying in Hatherleigh, one quickly gets drawn into the town and its community as the friendly locals are very proud of their home.

Not everything is as old as it seems here. **The George**, on Market Street, is thatched and *looks* medieval but what you see today is a stunning replica. The building was once the courthouse for the Abbots of Tavistock, becoming a coaching inn after their dissolution in 1539. In December 1980, it was set alight by a disgruntled chef and, despite the efforts of 100 firefighters, the hotel burnt to the ground; it was carefully rebuilt using traditional materials and craftsmanship at an eye-watering cost of £2.5 million. It's possible to stay here (page 249), and the restaurant serves good food.

Hatherleigh was once home to a whopping 17 pubs – most of which have converted into housing – look out for house names like The Royal Oak on Bridge Street that hint at the property's former life. Working in the market was clearly thirsty work and the lovely old police station in South Street, also now a private house, was doubtless where some sobered up. Further up Market Street, opposite the square, is the town's other surviving pub, **The Tally Ho** (✆ 01837 810306). Dating back to the 15th century, it boasts its own brewery, located in the town's old bakery. The local hunt, the Hatherleigh Harriers, always met here – which may explain why it changed its name in the 1950s from The New Inn to The Tally Ho.

"Hatherleigh was once home to a whopping 17 pubs – look out for house names like The Royal Oak on Bridge Street."

Continuing up Market Street, you'll find **Hatherleigh Pottery** (⌂ hatherleighpottery.co.uk) where potters Jane and Michael do all their work on-site. Jane makes everything from tableware to wall hangings, while Michael's work is more exuberant – large platters, bowls and dishes glazed in dramatic colours. There is a lot of **art** dotted around the town; near the market carpark is our favourite piece, Roger Dean's wonderful sculpture commemorating the old sheep market. Hatherleigh also holds an annual **arts festival** in July with workshops, exhibitions and music (⌂ hatherleighfestival.co.uk).

LOCAL PRODUCE

Mid Devon is renowned for its good food and drink which is a real delight for both locals and visitors. Locally made produce can be found in the pannier markets (see box, page 180) and most local shops, restaurants and pubs. Many products are not branded and just have a label describing them, for example 'Meryl's Red Velvet Cake'. The suppliers below have grown into small businesses and their brands are worth looking out for.

FOOD

Black Dog Eggs ⬧ blackdogeggs.co.uk. An odd name but Black Dog is the name of the village where these free-range eggs are laid by hens whose welfare is assured by the RSPCA. The eggs are guaranteed to be less than 48 hours old and can often be found in farm shops and butchers.

Crediton Dairy ⬧ creditondairy.co.uk. Arctic Iced Coffee and Moo Milkshakes may not make you think of Mid Devon but this dairy, next to the church in Crediton, has been running since 1947. They are still dedicated to using milk from local, family-run, dairy farms.

Curworthy Cheese ⬧ curworthycheese. co.uk. Award-winning cheese has been made at Stockbeare Farm since 1996 but the recipe dates from the 17th century. Curworthy is a full fat hard cheese that's creamy when young and has a fuller flavoured when aged. If you like a bit more heat, try their chilli cheese – the chillies are grown on Dartmoor.

Farmer Tom Ice Cream ⬧ dunstaple.co.uk. Forty delicious flavours of ice cream and sorbet produced from the milk of their own cows on Dunstaple Farm near Holsworthy. The lemon crunch is excellent, as is the tutti frutti, the double choc and ...

Foxcombe Bakehouse ⬧ foxcombebake house.co.uk. Helen started making cakes for the local pannier market at her kitchen table. Now, at her farm near Holsworthy, Foxcombe Bakehouse produces a small range of cakes and biscuits, all hand-baked and using local ingredients with no added preservatives. We love the walnut brownies. Plastic-free packaging and a good gluten-free range.

Quicke's Cheese Newton St Cyres EX5 5AY ⬧ quickes.co.uk. Quicke's is cheesemaking at its best: the Quicke family have been farming here since Henry VIII and they have been cheesemakers for over 50 years.

The old cattle and sheep market closed in 2018 but the community **pannier market** (⊙ 09.00–13.00 Tue), dating from 1693, is still a big draw. It is worth seeking out, with a great selection of local produce. At the time of writing, a new purpose-built market building was just opening – it's located just beyond the new housing at the rear of the market carpark along Old Market Way.

Back in the square, where you may be lucky enough to catch the town's silver band playing, take the narrow little lane that leads to the

Their outstanding clothbound cheddar is traditionally made by hand and then slowly matured; they also produce whey butter, which is tricky to make but a healthier alternative to normal butter. There is a small on-site factory shop (◷ 10.00–16.00 Mon–Fri).

The Red Ruby Farm Shop Clannaborough Barton EX17 6DA ◿ redrubydevonbeef.co.uk ◷ 09.30–17.30 Wed–Sat. Red Ruby Devon beef, naturally grown and hung on their farm near Copplestone. Peter can tell you exactly where your beef came from and how it was reared, so you can buy with full knowledge of the meat's provenance.

Taw Valley Creamery North Tawton EX20 2DA. Taw Valley uses traditional cheese-making techniques to produce award-winning cheeses from their plant near Sampford Courtenay. Their range includes favourites like cheddar, red Leicester and double Gloucester. There is a small shop at the creamery (◷ 09.00–17.00 Mon–Fri).

DRINK

Gotland Gin (page 189)
Hanlons Beers (page 224)

Holsworthy Ales ◿ holsworthyales.co.uk. Holsworthy Ales was started just ten years ago in a micro-brewery in Clawton on the outskirts of Holsworthy. Their four main beers are all vegan friendly, with no chemicals added to the beautiful Devon water they use. We like Muck 'n Straw best but recommend taking the time to check them all out.

Sam's Cider ◿ winkleighcider.co.uk. The company is named after Sam Inch who, in 1916, started to make cider in Winkleigh. David Bridgman is at the helm today, having joined the company at the tender age of 15, over 50 years ago. Sam's produce a full range of ciders and autumn scrumpies.

Sandford Orchards Cider (page 220)
Taw Valley Ale ◿ tawvalleybrewery.com. Amy and Marc left Brighton six years ago with the dream of drawing water from their own well, mixing it with malted barley and English hops in their 17th-century thatched cob barn and making beer. It all sounds pretty crazy – but they now brew excellent ales that are often featured as the guest ale in local pubs.

Ten Acres Vineyard (page 249)
Torview Wines (page 186)

churchyard, passing the old vestry on your right. The 15th-century **Church of St John the Baptist** is well worth a visit for its impressive medieval interior, with a host of angels looking down from the barrel roof, and a 12th-century font. In 1990 the church became famous when, during a great storm, the spire fell and crashed through the nave roof. It has all been beautifully restored.

From the church, there is an interesting two-mile **walk** on tracks and lanes that offers some great views over the moors to Dartmoor. Take the

HATHERLEIGH CARNIVAL

Hatherleigh seems to thrive on festivals, all announced by the town crier. Perhaps the most exciting is the annual carnival (⊘ hatherleighcarnival.co.uk) that dates back to 1903, though its flaming tar barrels date back much further. In pagan times, effigies of townsfolk who had misbehaved in the previous year were burnt around Halloween. Now, on a Friday night in November, the town's children, led by the Hatherleigh Silver Band, pull the unlit tar barrels on sledges to the top of the town. At 05.00 the next day, the tar barrels are set alight and dragged, ablaze, through the streets and the carnival begins. There follows a day of fun and music, with everyone in fancy dress. In the evening, there is a traditional carnival parade with floats and a carnival queen and, since this is Hatherleigh, flaming torches. The evening climaxes with even more tar barrels being set alight.

path diagonally uphill across the churchyard and then keep ahead on Church Lane, passing the old rectory, and on into Sanctuary Lane. After passing the farm, keep right up the marked track and you will soon pass the **Belvedere Tower**. Erected in 1879, this folly was used as a lookout point in World War II and is now run as a tiny, one-room romantic holiday home for two (⊘ holidaycottages.co.uk) with a private decked area on the roof giving 360° degree panoramic views.

Continuing on, you come to a road. Turn left and soon, on your left, you'll see the impressive **obelisk to Lt Colonel William Morris**. Born in Hatherleigh, Morris served in Crimea and led the charge of the Light Brigade (he's the one married to Vanessa Redgrave in the 1968 film, *The Charge of the Light Brigade*). He survived to tell the tale but died in India in 1858, aged just 37. From the obelisk you can look across Hatherleigh moor to the tors of Dartmoor. In the 14th century, the householders of Hatherleigh were given 500 acres of this moor to graze their stock and collect gorse for their fires. These rights continue today and entitled householders are known as 'potboilers'. You can return the way you came or just follow this road back into the town.

¶¶ FOOD & DRINK

One Market Street Cafe 1 Market St ✆ 01837 810582 ⊘ onemarketstreetcafe.com ⊙ 09.00–16.00 Tue & Thu–Sat, 09.00–14.30 Wed. Tom and Hannah's welcoming café serves excellent coffee and truly wonderful homemade cakes. Breakfasts, light lunches and cream teas make use of local and seasonal ingredients.

2 WAR HORSE VALLEY COUNTRY FARM PARK

Iddesleigh EX19 8SN ✐ 01837 810318 ⬧ warhorsevalley.co.uk ☉ Easter–end Sep
14.00–18.00 daily

Just over three miles northeast of Hatherleigh, War Horse Country Park
is a wonderfully eclectic mix of interesting sights, including a family-
friendly farm and a museum with exhibits covering everything from
farming history to World War I.

A 400-year-old cob barn houses the World War I and War Horse
exhibitions, focusing in particular on the effect that war had on this part
of Devon and the invaluable part horses played in the conflict. You can
even walk along a replica World War I trench, complete with the horrific
sounds of the battlefield. Also featured is the puppet horse, Joey, from
the stage adaptation of Michael Morpurgo's novel *War Horse* (see box,
below); the author lives next door. Another exhibition focuses on local

WAR HORSE

It was as a series of chance encounters that
piqued Sir Michael Morpurgo's interest in
the role horses played in World War I. While
drinking in The Duke of York in Iddesleigh he
got talking to World War I veteran Wilfred
Ellis who explained how horses were used in
France during the war. Soon after he met both
Captain Budgett, who had been a cavalry
officer in the same war, and Albert Weeks,
a local farmer who remembered the army
coming to Mid Devon to buy horses. (There
is a photograph of horses being bought in
Hatherleigh town square in the museum at
War Horse Valley Country Park; see above).

It was after these conversations that Sir
Michael, already a successful children's
author, decided to tell the story of the Great
War from a horse's perspective. His book
focuses on a young horse, Joey, who lives on a
Mid Devon farm. At the outbreak of war, Joey
is sold to the army. He initially serves in the
mounted infantry before being captured and
used to pull a German ambulance cart and,
later, an artillery wagon. When the Allies
advance, Joey changes sides once again and,
by chance, is reunited with his original owner
who has been called up to serve in a military
hospital. Joey has many further adventures
before ending up, once again, back at his Mid
Devon farm.

Over a million horses were bought by
the British Army during World War I. They
served on all fronts and suffered along with
the soldiers on both sides, with only 65,000
horses returning at the end of the war. These
surviving horses were often auctioned off to
the highest bidder and few returned to their
original homes.

War Horse was made into a play by the
National Theatre which has toured worldwide
and, in 2011, into a very successful film by
Steven Spielberg.

farming history with a 1915 Mogul, one of the oldest tractors in the country. It all makes one realise how slow and manual farming was a hundred years ago; cutting a field of grass with a scythe rather than a machine must have taken forever.

"There is a half-mile farm trail or, if your legs are weary, you can opt for owner Graham's 30-minute trailer ride."

Once you've had your fill of history, make time to explore the farm itself. Animals include pygmy goats, huge Kunekune pigs, and sheep – in spring you might be lucky enough to see lambing. Year-round you can feed the alpacas, pat the Shetland ponies and collect eggs from the hen house. There is also a circular half-mile farm trail that explores the site or, if your legs are getting weary, you can opt for owner Graham's 30-minute trailer ride (⊙ 15.45) instead. A small on-site **café** serves cream teas and kids can entertain themselves on the tractor go-karts.

3 EASTER HALL PARK

🏠 **Easter Hall Park** (page 249)

Petrockstowe EX20 3HP ✐ 01837 810350 ⊘ easterhallpark.co.uk; booking essential

Five miles north of Hatherleigh, Easter Hall is a must for horse lovers. Friendly owners Nick and Gail have enormous experience in carriage driving and offer carriage rides to visitors. They offer lessons with British Horse Society (BHS) qualified instructors, in the basics or to help you improve your skills, in their arena.

There is livery available for visitors to stable their own horses and an impressive four-person log cabin if you would like to stay on-site, with or without your own horse. As the equestrian centre is set on a 200-acre farm of pasture and woodland, there is plenty of scope for leisurely rides across the rolling Devon countryside.

4 TORVIEW WINERY & VINEYARD

Sheepwash EX21 5PB ✐ 07977 408829 ⊘ torview.co.uk ⊙ guided tours Apr–Oct 11.00 & 14.00 Fri, Jul & Aug also Thu & Sat; booking essential

Devon has an ever-increasing number of vineyards, but there are few that you can visit and be guided by a really passionate expert. At Torview, just a mile north of Sheepwash, Tim will take you around his vineyard and explain the site's 15-year history, where he now has over

THE DEVIL'S STONE

Five miles west of Sheepwash lies the village of Shebbear and its newly renovated 17th-century inn, The Devil's Stone (page 249). Locals and travellers alike are welcomed in the cosy bar with its low wooden beams, flagstone floors and open fires. Some say that the inn is haunted by three different ghosts and that a secret tunnel links the inn to the church. Yet it's the pub's name that hints at the village's greatest legend – the devil's stone.

On 5 November, when many people are setting off fireworks to celebrate Bonfire Night, the villagers of Shebbear are more concerned about the devil and a huge one-ton boulder.

At 20.00, the church bells are rung and then the vicar appears on the village green to recount the tale of the devil's stone. The story goes that the devil went up to Heaven to challenge God and cause trouble, but St Michael and his angels intervened and forced the devil back. As the devil looked down at the earth, he spied the sleepy village of Shebbear and decided to make trouble there, but St Michael could see what was happening and threw a rock that hit the devil on his back. The devil fell and was crushed, trapped beneath the rock.

Concerned for their safety, every year the villagers, holding lanterns aloft, surround the stone, declaring God's triumph. Fearful that the devil may be trying to dig his way out, the church bell ringers, armed with crowbars, roll the stone over to ensure that the devil remains trapped, and the village stays safe for another year.

7,000 vines of three grape varieties – Pinot Noir, Rondo and Dornfelder. In the winery, Tim will show you how he produces award-winning red wines, all on site, so you can see the complete process, from vine to glass. Speaking of which, the hour-long tour concludes with a tasting of three Torview wines.

5 SHEEPWASH

🏠 **Devil's Stone Inn** (page 249), **Half Moon Inn** (page 249) 🏕 **Syncocks Farm** (page 249)

Five miles northwest of Hatherleigh, the tiny village of Sheepwash has a population of only 253. It is the epitome of a Devon village and is as quiet and serene as they come. Life centres around the market square with its old hand-operated water pump, some fine cob and thatch cottages, a post office and store and the popular Half Moon Inn; just beyond the square is the parish church of St Lawrence .

This peaceful scene disguises the turbulent history of a strong community that has survived many changes. First documented in 1166,

A GOOD HAT & A GOOD PAIR OF SHOES

Cob cottages can be seen throughout Devon with their characteristic smooth walls and thatched roofs. The term 'cob' was first used around 1600 and, while the building technique has now largely died out, there are still a few cob cottages being built today. This edited extract from *An Encyclopaedia of Cottage, Farm, and Villa Architecture* by John Claudius Loudon (1839) describes how these cottages were traditionally built.

The cob walls of Devonshire are composed of earth and straw mixed up with water, well beaten and trodden together. These walls are made two feet thick and are raised upon a foundation of stonework. The higher the stonework is carried the better, as it elevates the cobwork from the moisture of the ground. After a wall is raised to a certain height, it is allowed some weeks to settle before more is laid on. The first rise is about four feet; the next not so high. In forming cob walls, one man stands on the work to receive the cob, which is pitched up to him by a man below.

The solidity of cob walls depends much upon their not being hurried in the process of making them for, if hurried, the walls will surely swag from the perpendicular. In Devonshire, the builders of cob-wall houses like to begin their work when the birds begin to build their nests, in order that there may be time to cover in the shell of the building before winter.

Cob houses are considered remarkably warm and healthy and they are generally covered with thatch. The durability of cob is said to depend upon its having 'a good hat and a good pair of shoes'; that is, a good roof and a good foundation.

the village was named 'Schepewast', meaning 'the place where sheep are washed before shearing'. Shepherds would drive their sheep off the surrounding moors and wash them in the local beck, a small stream feeding the River Torridge. A settlement grew up around the beck and throughout the Middle Ages sheep farming prospered and the village grew. A market was regularly held in the square attracting people from all the neighbouring farms.

Disaster struck in 1743 when a great fire destroyed much of the village, including the church which was so badly damaged it had to be demolished. The market was consequently relocated to Holsworthy and many people moved away; it was ten years before the village was rebuilt and people returned.

Rural life progressed quietly until 1834 when the new Poor Law was brought in, depressing already low agricultural wages. The villagers of

Sheepwash rioted, setting alight several hayricks. Despite the efforts of a hostile crowd, the five ringleaders were arrested by the North Devon Yeomanry, tried in Exeter and jailed for three months.

Though a temporary church had been hurriedly constructed after the 1743 fire, it wasn't until 1880 that a new parish church was commissioned, at a cost of £1,900, by the splendidly named lord of the manor, Charles Henry Rolle Hepburn-Stuart-Forbes-Trefusis. It is worth a visit inside to admire the splendid stained-glass windows which depict many lesser-known saints including St Petrock and St Alban. Amazingly, Sheepwash now has three churches: the parish church of St Lawrence, a Methodist chapel and a Baptist church.

In the 18th century there were four pubs in Sheepwash, today only **The Half Moon Inn** (page 249) remains. This inn, situated in the village square, offers rooms, food and drink, and excellent fishing: the River Torridge runs just a quarter of a mile south of Sheepwash and the inn has its own exclusive beats on the river for trout and salmon fishing and Charles Innes, the guru of the Torridge, is available to offer guidance. Charles has been fishing the river since he was a boy and wrote *Torridge Reflections*, a definitive guide to game fishing.

⁕ FOOD & DRINK

The Black River Inn Black Torrington EX21 5PT ✆ 01409 231888 ⌂ blackriverinn.co.uk ◷ drinks 17.00–23.00 Mon–Wed, noon–23.00 Thu–Sat, noon–18.30 Sun; food noon–14.30 & 18.00–21.00 Thu–Sat, noon–15.00 Sun. Locals recommended this excellent pub to us, just a couple of miles west of Sheepwash. Alex and Gill serve Devon beer and cider and delicious food. Everything is cooked without gas hobs or electric ovens; instead, they have a wood-burning oven that also produces the embers and coals for use under pan rings, grills and the stove top. They try to source local produce, some from their own garden, and even the wood comes from just up the road. While Black River has a selection of main courses, it was their tapas that really impressed us. These are great for sharing and there is a huge selection – don't miss the trout gravlax or their padron peppers. Many vegan, dairy-free and gluten-free dishes.

Gotland Gin Highampton EX21 5LS ✆ 07764 277038 ⌂ gotlandgin.co.uk ◷ noon–18.00 Thu–Sat & bank hols or by appointment. See ad, page 200. An outdoor, covered bar with a sunset view, serving Gotland's wonderful gin, made on site, and other drinks too, situated just over a mile south of Sheepwash. The bar can be booked for your exclusive use or you can just turn up; you can also book food platters in advance to accompany your drinks. In their tiny distillery, Dawn and Mark can explain the process of making their hand-crafted gin. The shop sells gin, of course, plus sheepskins and local crafts.

6 SAMPFORD COURTNEY

🏠 **The Cow Shed** (page 249)

This village five miles or so north of Okehampton is known mainly for its involvement in the Prayer Book Rebellion of 1549 (see box, below). It's also a stop on the Dartmoor Railway, so is accustomed to visitors and presents itself well, having 70 or so listed buildings and monuments. As Arthur Mee wrote 70-odd years ago: 'It is charming, with white cottages and thatched roofs and a lofty pinnacled tower. Old crosses keep watch by the road, and another guards the 15th-century church.' That **church**, St Andrew's, rebuilt from an earlier building in 1450 and mentioned in Simon Jenkins's *England's Thousand Best Churches*, has some fine bosses in its wagon roof, including a sow suckling seven rather elongated piglets, and a permanent descriptive display about the Prayer Book Rebellion. There's also a venerable old oak chest, made from a single block of wood, and a rare walnut pulpit.

THE PRAYER BOOK REBELLION

Janice Booth

As part of the Protestant reforms instigated under the boy king Edward VI, the familiar prayer book in Latin was declared illegal and, from Whit Sunday 1549, churches in England were required to adopt the new *Book of Common Prayer* in English and to adapt their traditional rituals. Resistance to this was particularly strong among the villagers of Devon and Cornwall, as people saw their traditional methods of worship under threat. At Sampford Courtenay they likened the English prayer book to a 'Christmas game', something like a Nativity play without true substance; initially their priest obeyed orders, removed his robes and conducted the 'new' Sunday service, but vocal parishioners quickly forced him to revert to the Latin form. Others dissented, a fracas developed, and in the mêlée a local man was stabbed with a pitchfork on the steps of the Church House and then hacked to death.

Villagers in their thousands, armed with no more than farm implements and staves, then rose in support and marched to Exeter, laying siege to the city and demanding the withdrawal of the English version. The siege lasted six weeks, but in the end the rebels were no match for the well-armed military force sent to quell them: more than 3,500 died in skirmishes in Devon, including 1,300 in a final stand at Sampford Courtenay. The militia continued into Cornwall and, by the time the rebels were crushed, some 4,000 from both counties had died – and to little eventual purpose, as when Edward's half-sister Mary, who was a devout Catholic, succeeded him in 1553 she re-legalised the Latin version anyway.

Less than two miles north is **Honeychurch** (see box, page 192) where you will find another little gem of a church.

¶¶ FOOD & DRINK

New Inn Sampford Courtenay EX20 2TB ⟳ newinnsampfordcourtenay.co.uk ⊙ Tue–Sun. Owners Debbie and Jason have breathed new life into this very old inn which now serves good beer and local food, including excellent fish and chips. There is a beer garden hidden at the rear and grass paddocks for those who wish to play.

7 WINKLEIGH

Å Ten Acres Vineyard Camping (page 249)

This unassuming village lies quietly off the busy A3124, seven miles east of Hatherleigh. Apart from the flamboyant church (see box, page 193), it repays a visit for its narrow streets of pastel-coloured houses. There are two pubs, the beautifully thatched Kings Arms (see below) and the Seven Stars (⟳ sevenstarswinkleigh.co.uk), which has live sport and typical pub fare. On South Street there is a friendly coffee shop, **Wright and Proper** (⟳ 01837 83038; no dogs), serving cakes and light lunches.

The village pump has a brass plate explaining that it was put there to commemorate the passing of the Great Reform Bill of 1832 which allowed more categories of citizens to vote in parliamentary elections: small landowners, tenant farmers and shopkeepers. No women, of course. The pump was in regular use until the arrival of mains water around 1940 and was needed again during the great drought of 1976.

¶¶ FOOD & DRINK

The Kings Arms Winkleigh EX19 8HQ ⟳ 01837 682681 ⟳ kingsarmswinkleigh.co.uk. A thatched 17th-century pub serving local food and a great selection of ales and ciders. **Cecilia's Tea Room** ⊙ noon–15.00 Fri & Sat. Part of the same building as the Kings Arms, this tea room serves excellent cream teas.

8 WOOLLEY ANIMALS

Winkleigh EX19 8AN ⟳ 01769 520300 ⟳ woolleyanimals.co.uk ⊙ 10.00–16.00 Sat, Sun & school holidays; booking recommended for walking with the alpacas

We're not sure whether it was the Swiss Valais Blacknose sheep that did it – sheep that look rather like teddy bears. It might have been the baby alpacas, black as night and with the softest woolly coats, or Alvin, the pygmy goat who knew that if he bit the bottom of my animal food bag,

TWO SPECIAL MID DEVON CHURCHES

Hilary Bradt

Even the name is irresistible: **Honeychurch**. And it is indeed the sweetest little church in Devon. I knew that before even seeing the weathered, worm-eaten oak door pockmarked with the nail scars from centuries of posted notices. I knew it after reading Simon Jenkins's eulogy in *England's Thousand Best Churches*, and it was confirmed when I stopped a cyclist to ask for directions. 'Oh you're not going to the *church*!' said Richard, his face suffused with delight 'I'm going there myself – follow me. It's perfect'.

The secret of this perfection is told in the informative leaflet about St Mary's Church. 'Honeychurch is one of the simplest and most unsophisticated country interiors in the whole of England. It owes its preservation from any kind of rigorous Victorian

"restoration" to the fact that it has always been a small parish without a squire, and without the money to ruin it by reckless alterations...' So there was no money to pay for varnish or wood preservatives. The pale oak pews are rough and worm-eaten, no money for stained glass in the windows, and no money to supply electricity. Paraffin lamps do the job of lighting the church.

Where money has been spent on this essentially Norman church, it was done modestly and elegantly in the 15th and 16th centuries with the addition of a bell tower and a lovely barrel roof with carved ribs and bosses on a white background. On one wall are the remains of a mural that once depicted the Royal Coat of Arms of Queen Elizabeth I, opposite the more modern Lion

---

then all the food would fall at his feet. One way or another, Woolley Animals is one of those places that makes you smile.

About ten miles northeast of Hatherleigh, this farm park has a vast array of animals, all in large enclosures so that visitors can interact with them but feel very safe. Every single animal seems to have a bit of attitude, from aloof Stinky Pickle, the Guernsey billy goat, to Max, a chilled-out alpaca. And every animal is your friend when they spy that you have grass pellets to feed them. As well as being able to meet the animals, you can take an alpaca for a walk around the lake and through the extensive farm grounds. A **small shop** serves drinks and snacks and sells everything woolly, from socks to hats.

HOLSWORTHY & AREA

The western half of Ruby Country borders Cornwall and the River Tamar. Even though the market town of Holsworthy is only nine miles

and Unicorn. A simply carved Norman font completes the scene.

For a contrast, head off to the neighbouring village of **Winkleigh** (page 191). The Church of All Saints owes its interest to the enthusiastic restoration undertaken in the 20th century by John Ford Gould, with the financial help of George Henry Pinkard, whose marble bust stands near the tower. Money was clearly no object: every inch of wall is decorated with Minton tiles and other designs, the floor is inlaid with memorials (look out for the rather cute skull next to a crenellated tower which is evidently part of a coat of arms). The tightly spaced ceiling ribs are richly painted and end in a heavenly host of gilded angels. You won't see a more colourful roof – or walls – in Devon. And that's not all that Mr Gould

turned his attention to. Take a look at the pulpit. Instead of the carved wooden affair that graces most churches, this is a splendid creation of coloured alabaster and marble, which dominates the church. Or it would, if it were not competing with so much other ornamentation.

There's plenty to look at outside as well. An angel on the roof trumpets the resurrection, and there is a good lion or dog gargoyle spouting water, but nearby is an altogether more curious carving: a 'pumpkin head'. Looking all the world like a Halloween decoration, the stone sphere is carved on three sides with grinning faces. Todd Gray, author of *Devon's Fifty Best Churches*, speculated that it might be a death's head. No-one knows… that is one of the delights of our village churches.

from the coast, there is no sense of being near the sea. The gently rolling countryside is a mixture of hedged fields, unenclosed heath and Culm grasslands, crossed by many shallow streams, all heading southwest to the Tamar. Sparse hamlets and isolated farms are connected by a network of narrow lanes and bridleways.

9 HOLSWORTHY

⌂ **Forda Farm** (page 249)

Tourist Information North Rd, EX22 6DJ ✆ 01409 254185 ⊙ 10.00–13.00 Mon & Wed–Sat

Thirteen miles west of Hatherleigh, Holsworthy is a traditional market town serving a widespread rural community. It's a small place, with a population of just 3,400, but it has a busy working community. The town is known for its thriving **cattle market** – the largest in the southwest. Held every Wednesday from 06.00, the market sees the auction of more than 2,000 cattle each week and is attended by perhaps

500 buyers, sellers and onlookers. Specialist auctions of pigs, poultry and machinery may attract even larger crowds. The market is situated on the southern edge of town and has an on-site café, the **Cow Shed** (☉ 08.30–14.30 Mon–Fri), which serves good, reasonably priced breakfasts and lunches.

The town is centred around the old Market Square where the **pannier market** (see box, page 180) is still held on Wednesday mornings. This square originally housed not only the pannier market but cattle, sheep and horse sales too – it must have been chaotic, especially as livestock regularly escaped to run amok in the town. Until the mid 20th century, all cattle and sheep would have come to market on foot, with farmers driving their livestock along the country lanes. The traditional drovers'

"There is a room upstairs where the shepherds slept, complete with recesses for their sheep dogs."

inn is the **Golden Fleece** in Bodmin Street (☎ 01409 253263), still very much a locals' pub. There is a room upstairs where the shepherds slept, complete with recesses for their sheep dogs. There were originally three pubs on Market Square: the Globe at number 21, which is now a Hospice shop; the Huntsman, at number 28, which is now a greengrocers; and the only remaining pub, the **Kings Arms** (⟁ kingsarmshotelholsworthy.co.uk). There has been an inn on this site since the 11th century and it has hardly changed inside since the early 1900s.

Just north of Market Square is **Holsworthy Museum** (⟁ holsworthymuseum.co.uk) in a 17th-century manor house – the kitchen has been kept with a display of household wares. Four further rooms display interesting aspects of the area's local history, including how Holsworthy doctor Stuart Craddock worked alongside Alexander Fleming when penicillin was discovered. Across the road from the museum is **St Peter's parish church** with its impressive granite tower built in 1450. It houses a carillon of eight bells that chime throughout the day and, sometimes, all night. The church's organ is positively venerable, having been built in the late 1600s for All Saints, Chelsea, and sold to Holsworthy in 1865.

◀ **1** Roadford Lake, Wolf Valley. **2** Common spotted orchid, Dunsdon's Culm grasslands. **3** Super Dodgems dating back to 1932 at Dingles Fairground Heritage Centre.

HOLSWORTHY'S PRETTY MAID

Every July since the 12th century, Holsworthy has held **St Peter's Fair**. It starts on the Tuesday evening with the town crier leading the local band and an increasingly merry group of ale tasters around the town. Ale is drunk in every hostelry and an ivy branch, 'Fair Ivy', is awarded to those meeting with the tasters' approval.

On Wednesday the Pretty Maid is crowned, a tradition that to many outsiders may seem quite out of date but which continues to be heartily embraced by the locals. The Pretty Maid's Charity was gifted by Rev Thomas Merryck in 1841 and under the terms of his will the income from his legacy is paid annually 'to the young single woman resident in Holsworthy under 30 years of age who is generally esteemed as: the most deserving, the most handsome, the most noted for her quietness and attendance at church'. Before the ceremony, the identity of this year's Pretty Maid is a closely guarded secret. On the stroke of noon, the chosen maid appears with the rector at the door of the church to be presented to the town. The criteria for the Pretty Maid have changed little; the girl must still be a church-goer and a good example to Holsworthy's young people.

Thursday sees the town's brass band lead the Furry Dance, a local version of the Flora Dance, long celebrated in the West Country. The procession of dancers hop, skip and twirl their partners along the streets and even through some pubs. All the local clubs join in, from the Theatrical Society to Cub troops. The dance finishes in the town square, where live music is held throughout fair week.

Look out for the Art Deco theatre on Bodmin Street. Built as a cinema in 1932, it closed down in the late 1950s and was used as a warehouse until it was rescued in 1969 by HATS. Their volunteers lovingly refurbished the theatre and now stage an annual pantomime and two or three other productions each year. To find out what is on, look out for posters or check their website ⊘ holsworthytheatre.co.uk.

⚍ FOOD & DRINK

South of St Peter's on Fore Street are **Filter Through** and **Posh Totties**, two reasonably priced cafés right in the centre of town. Both serve good teas, coffees, snacks and cakes; Posh Totties opens at 08.00 so it is good for breakfast too. Dinner options are limited but there are good alternatives in the local villages.

Molesworth Arms Pyworthy EX22 6SU ☏ 01409 259966 ⊘ moleswortharmspyworthy. co.uk ⊙ 17.00–22.00 Wed–Sun. This historic pub with flagstone floors, a large open wood fire for the winter and a beautiful outdoor garden for the summer is just two miles west of Holsworthy. Homemade food and real ale.

10 DUNSLAND

Brandis Corner, Holemoor EX22 7YE; National Trust

'Devon's most tragic loss since the last war.'
Devon by Nikolaus Pevsner

Just five miles west of Holsworthy is the National Trust's Dunsland Estate, bought in 1954. The Trust spent 13 years, and an enormous amount of money, restoring the grand stone-built mansion but in November 1967 – shortly after restoration was complete – the house caught fire after a formal dinner and musical recital. Within a few hours the house was reduced to a smoking ruin. Today, nature is slowly reclaiming the estate and a walk through the park gives you a sense of what once was and what might have been.

From the parking area, the impressive gateway leads to the old carriageway that sweeps down to pass the fish ponds and then gently climbs to the house. The park is home to a variety of trees, including 700-year-old sweet chestnuts and many old fruit trees. As you climb the slope, take the left fork though a gate. This soon leads to a meadow on your right, the site of Dunsland House. You may spot, on your left, the steps down to the terrace but almost nothing else remains. Keeping ahead, the path curves right to reach the only building to survive the fire, the coach house. Opposite this is a crumbling wall, once part of the kitchen garden, and an interpretation board with pictures of the house as it once was.

If you turn right on to the track here, it will lead you back down the carriageway. There is a slightly unreal quiet to Dunsland; it feels as if someday it will awake from its slumber and once again carriages will roll up the driveway and ladies and gentlemen in evening dress will dance on the terrace.

✳ ✳ ✳

🚶 A WALK FROM DUNSDON TO VEALAND

❄ OS Explorer map 111; start: Dunedin carpark EX22 7JW ♀ SS302081; 3 miles; easy (one muddy section).

This walk links two nature reserves along a disused canal that has, itself, returned to nature. It is best walked from May to September when the meadow flowers are blooming.

From the carpark walk down the boardwalk into the Culm meadow. Follow the path which curves left around the meadow's edge.

Dunsdon is Devon Wildlife's flagship Culm grassland site and arguably the county's most important habitat. Culm is characterised by purple moor grass, tussocky deciduous grass and patches of sharp-flowered rush. This makes for a rather uneven, muddy field but the reward, when we visited in June, was a profusion of early purple orchids, yellow flag irises, blue devil's-bit scabious, buttercups and cream meadowsweet.

Take the small bridge across the canal and turn left along it. Now just follow the canal towpath, crossing two small farm tracks as you do so. Damselflies, dragonflies and butterflies were everywhere when we walked, and the mixed hedgerows were full of the constant chatter of small birds.

This small canal is a branch of the Bude Canal, built around 1820, and originally designed to feed water into the main canal. It was soon upgraded so that tub boats could use it to carry lime-rich sea sand from the coast to fertilise the land and then to take agricultural produce back down to the coast. The tub boats had wheels and were hauled up two inclined planes as they came inland. There is an information board part way along the towpath. If you look across the canal at this point you may spot a wide ditch that was the Holsworthy branch. Unfortunately, the canal had limited success and closed in 1901 when the railway reached Bude. The system was, however, used to supply water for another 50 years. When you reach a bridge with a sign to Vealand, turn right into the carpark and then left through a gate to continue parallel to the canal. Passing through a second gate, you enter Vealand Farm Nature Reserve with its newly restored ponds, hedges and meadows. Again, the profusion of flowers and grasses is wonderful. Return along the same route. This walk can, obviously, also be walked from Vealand Farm carpark (EX22 7JY ♀ SS288068).

✳ ✳ ✳

11 ROADFORD LAKE

⌂ Hideaway Camping (page 249), **Wild Spaces** (page 249)
Broadwoodwidger PL16 0RL ◈ swlakestrust.org.uk/roadford

Nestled among the beautiful surroundings of the Wolf Valley, ten miles south of Holsworthy and with the dramatic tors of Dartmoor as a backdrop, Roadford Lake attracts both those seeking exercise and those just looking for good coffee.

The Activity Centre (✆ 01566 771930 ○ summer 10.00–16.00 daily; winter 10.00–16.00 Fri–Mon) offers a huge range of watersports. You can kayak, canoe, paddleboard or sail and the centre can provide all the equipment you need if you do not have your own. Other sports are available, including archery, climbing and fishing. Booking is recommended and qualified instructors are on hand if you would like to improve your skills. At the southern tip of the lake is a carpark, a shop and a good **café**, for those who just want to watch. The **Jubilee Sundial** and the **bird hide** are both a short walk north of the café, and there are five **interesting nature walks and cycle trails**, from one to five miles, along the lake shore and in the woods, all well signed.

The northern part of the lake is a **nature reserve** with its own parking area near Southweek (EX21 5BB ♀ SX43499305); a bridleway takes you into the reserve from here, and the second bird hide on the lakeside makes it worth the walk. As well as many common water birds, in summer you may be lucky enough to see osprey hunting and, in winter, whooper swans.

12 DINGLES FAIRGROUND HERITAGE CENTRE

Milton Lifton PL16 0AT ☎ 01566 783425 ⊘ fairground-heritage.org.uk

Just three miles south of Roadford Lake is Dingles, a complete working fairground with rides dating from the 1920s to the 1970s and housed in two giant hangers. Never was a heritage centre so much fun. Music and coloured lights set the atmosphere as the riders scream on Moon Rocket, the ultimate 1930s white-knuckle ride, while Harry Tuby's Victory Horses roundabout is a little more sedate – built in 1920, it is resplendent in its original colours and wooden horses.

Every ride has its own history, explained on an information board. The Ghost Train was built in 1947 and owned by Joe Stevens, son-in-law of Billy Smart of circus fame; it has its original decoration which contains some fantastic and amusing cartoon scenes. The Super Chariot Racer was one of the first white-knuckle rides and proved very popular in the 1930s, costing £1,750 to build. Decorated with a Roman chariot theme, it is as scary today as it was nearly a hundred years ago. Then there are the Super Dodgems which date from 1932 and toured England until 1980. A contemporary newspaper described the dodgems as 'A game of indoor motoring, in which collisions call forth no bad language'.

There are so many rides, as well as traditional sideshows and even the caravans used by the showmen as they toured the country. In 2021 a **new shop and café** were added, much of the work being carried out by passionate volunteers. It is a wonderful place, we loved our time there and will be back; don't miss it.

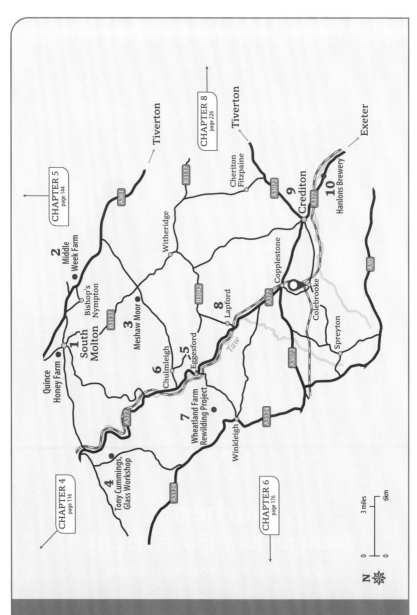

THE HEART OF DEVON

7
THE HEART OF DEVON

Between Dartmoor and Exmoor lies the very heart of Devon. Narrow hedged lanes wind their way through this verdant countryside, linking farms and villages. The red Devonian sandstone in the soil makes for lush pastures and fruitful orchards, while the proximity to good roads and railways has enabled the growth of a small food and drink industry – from beer and cider to cheese and milkshakes.

South Molton and Crediton are the largest towns in this area, both of which grew prosperous on the wool trade which was the driving force of their medieval economy for over 200 years. Today, in the villages and countryside, green business is booming. Orchards have 25-year contracts to supply their apples for cider, small farms now take in guests and use this income to rewild their lands, while in many villages there is the opportunity to see traditional crafts making a comeback, such as glass-blowing, thatching and candle making. The heart of Devon continually surprises us. We enjoyed a breakfast of fresh croissants surrounded by shiny Harley-Davidson and Triumph Bonneville motorbikes, a lunch in a pannier market while catching up on the local gossip, and an evening eating pizzas in a cider mill.

"This is the very heart of Devon: narrow hedged lanes wind their way through this verdant countryside, linking farms and villages."

WET-WEATHER ACTIVITIES

GETTING THERE & AROUND

There is good access to the area for the motorist, with the M5 not far to the east and the A30 bordering it to the south. Once off these arteries, roads are slow, encouraging one to take the opportunity to walk, ride or cycle.

SPREYTON & OLD UNCLE TOM COBLEY

Tom Pearce, Tom Pearce, lend me your grey mare.
All along, down along, out along lea.
For I want for to go to Widecombe Fair,
With Bill Brewer, Jan Stewer, Peter Gurney,
Peter Davy, Dan'l Whiddon, Harry Hawke,
Old Uncle Tom Cobley and all,
Old Uncle Tom Cobley and all.

Devon's best-known folk song tells the tale of seven men borrowing a horse from Tom Pearce to travel to Widecombe Fair – the old grey mare unfortunately dies before she returns home and later appears to the men as a ghost.

The events in the song are believed to have taken place in 1802 with the group of seven men walking and riding over the moors from Spreyton, ten miles west of Crediton, to Widecombe in the Moor on Dartmoor for the annual fair and livestock sale (a distance of 12 miles).

Tom Pearce was a mill owner who lived in nearby Sticklepath – you can find a grave in the village to a Tom Pearce who died in 1875 – and Bill Brewer also lived there. Gurney, Davy, Widdon and Stewer were all common names in the area at that time, as a walk around any churchyard will show.

The original Uncle Tom Cobley lived near Spreyton in the early 1800s. He had bright red hair and was a lively bachelor, known for having many female companions whose children he would only support if they had inherited his tell-tale red hair. Cobley died in 1844; his grave is just outside the south door of Spreyton church. If you visit the church, look up above the altar at the medieval ceiling boss. It depicts three running hares with shared ears, a popular emblem in Dartmoor. They are commonly known as 'tinners' rabbits' although any connection with the tin trade is uncertain. There is also an impressive modern stained-glass window of St Michael.

The tavern in Spreyton the men set out from, now predictably called the **Tom Cobley Tavern** ($\mathring{\partial}$ tomcobleytavern.co.uk) is still open; it's a small, family run, dog-friendly pub serving local ales and cider and good food. (It's also the only pub we've been to that has a thatched bar!) No doubt the seven men who set out for Widecombe from here would be amazed that their names are still being sung over 200 years later.

The **Tarka Line** is an ideal and picturesque way to travel (⊘ greatscenicrailways.co.uk/lines/tarka-line; page 211); it runs more or less hourly from 05.30 to 21.30, a little less on Sundays. There are thirteen stations on the line; the five smallest are only stopped at by some trains and then only if you make a request to the conductor. To board at one of these five stations, you stand on the platform and wave frantically at the driver – it seems to work.

There are a myriad of **bus** companies offering a good network of routes across the area, though some are rather infrequent. Particularly useful are bus 5, which runs from Exeter to Crediton (30 minutes, every hour), and the 5B and 5C that carry on from Crediton to serve Winkleigh and Chulmleigh, respectively (each a further 40 minutes, every two hours). Another useful route is the 155, linking Barnstaple in the north with South Molton (40 minutes, hourly) and then carrying on to Tiverton (a further 50 minutes, every two hours) in the east.

SELF-POWERED TRAVEL

Two long-distance **walking trails** cross the heart of Devon's rolling countryside. One is the final 15-mile section of the Tarka Trail which hugs the River Taw from Sticklepath to Eggesford. The second is the central 30-mile section of the Two Moors Way, also known as the Devon Coast to Coast, which wanders from Drewsteignton in the south through Witheridge and Knowstone. A new short trail is the **St Boniface Way**, one of three short pilgrim routes in Devon (⊘ devonpilgrim.org.uk), running for 14 miles from Crediton to Exeter.

The network of tiny lanes provides ample scope for the **cyclist** while locations such as Eggesford Forest (page 214) have waymaked off-road cycling routes.

Horseriding offers another way to travel slowly and the hills are certainly easier on four legs.

RIDING & TREKKING STABLES

Boldtry Riding Stables Leigh Rd, Chulmleigh EX18 7JN ✆ 01769 580366 ⊘ boldtrystables-chulmleigh.co.uk. Boldtry Riding Stables offer tuition and recreational riding, with a range of ponies and horses to suit everyone, from beginners to more confident riders, irrespective of age.

Collacott Kings Nympton EX37 9TP ✆ 01769 572491 ⊘ collacott.co.uk. A riding school, indoor and outdoor, as well as riding breaks and even tuition on how to care for a pony.

Collacott also offers a holiday livery so you can bring your own horse, and it's possible to stay nearby at one of their eight holiday cottages. There is even an outdoor heated swimming pool (for you, not the horse).

SOUTH MOLTON & AREA

Just south of Exmoor is the active market town of South Molton, where traditional values and skills are still strong; here you can journey back in time on a hay cart or spend a day learning to blow glass. On the edge of town is the remarkable Quince Honey Farm where there is nothing they do not know about bees. Further south, Meshaw Moor nature reserve is a haven for wildlife and wildflowers.

1 SOUTH MOLTON

🏠 **The George** (page 249) ⚑ **Welcombe Meadow** (page 250)

South Molton has been a market town since Saxon times and has retained so much of its charm that one is not surprised to find that there is still a real butcher, a real baker and, up the road at Quince Honey Farm, a candlestick maker. Indeed, the main streets are full of interesting independent shops including a saddlers, a cheese merchant, a clock shop and a seller of vintage clothing. Right in the centre of town, on Broad Street, you will discover the undercover **pannier market**. Every Thursday and Saturday (◷ 08.00–13.00), up to 70 stalls sell everything local: fruit and flowers, vegetables, jams and chutneys, arts and crafts, cakes and loaves. There is even a small café where you can catch up on local gossip. Next door to the pannier market is the **museum** (◷ 10.30–16.00 Mon & Tue, 10.30–13.00 Thu & Sat), in the old Guildhall. Focusing on local history, it provides an interesting glimpse of South Molton's past; there are three old fire engines, horse drawn and with buckets hanging off, a penny farthing bike, a large cider press made from oak and elm, and even a medieval huntsman's whistle which was discovered locally. You can also pick up a heritage trail guide here which will guide you around the town's 30 heritage plaques, enabling you to see the many grand buildings that were the result of a thriving wool trade which started in the 12th century and continued for 700 years.

◀ **1** Town Hall, South Molton. **2** Quince Honey Farm. **3** At Middle Week Horse-Powered Farm visitors can ride on a variety of horse-drawn wagons and carriages.

In front of the museum and the pannier market, in the middle of the road, sits the impressive **Medical Hall** which has been a pharmacy for around 200 years. A cast-iron balustrade proclaims that Mr Currie sells wines and spirits as well as being a chemist. Alas, Mr Currie, the wine and the spirits are long gone but the pharmacy still remains. After crossing Broad Street, you can walk up to the impressive medieval parish **Church of St Mary Magdalene**. Its tower dominates the town and a peal of eight bells is rung regularly. Built in the 15th century, the church was extensively restored in the 19th century, when large stained-glass windows were installed. To the left of the chancel arch there is an unusual carving of a green man, thought to be an ancient symbol representing fertility.

"There is an unusual carving of a green man, thought to be an ancient symbol representing fertility."

Behind the pannier market you will discover the pens and buildings of the **livestock market**. Every Thursday, 2,000 sheep are auctioned in a traditional covered ring, surrounded by buyers and overseen by the auctioneer. Alternate Wednesdays are reserved for cattle. The auctions are noisy affairs, with hundreds of animals penned up awaiting their turn to be auctioned; every so often you hear the thump of the hammer as a deal is struck.

Quince Honey Farm

North Rd, EX36 3RD   01769 572401   quincehoneyfarm.co.uk   09.30–17.30 daily

Everything is hexagonal in this truly amazing park and exhibition, just two miles northwest of South Molton. If you thought you already knew quite a bit about bees, here you will find that you have only scratched the surface: you can learn about the history of beekeeping, which goes back some 10,000 years; the different species of bees; and where and how they make their homes in other parts of the world. Twice a day, talks lead you through the honey process from flower to hive, with a demonstration of beekeeping and a tour of the honey factory. There is also the opportunity to watch candles being rolled and to taste different honeys. It really is amazing how much effect the flowers visited by the bees has on the flavour of the honey they produce.

The farm was created in 1949 by George Wallace; his grandson Ian now runs the farm and more than 1,500 hives that they keep on site.

A fun environment, with super-enthusiastic young experts, learning about these remarkable creatures here is absorbing. Little children can tumble around in the Play Hive and climb the outdoor play area, while older ones will be fascinated by watching and learning about the bees' behaviour. There are also **tractor tours** – although you may prefer to walk the meadow and garden trails. The **shop**, as you might expect, sells every possible product connected with bees, while the Nectary **restaurant** has plenty of seating inside and outside, serving delicious homemade meals and snacks with views over the garden.

2 MIDDLE WEEK HORSE-POWERED FARM
Ash Mill EX36 4QD ✂ 01769 550880 ◴ Mon–Sat; booking essential

Middle Week farm is just five miles southeast of South Molton but a world away in time. Farmer Stuart has been using horses to work his 12-acre smallholding for more than 40 years; there's no modern machinery or tractors here, just three heavy horses – Albert, George and Bella – and ancient, lovingly restored farming equipment. Stuart and his horses live a simple life – what we now call a green sustainable life – enjoying nature and limiting their impact on it. Not only does he farm using horsepower but he takes his produce to market by horse too.

Middle Week Horse-Powered Farm offers visitors a variety of old-world horse-drawn experiences, from carriage rides to wedding transport. You can book a carriage, or even a hay wagon if you are a larger group, and ride off to visit a 13th-century country pub or perhaps somewhere special for a Devon cream tea. Ambling through the countryside, high up in your carriage, is a trip back in time to a way of life that has been almost entirely lost.

3 MESHAW MOOR
EX36 4NL

Meshaw Moor is a timeless place a little over seven miles south of South Molton. A Devon Wildlife Trust **nature reserve**, its patchwork of fields reflects how large parts of Devon once looked – even the sounds and smells are those of a bygone era. This area of pasture had always been traditionally farmed, so instead of being neat and tidy it's rather scruffy; yet stand still for ten seconds and you will soon be aware of the diversity of nature that surrounds you. The fields are full of wildflowers, reeds, rushes and grasses. When we visited in summer, we saw yellow greater bird's-foot-trefoil, tall purple thistles, white marsh valerian, purple knapweed and creamy meadowsweet; below these, tiny yellow tormentil flowers and violet selfheal. In July and August, the splendidly named and very unusual, white and yellow sneezewort flowers may be spotted. This plant not only has the reputation of making you sneeze but was also used in herbal medicine; when chewed, the leaves have a peppery taste and cause a numbing or tingling effect in the mouth. For this reason, the leaves were traditionally used as a cure for toothache.

In summer, the whole marsh is alive with butterflies, day-flying moths and dragonflies. These pastures are no longer farmed but the Trust do harvest the flower and grass seeds at the end of the summer, using the seeds for other restoration projects. The marsh is best visited between May and September, but come at twilight at any time of year to spot the barn owls heading out to hunt – this is a habitat full of small mammals including mice and field voles.

There is a well-waymarked **path** that is only about a mile long – but allow yourself plenty of time as the path takes you around much of the wildlife reserve and there is a lot to see. It is fairly flat but muddy in places, though there are a few boardwalks to help with the worst sections.

4 TONY CUMMINGS, GLASS WORKSHOP

Old Post Office, High Bickington EX37 9AX ✐ 01769 560201 ⬙ tonycummingsglass.com; booking essential; see ad, page 225

The Old Post Office in High Bickington, ten miles west of South Molton, has some beautiful glasswork on its shelves. They are a clue to the fact that this unspoilt and isolated village hides Tony Cummings's glass workshop. Here Tony not only makes bespoke, free-blown glass items but also enables others to experience the thrill of making their own pieces.

"Tony not only makes bespoke glass items but also enables others to experience the thrill of making their own pieces."

Tony and his wife Lorraine are a joy to be with. Tony started working with glass at 15 and is a true craftsman. The methods he uses may date back over 3,000 years but the equipment is that of a modern workshop. Every piece is individually free-blown, using nothing but hand tools; as a result, each piece is unique.

You can work with Tony for a full day to try all the techniques: gathering molten glass from the furnace on to the rod; shaping and working it; and blowing the glass vessel. It is all hands-on and, by the end of the day, you can expect to have made several glass items. What you make is up to you – with a little guidance from Tony as to what is possible! – and no previous experience is necessary. It takes a day or so for the glassworks that you have made to cool down from molten hot, so your handiwork is posted to your home as soon as it is safe to do so.

ALONG THE TARKA LINE

The scenic 39-mile Tarka railway line bisects the heart of Devon, running from Exeter to Barnstaple and following the gentle river valleys of the Yeo and Taw. The line's 13 stations offer great opportunities to explore the area, giving access to several historic villages including Eggesford's forests and walking trails, Chulmleigh with its unusual architecture and ancient buildings, and Lapford with its strong community and ghost stories.

THE HISTORY OF THE TARKA LINE

It is amazing that the Tarka Line still exists, let alone thrives, as its building was beset with difficulties. In the early 19th century, rail companies were competing to build new railways all over England. Two rail routes to Barnstaple were proposed as early as 1831 – one from Exeter via Crediton and the other from Tiverton via Bideford. The latter was favoured by the government and Isambard Kingdom Brunel was recruited as its engineer. However, the company failed to meet parliament's deadlines and, in 1845, the Exeter route via Crediton won the day.

There then followed years of argument over the gauge of the railway and funding became an increasing issue. After years of 'railway mania' when money was no problem, investors' enthusiasm had declined and money was hard to come by. Work first started on the Exeter to Crediton passenger line nearly six years after getting parliamentary approval, with the first trains departing from Exeter in 1851. Work on the line from Crediton to Barnstaple began later that year and this extension opened three years later.

The line was taken over by Great Western Railways in 1876 and then nationalised in 1948. Despite many railways being closed in the 1960s, the Barnstaple to Exeter route survived, the only remaining rail line out of Barnstaple. Fearing for its future, local organisations rallied to support the line and it was one of the first to be given an identity as a tourist railway, sponsored by North Devon tourist board.

Today, the Tarka Line is operated by First Great Western, and the number of passengers has trebled in the last 20 years.

The southern end of the Tarka Line serves the town of Crediton, which sits at the confluence of the River Yeo with the River Creedy. Its location in the centre of great farming land plus good transport links to Exeter and the M5 has lead to the establishment of many local food industries – cider mills, breweries, creameries and dairies.

5 EGGESFORD

🏠 **The Fox & Hounds** (page 249)

Set in the valley of the River Taw below the town of Chulmleigh, tiny Eggesford once sat at the heart of the Earl of Portsmouth's estate. As a condition of the railway passing through his land, the earl demanded his own station, and for every train to stop here, something that continues today. Eggesford is hardly even a hamlet – but it does still have that railway station on the Tarka Line, a church, a stately home on the hill, numerous woods and a coaching inn.

Eggesford's **All Saints Church**, half a mile from the station, is not to be missed – to get there, cross the level crossing and turn left after about quarter of a mile. This isolated church was originally the Eggesford estate church and, although it was built in the 15th century, it was completely re-modelled in 1867. The church has an unspoilt view across the Taw but it is inside that wonder awaits. Monuments, the scale of which would be more suited to a cathedral than this little church, dominate the interior.

Facing the entrance door is a life-size Arthur, 2nd Viscount Chichester, carved in alabaster and with his two wives lying on either side of him. The second wife, Lady Mary (on the right), has her still-born eighth child with her. Below are her other seven children – James, Digby, Arthur, Edward, Beatrix, Arthur and John. All died before their parents. On the north wall is a memorial to Edward, 1st Viscount Chichester, and his wife Anne. If you look carefully you may see traces of the original colour on the white marble. Anne does not have a coronet as Edward was not ennobled until after her death. Many monuments of this type were destroyed in the Victorian era but, luckily, these two were merely boarded up and so have survived.

The Eggesford estate was sold by the Chichesters in 1718. The monuments to the new lords of the manor – the Earls of Portsmouth

◀ **1** Eggesford, on the Tarka Line. **2** Flashdown Wood, part of Eggesford Forest.
3 The Church of St Andrew, Colebrooke, is notable for its carved bench ends.

and their families – are much more modest and can be seen on the north wall of the church. Beneath the church is a vault that belongs to the Portsmouth family, last opened in 1932 for the burial of Lady Henrietta Evans.

In the station's good's yard is the small **Eggesford Crossing Café** (☉ 09.00–14.00 Thu–Sat) and a farm shop, **The Plant Shed** (☉ 10.00–18.00 Tue–Sat) that sells local food, fruit and vegetables as well as plants. A short distance north up the A377 is the **Fox & Hounds** (page 249), the perfect place for a coffee, a meal or to spend the night.

Eggesford Forest

Eggesford is surrounded by woodlands, all owned by the Forestry Commission. Most have parking, good walking and often some interesting history. Note, however, that it is not easy to walk between the woods.

Starting at the carpark in **Heywood Wood** (EX18 7QR), to the west of Eggesford station, a path goes through a forest of Douglas firs, many of which are approaching 200 years old. The path leads to the motte and bailey of Heywood Castle which was built by the Normans and occupied from the 11th to 13th centuries. The conical mound of earth and rubble is about 30ft high and it is worth climbing the steps to get a sense of the scale of these earthworks: the mound is over 160ft in diameter and from the top you can work out the ups and downs of defensive ditches and a causeway crossing them. Before the trees were planted, the castle would have had a clear view of the Taw River valley and anyone passing through the area.

A short distance to the south of Heywood lies **Flashdown Wood** (EX18 7RZ), home to the very first trees planted by the Forestry Commission, which was formed in 1919 to replant Britain's woodlands. Immediately after the first meeting in London, founding members Lord Clinton and Lord Lovat challenged one another to plant the first trees. Lord Clinton had assembled a small team of foresters to be ready as soon as he disembarked from his train at Eggesford Station; when Lord Lovat arrived home, he was handed a telegram announcing that the first trees had already been planted in Flashdown Wood. Today, some of the same Douglas firs, larch and beech trees stand at around 130ft tall. On the left of the parking area is an avenue of copper beach planted in 1969 to celebrate the Forestry Commission's 50th anniversary, as a fine stone and plaque on the right attest. A pleasant walk, through the gate to the right of the carpark, leads up a second 500yd-long avenue of trees, planted in 2019 to celebrate the commission's 100th anniversary. Another stone and plaque can be found halfway up and on your left; it was unveiled by the current Lord Clinton, grandson of the Lord Clinton who planted the first trees. The avenue's verges are full of wildflowers and wildlife; butterflies and hoverflies abound.

6 CHULMLEIGH

Just two miles north of Eggesford but 300ft above is the charming hilltop Saxon town of Chulmleigh, overlooking the Little River Dart. With its narrow cobbled lanes, courtyards and welcoming inns, it is a pleasure to wander around this unspoilt corner of Devon. The centre of the town is a conservation area, with beautiful cob and thatch cottages and 200 listed buildings. Watch out for the keystones and carved heads above the doors and the unusual cast iron pump-cum-lamppost in the centre of the road.

Chulmleigh once prospered on wool trading, but the development of the turnpike road between Barnstaple and Exeter in 1830, which bypassed the town, plus the advent of the railway in 1854, resulted in this trade moving elsewhere. Today, Chulmleigh is a busy town with many independent shops, including a traditional bakery, a deli and a family-run butcher's.The town's big event is the annual Chulmleigh Old Fair (⊘ chulmleigholdfair.co.uk; see box, below). Just south of the town

CHULMLEIGH OLD FAIR

Chulmleigh Old Fair (⊘ chulmleigholdfair. co.uk) has taken place every year since Henry III granted a Royal Charter to the town in 1253. The annual five-day festival starts on the first Tuesday after 22 July when the Fair Queen is crowned; in the evening, coins are tossed from the upstairs window of the Town Hall and a money scramble ensues. (The coins used to be red hot but safety concerns have now put a stop to that.) A large white glove, symbolising the King's gauntlet, is then paraded through town and displayed at the Town Hall. Over the subsequent four days the town takes on a carnival feel with more than 30 events, including a road race, golf, orienteering, football, a scarecrow competition, skittles, a flower festival, a craft market, a history walk around the town and a street party. It is quite amazing that such an ancient fair still takes over the whole town for five days, attracting hundreds of people from miles around.

centre, the **Parish Church of St Mary Magdalene** is impressive from the outside but inside it is spectacular, with beautiful stained-glass windows, a 15th-century carved and painted oak rood screen that stretches the full width of the church, and a medieval wagon roof resplendent with painted and carved bosses and exquisite little angels.

The town's two pubs date back to the 17th century. In the centre of town, **The Red Lion** (⊘ theredlionchulmleigh.co.uk) has welcoming open fires and beamed ceilings, and serves local ales, pizzas and burgers. Charles I stayed at the thatched **Old Courthouse** (⊘ oldcourthouseinn.co.uk) on South Molton Street, just north of the town centre, during his first tour of the West Country in 1633; they serve good home-cooked food, real ales and cider, and have rooms and a cobbled courtyard garden.

7 WHEATLAND FARM REWILDING PROJECT

🏠 **Wheatland Farm** (page 249)

EX19 8DJ ⊘ 01837 83499 ⊘ wheatlandfarm.co.uk

Despite its name, Wheatland Farm is really a nature reserve rather than a farm. Today the terms 'eco' and 'green' are everywhere but in 2006, when Ian and Maggie took over Wheatland's 21 acres, three miles west of Eggesford, these were little known concepts. The idea of taking a failing farm and returning it to its natural state ran contrary to the normal ideas of progress. They decided that they would not exploit the land but work with it to improve and restore it. One of their first projects was to put up a wind turbine to provide their own green electricity – it has been so successful they are now contemplating a second turbine.

All their new eco lodges are made with re-use and recycling in mind: they have solar-heated water; and their walls are made from straw cut a couple of fields away, clad with local wood. All their free-to-use bikes have been repaired many times – reduce, re-use, repair, recycle are not just slogans here. They've twice won Visit England's top award for sustainable tourism – something that doesn't surprise us, having visited.

Ian and Maggie are inspirational and straight forward about their approach. The eco lodges make the nature reserve possible and pay the bills for this ongoing conservation project. So far, the couple have replanted the old orchard, reinstated the traditional summer grazing moors, reshaped and replanted the ponds, and started traditional management of the hedges. Wildlife has, as a result, moved in: butterflies, dragonflies and damselflies; frogs, toads, voles and water shrews; barn owls, songbirds, dormice and bats.

Ian and Maggie welcome visitors and will be happy to show you around – booking is essential. When we visited, Ian said, 'We hope you love this special place as much as we do.' And we do.

8 LAPFORD
🏠 **Hidden Chapel** (page 249)

Steeped in history and legend, the thriving village of Lapford – the next stop south from Eggesford on the Tarka Line (though note it is only a request stop) – has an inspiring community. This is perhaps best seen at the **Community Church**, held at the Victory Hall in the centre of the village and one of three churches in Lapford. When we visited they were just finishing their Sunday meeting and we were warmly welcomed. This church has converted an old village shop into a community hub called **The Ark**, just down from the Victory Hall. Staffed entirely by volunteers, The Ark runs a food bank, along with a library, a meeting place for the village and, on Tuesdays and Fridays, a café where everyone is welcome, including visitors. Another of Lapford's three churches can be found next door. This is the **parish church** of St Thomas of Canterbury, worth visiting to see the exquisitely carved 15th-century rood screen and skilfully carved Tudor bench ends.

"The Ark runs a food bank, a library and a café where everyone is welcome, including visitors."

Across the road from the churches is **The Old Malt Scoop Inn** (page 218), which has been serving ale since the 16th century. Adapted over the years – it was even used as an undertakers in 19th century – it still retains an old-world charm with exposed beams, the original stone walls and floors, and comfy leather armchairs to sink into by the wood burner.

The village is said to have two ghosts that haunt it, although nobody we spoke to here admitted seeing one. One is a former vicar at the parish church, John Radford, who murdered his curate in 1860. John was spared the gallows by a jury consisting of many of his parishioners; in fact, he even returned to his parish duties. His dying wish was to be buried in the church chancel, threatening that he would haunt the village forever if his wishes were not carried out. The church authorities would not allow it and John was buried outside the vestry door (you can still see his grave there today); true to his word, John's spirit is believed to still wander around the village.

The village's other ghost is said to be the spirit of Thomas Becket, The Archbishop of Canterbury, who was murdered in Canterbury in 1170. It is said that on 29 December, the anniversary of his death, he gallops through the village on his white horse to confront Sir William de Tracy, the lord of the manor and one of the four knights involved in his murder.

¶¶ FOOD & DRINK

The Old Malt Scoop Inn EX17 6PZ ℘ 01363 83330 ⊘ theoldmaltscoopinn.co.uk ⊙ food noon–14.30 & 18.00–20.30 daily. Once a coaching inn, The Old Malt Scoop serves home-cooked food, local ales and lagers (one of which is brewed at the end of the road), and local ciders too. B&B rooms are also available.

9 CREDITON

🏠 **The New Inn** (page 249), **Warrens Farm B&B** (page 249) 🏡 **Holly Water** (page 250)
⛺ **Orchard Retreat** (page 250), **Upcott Roundhouse** (page 250)

Once a prosperous wool-trading town, Crediton sits on the Tarka Line, just seven miles northwest of Exeter. The town now attracts light industry, particularly the manufacture of food and drink products. It is a town with a few surprises – the first being that it is the birthplace of a saint. St Boniface was born here, back in AD680; today, following the **Boniface heritage trail** (⊘ creditontownteam.org.uk/st-boniface) is a good way to see the town, taking you past eight extraordinary, 6ft-high, stained-glass panels and ending at the St Boniface shrine.

Market Square in the centre of town is a good place to head if you need a coffee or a snack. The square still hosts a **market** (⊙ 10.00–13.00) on first and third Saturdays of the month. Stalls sell a wide selection of local produce and you can sample before you buy – keep your eye out for the lady with the cinnamon buns. The Market Square is also the venue for the town's food and drink festival (⊘ creditonfoodfestival.co.uk), held every June, with cooking demonstrations and music into the evening.

West of Market Square, on the main street through town (the street has five names along its length), is the old Town Hall. This is now occupied by the **Crediton Museum** (⊙ Apr–Oct), which focuses on local history and is run entirely by volunteers with a wealth of local knowledge. There is a fascinating model of the town before the great fire of 1743 – the fire destroyed 460 homes, many containing the weavers' looms that provided the families' income.

At the east end of the main street, the **Church of the Holy Cross** is surprisingly large for such a small town. It was built as the cathedral for Devon and Cornwall in the 10th century; the bishop moved to Exeter after 140 years and the church became collegiate with 36 canons and vicars, until it was dissolved by Henry VIII in 1545. Largely restored in the 19th century, the building still retains some of its Norman character. Inside, one is immediately struck by the immense nave and the stained glass at the east and west ends. As befits a church of this size, there are plaques and wall hangings everywhere, some ancient and some very modern. The effigy of Sir John Sully, in the south aisle, is not to be

THE CHURCH OF ST ANDREW, COLEBROOKE

Hilary Bradt

An ancient cobblestone path, one of the few remaining originals in the county, leads you to the door of this lovely church. Inside you are struck by the fine barrel roof and an unusual pulpit at floor level which seems more like a corral for the priest than a stage for his sermons. Nearby are two extraordinary carved bench ends, depicting a wildman or woodwose, clothed in feathers and holding an escutcheon for his master, and a more benevolent-looking and clothed man (although he has a pig's nose) wielding a club. They bear the coats-of-arms of the Coplestone and Gorges families who combined in marriage in 1472, so it is likely that the bench ends date from that time.

Enclosed behind a very lovely screen is the Coplestone Aisle or Chantry, built by Philip and Walter Coplestone in memory of their father who died in 1457. In it is an ancient prie-dieu carved with the family coat of arms and a bricked-up fireplace that will have kept the Coplestone family warm during winter services.

At the north end is something much newer: the Penstone Patchwork, created to commemorate the millennium by the villagers of Penstone, a hamlet of 22 houses that is on the route of our walk (page 222). As the explanatory folder tells us, the hamlet is proud to be insignificant, a place where 'summer days pass unmarred by droves of tourists'. The text ends with the hope that the Penstone Patchwork 'will give you a flavour of this little place at this time in its history and perhaps an insight into the people who shared and relished its peaceful insignificance for a small fraction of its lifetime'. It does. Thank you Mary Stephenson for explaining what this delightful patchwork, depicting the history, flowers and wildlife of a Devon hamlet, is all about. It could easily represent so many 'insignificant' but much-loved places in this county.

missed; he died in 1388 at the ripe old age of 106. In the north aisle is a magnificent organ dating back to 1921 and designed, fittingly, by Harold Organ, the church organist.

Opposite the church is **Union Road Moto Velo** (⊘ unionroadmotovelo. com) – a café, a motorbike shop, workshop and B&B; it's a magnet for bikers. On Thursday evenings and at weekends you can join them in admiring their shiny machines parked along the kerbside and pop inside for a beer or a coffee.

The range of accommodation in this area is extraordinary – roundhouse, tree house, shepherd's house or yurt, you'll find it on a hilltop or hidden in a valley near Crediton.

Sandford Orchards Cider Mill Tours
Commonmarsh Ln, EX17 1HJ ✎ 01363 777822 ⊘ sandfordorchards.co.uk ⊙ shop 09.00–17.00 Mon–Fri, 10.00–14.00 Sat; cider & pizza 17.00–21.00 Fri & Sat; tours monthly, see website

Sandford Orchards, up on the hill above Crediton, has come a long way since Barny first started making cider in his shed. Here, local apples are collected and pressed over a two-month period in the late autumn before the juice is fermented for around 14 days, with nothing added: no artificial flavours or aromas, no added concentrates. The three cider makers – Andy, Barny and Dave – then blend these single-orchard ciders together to produce their award-winning flavours. It all takes time but, as they told us, there is no hurry; they just want to make great cider.

There is a **shop** at the cider mill; customers are encouraged to bring their own bottles in order to be more ecofriendly. On Fridays and Saturdays you can join them for a cider and pizza either in or outside the factory, depending on the weather. We really recommend taking the monthly **tour** around the cider mill; it's the oldest working one in Britain and has been here for 75 years so there are many stories to be shared. Your guide, probably Barny, will explain how they commit to a long-term relationship with the apple growers; the cider making relies on over 400 acres of apple orchard around Crediton. Tours end with a tasting of six of Sandford's ciders, with an explanation of why they have such a range of flavours.

---

1 Crediton, birthplace of St Boniface. 2 Church of the Holy Cross, Crediton. 3 A traditional cob and thatch house, Chulmleigh. ▶

¶¶ FOOD & DRINK

Ashton's Coffee Lounge Market Sq ⬦ ashtons-coffee-lounge.business.site ⊙ 07.45–
17.00 Mon–Fri, 09.00–14.00 Sat. A modern coffee shop with lovely cakes.
Crediton Coffee Company Market Sq ⬦ creditoncoffee.co.uk ⊙ 10.00–16.00 Mon–Sat.
Roasts speciality coffee every day and serves an excellent cappuccino.
The Duck Yeoford EX17 5JD ✆ 01363 85273 ⬦ theduckatyeoford.co.uk ⊙ 17.00–23.00
Wed, 11.30–23.00 Thu–Sat, 11.30–17.30 Sun. Five miles west of Crediton, this is a thriving
village pub with a huge garden. There is good local food (try the duck cassoulet), local beer
(including their own Muddy Duck) and cider, and a choice of 20 wines by the glass.
Lamb Inn Sandford EX17 4LW ✆ 01363 773676 ⬦ lambinnsandford.co.uk. A 16th-century
posting house with open fires, low ceilings and comfy sofas just two miles north of Crediton.
They win awards every year, from 'best pub in Devon' to 'prettiest UK pub garden'. Parking is
further along the road and they also have rooms.
Three Little Pigs Market Sq ⬦ thethreelittlepigscrediton.com ⊙ 11.00–23.00 Mon–Sat,
11.00–22.00 Mon–Sat. An eclectic mix of memorabilia hangs from every space in this bar
and restaurant, which is very popular with locals and a good choice for lunch.

* * *

🥾 FOUR HAMLETS: COLEBROOKE, COLEFORD, KNOWLE & PENSTONE

❀ OS Explorer map 113; start: The Church of St Andrew, Colebrooke EX17 5JH
♀ SS77030005; 4 miles; moderate

This circular walk from Colebrooke links four hamlets – Colebrooke, Coleford, Knowle
and Penstone – all once part of the Eggesford estate (page 213). This is quintessential
Devon, with quaint thatched cottages and huge views across rolling pasture. The walk is on
good paths with some gentle hills but a couple of sections can be muddy. Coleford has a
pub with a small garden that's perfect for a rest – and for lunch if you time it right.

1 The walk starts at the door of The Church of St Andrew (see box, page 219), which
dominates the local landscape, sitting 200ft above the valley. Take the paved path that passes
under the clock and sundial to go through the churchyard and then past the Parish Hall, the
Old Post Office and Bell Inn Cottage. The track becomes a footpath and, eventually, passes
through a gate from where there are great views across the valley. Keep straight ahead then
turn right after the next field boundary and pass through two more gates. The path continues
to descend; in the field before the railway, turn left across the middle of the field to reach, in
the far corner, a tunnel under the railway.

2 Pass through the tunnel and keep straight ahead, turning right at the road. Follow the road to cross a stream and then immediately take the footpath on the right, along the stream. This path soon turns left and rises before turning right through a gate on to a narrow path. Pass through two more gates as the path becomes a green lane. Soon after the second gate, take the left turn on to a bridleway; follow the field edge.

3 Turn right on to a signed footpath to cross a stream and head uphill. Turn left to go through a gate. At the next gate, turn right and cross a field dotted with smallholdings. At the lane, turn left and then almost immediately right to descend into the beautiful hamlet of Coleford. Keep ahead at the crossroads to reach the New Inn (page 249), a useful place for refreshments.

Curve left around the New Inn and, where the road curves right uphill, keep straight ahead on a footpath and cross the stile. Follow the path across the field to pass under the railway, then fork left through a gate and follow the path through four more gates, leaving the woods for pasture before entering a hedged lane. This passes two farms before arriving in the minute hamlet of Knowle. Here, the route turns right but it is worth detouring to see the simple Chapel of St Boniface, ahead. There is a wonderful tapestry, produced by a local lady, behind the altar.

4 Back on the route, climb the road to the south of the chapel, up the wonderfully named Goblin Hill, and then turn right, signed Colebrooke, walking for about 400yds to find a bridleway on your left, signed to Lower Combe Cottage. There is another great view across the Devon countryside, with Colebrooke church clearly visible.

5 Of the two tracks here, follow the rightmost downhill and then, at the cottages, turn right and then left to cross a stream. Walk along the green lane, almost a tunnel at this point, that takes you over the hill to the hamlet of Penstone. At the road in Penstone, fork right to go under the railway once again and then over a stream.

6 After crossing the stream, fork left on to the signed footpath. The path soon crosses the railway tracks but do so with care as this is the newly reopened line to Okehampton. Follow the path back to Colebrooke; when you reach the village, go through the gate and turn left on the road to return to the church.

* * *

10 HANLONS BREWERY

Newton St Cyres EX5 5AE ✆ 01392 851160 🖥 hanlonsbrewery.com ⊙ food 16.00–22.00
Thu & Fri, noon–22.00 Sat; tours monthly, see website

John O'Hanlon started brewing beer behind his pub in Clerkenwell, London, in 1996 and was soon selling more beer wholesale than in the pub. The brewery moved to Devon in 2000 and today they brew a range of award-winning beers here, just five miles southeast of Crediton. The water comes from their own spring and the other ingredients are all as local as possible. Hanlons is still a family concern and they are clearly passionate about their beer.

The kitchen is open at the factory from Thursday to Saturday, serving beer, burgers, fish and chips, and a range of smoked meats from their very own smoker, 'Peggy Sue'; lots of the ingredients are from the Crediton area. Once a month, you can combine food and beer with a tour of the brewery and get a real insight into how Hanlons brew beer. Some say their Port Stout is better than Guinness, but Yellow Hammer is our personal favourite.

TONY CUMMINGS GLASS

Come and learn the art of glass blowing and create your own unique
glass pieces during an experience day with tuition from master craftsman
Tony Cummings. Refreshments and homemade lunch included.
Glass blowing demonstrations also available for small parties.

Old Post Office
High Bickington,
Devon, EX37 9AX

✉ info@tonycummingsglass.com
🖱 tonycummingsglass.com
☎ 01769 560201

HOLLY WATER HOLIDAYS

A tranquil slice of rural paradise in the heart of Devon. Our Shepherd huts and
treehouse offer you the perfect base for exploring the area and the opportunity to
reconnect with nature. Stunning views and peace – the ideal place for relaxation.

Holly Water Holidays
Hill Farm, East Village,
Crediton, EX17 4DA

✉ info@hollywaterholidays.co.uk
🖱 hollywaterholidays.co.uk
☎ 01363 866240 📱 07970 007245

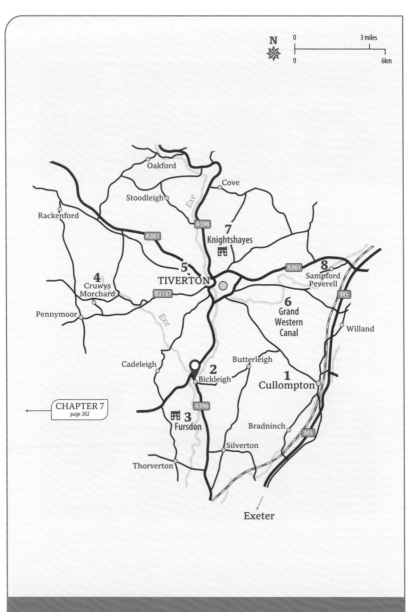

8
THE EXE VALLEY

> From this point [the lower Exe] we are in the real Devon of which so
> few visitors seem to know anything, the country of small rich fields,
> with massive hedges, innumerable villages of white thatched cottages
> clustering round a square-towered church, wooded knolls, and
> everywhere birds and flowers in great profusion.
>
> S P B Mais, *Glorious Devon*, 1928

This part of Devon was shaped by the wool industry: mills were
built; great churches were financed from wool wealth; and otherwise
inconsequential villages became important market towns. The area was
defined by Devon's major river, the Exe, which rises in Exmoor and
brought shipping and wealth to Exeter, up-river from Exmouth, and
provided the power needed by the wool industry. Synthetic fibres brought
a decline in the importance of wool, and nothing much happened in the
region until the arrival of first the railway, and then the M5 motorway
which gave easy access to the market town of Tiverton. The towns of
Tiverton and Cullompton give this region more of an urban feel than
other parts of Mid Devon – and make it particularly rewarding for bad-
weather touring with its exceptional churches, museum and the stately
home of Knightshayes. But the River Exe is still the place to be in fine
weather with its cycleways and footpaths, and the pleasures of messing
about in boats.

GETTING THERE & AROUND

The M5 allows easy access to drivers, and public transport isn't bad,
with regular **buses** heading here from Exeter and others serving
many of the villages. As always in Devon, check the latest routes and
timetables online in advance on ⊘ traveldevon.info. The interactive bus
map is particularly helpful. The railway from Paddington to Plymouth
and Penzance stops at **Tiverton Parkway**, an exceptionally hassle-free

station just off the motorway, with an hourly bus service into Tiverton (25 minutes away), Cullompton and Exeter.

CYCLING

This is a great area for cycling, with a stretch of the **Grand Western Canal** within minutes of Tiverton Parkway station. The canal forms part of the West Country Way (National Cycle Network Route 3), which runs along the canal from the Somerset border to Tiverton. The canal was closed as a commercial waterway in 1925; now a country park, it provides 11 miles of safe cycling for all the family. Bikes can be hired at the Globe Inn, Sampford Peverell (see below).

Much of the **Exe Valley Way** is ideal for cycling since it runs along small lanes for part of its lower length, as well as for an alluring stretch above Tiverton. And, since it follows the river, it's mostly blissfully flat – a rarity in Devon. However, the lower stretch towards Exeter has some relentlessly steep hills, which you can't avoid if you do a circular trip. NCN Route 3 runs fairly close to the Exe, so here you have a ready-made round trip: up the Exe

"Much of the Exe Valley Way is ideal for cycling since it runs along small lanes for part of its lower length."

Valley Way from Tiverton to the bridge at Cove and then back down NCN3, with a few steep hills to keep your muscles in shape. OS maps Explorer 114 and Landranger 181 cover this route, and an interactive cycle map of Devon can be downloaded from traveldevon.info.

 CYCLE HIRE

Abbotshood Cycle Hire The Globe Inn, Sampford Peverell EX16 7BJ 01884 821214
 abbotshoodcyclehire.co.uk. A wide range of bicycles available, including electric, plus child seats and trailers.

WALKING

Though this region lacks the views of a coastal path, walking the river valleys bring their own appeal, especially for less energetic walkers. The **Exe Valley Way** is relatively level, at least along the stretch that falls into this chapter: Bickleigh to Tiverton (page 237). In total it's about 45 miles long, running from the Exe estuary below Exeter to Exford in Exmoor. And the great thing is that you need only walk in one direction – there are always buses to take you back to your starting point.

WET-WEATHER ACTIVITIES

Church of St Andrew Cullompton (see below)
Devon Railway Centre & Bickleigh Mill (page 234)
Knightshayes (page 244)
Tiverton Museum (page 238)

1 CULLOMPTON

Tourist information Town Hall, 1 High St, EX15 1AB ✆ 01884 38249

This ancient Mid Devon market town was almost destroyed by a devastating fire in 1839. Only a few buildings survived, including the splendid church and the 16th-century manor house, now the Manor House Hotel. Another survivor was **The Walronds**, a recently restored Tudor building with some lovely wood panelling and plasterwork, and a spacious garden that is open to the public on the second and fourth Saturdays of the month, providing a good opportunity to look around the house and have tea or a light lunch in the café. It is used for a variety of community events too, such as the annual food and craft festival in October.

"The Shell Guide describes the top of the tower as 'pinnacled, crocheted, gargoyled and pierced."

The wide **main street** (Fore Street) is typical of an old market town, which has kept its rural roots: the farmers' market, held on the second Saturday of each month, is said to the longest-established in the southwest.

Cullompton's splendid **Church of St Andrew** stands as a landmark for miles around and is the main reason to visit the town. The Shell Guide describes the top of the tower as 'pinnacled, crocheted, gargoyled and pierced' and this lavish decoration continues on much of the exterior, although the gargoyles and carvings are so eroded it's hard to make out whether they are beasts or angels. Constructed of local red sandstone, this is a 'wool church' and wool merchant John Lane left his mark with carvings of sheep shears as well as ships.

The interior is stunning. The church was built in the perpendicular style, with two different families competing in their displays of wealth and piety. There is a Moore chapel, with lots of angels and the family coat of arms, and the Lane chapel which is really an entirely new aisle, with a fan-vaulted roof to rival King's College Chapel, and angels and twiddly carvings crammed into every space. Some angels are holding symbols of

the wool trade: cloth shears or teasel frames. While the Lane Chapel/aisle is all creamy-coloured sandstone, the rest of the church is done up in muted green, blue, red and gold. The barrel roof, with a criss-cross pattern of feathered wooden braces, is dull gold and sky blue, and wherever there's room for an angel you'll find one. The screen is very finely carved with entwined foliage and also painted (though with no saints in the panels). Every pillar is topped with vines or a figure – there is some very splendid facial hair in this church, particularly in the wood carvings on the organ screen. Of the stained-glass windows, one depicting the evangelists on the south side of the Lane Chapel stands out because of its rich colours: it's by the Pre-Raphaelite artist Edward Burne-Jones.

I almost missed what was, for me, the pièce de résistance. At the back of the south aisle is a trunk of oak, carved along its length with skulls, bones and rocks. The boldness of the carving looks modern, and is quite different from anything else in the church, yet it is said to be just as old. It is called **Golgotha** and supposedly once supported the rood. I'm glad it's now at eye level where it can be properly admired, as it's a stunning piece of sculpture in its own right.

❡❙ FOOD & DRINK

Bakehouse 3 High St, Cullompton EX15 1AB 🖉 01884 35222 ⬦ thebakehousecullompton. co.uk. ◷ 09.00–17.00 Mon & Tue, 09.00–17.00 & 18.00–23.00 Wed–Sat. This café is a popular place for lunch and tea, and a varied menu is on offer for dinner. The proprietors are enthusiastic about their food and service – and it shows.

The Olive Well 33 High St, Cullompton EX15 1AF 🖉 01884 38898 ◷ 11.00–15.00 daily, also 18.00–21.00 Mon, Wed–Sat. A seasonal menu, over 20 different pizzas and a good kids' menu, too.

BICKLEIGH, FURSDON & AROUND

🏠 **Silverton Park Stables** (page 250) ▲ **Exe Valley Glamping** (page 250)

2 BICKLEIGH

Picturesque Bickleigh draws visitors to its riverside setting with thatched houses and pubs and an impressive five-arch stone bridge over the Exe,

◀ **1** Mid Devon is characterised by its agricultural landscape. **2** The Church of St Andrew, Cullompton – one of Devon's wool churches. **3** The Golgotha, Church of St Andrew.

THE KING OF THE GYPSIES

Janice Booth

Bampfylde Moore Carew was born in Bickleigh in 1693 and buried there in 1759 after a life novelists would be hard put to create. A wild lad from a leading and reputable local family (his father was the Rev Theodore Carew), he is said to have run away from home and ended up with a wandering group of gypsies. He quickly learned to live off his wits and was apparently a consummate actor. At the scene of a shipwreck, plunging into the waves as if swimming desperately ashore, he conned rescuers into giving him food, money and clothing; wrapped in rags, he feigned madness and received alms; and when a fire occurred locally he would sprint to the scene, elicit some facts from onlookers, then rub ash into his clothes and claim to be a needy survivor. He begged skilfully (sometimes dressed as a woman) and stole when he could. When the gypsy king died he was elected a successor – hence his nickname 'King of the Gypsies'.

He also had a good line in religious mania, spouting the scriptures wildly until some devout believer took pity on him and parted with cash. He was imprisoned, escaped, was recaptured, was shipped to the USA, escaped, was recaptured and fitted with a heavy iron collar, escaped again and took shelter with a native Indian tribe. Back in England, having tricked well-wishers into paying his passage, he evaded re-arrest by pricking his skin and rubbing salt and gunpowder into the wounds, to simulate smallpox.

After involvement with the Jacobite rebellion his exploits gradually lessened. He devoted himself to helping the gypsies, until illness forced him to resign his 'kingship'. Tales of his exploits – no doubt embroidered – were widespread in the West Country, and Thackeray refers to him in *Vanity Fair*.

originally dating from the 16th century but rebuilt in 1809 following flood damage. **Fisherman's Cot** (✆ 01884 855237) serves good food by the river, where outdoor tables allow you to share your meal with smartly dressed mallards.

The village centre, just a collection of whitewashed thatched houses and the church, is some way from the river up a steep hill (signposted). The church is peppered with monuments to the powerful Carew family who spread over so much of Devon in medieval times. Those commemorated in the church lived in and after Queen Elizabeth's reign; outside, in an unmarked grave, is Bampfylde Moore Carew, the 'King of the Gypsies'

1 Riverside cottages at Bickleigh. **2** Bickleigh bridge across the River Exe where, on midsummer night, you might see the ghost of Sir Alexander Cruwys. ▶

(see box, page 232), one of the more colourful members of the family. In the 14th century one of the Carews had an unfortunate altercation on Bickleigh bridge with Sir Alexander Cruwys, Lord of the Manor at Cruwys Morchard (page 236). Sir Alexander smote him with his sword and dumped the body in the Exe. He was sentenced to be hanged for this murder but rich men don't hang and he bought his pardon. However, Mr Carew got his revenge since Sir Alexander, presumably stricken with remorse, is said to ride his charger over Bickleigh Bridge at midnight on midsummer's day. So if you happen to be on the bridge at this time, look out for a knight in full armour with a head under one arm. Exactly whose head is open to speculation.

Across the river are the Devon Railway Centre and Bickleigh Mill, an extensive gift shop and restaurant. The **Devon Railway Centre** (EX16 8RG ✐ 01884 855671 ⚭ devonrailwaycentre.co.uk ☉ Apr–Oct, days vary) is at the former Bickleigh railway station on the closed Great Western Railway branch from Exeter to Dulverton. It is the ideal place to bring small children, with short narrow-gauge train rides, an Edwardian model village and model railways to delight adult train enthusiasts as well as kids.

Bickleigh Mill (✐ 01884 855419 ⚭ bickleighmill.com ☉ daily, hours vary) is an 18th-century mill, which was working until the 1960s. It has been converted into a classy bistro and gift shop displayed on three storeys. There is a large selection of toys, jewellery and crafts. For a preview or to shop online, check the website.

3 FURSDON HOUSE

🏠 **Fursdon Cottage** (page 250)

EX5 5JS ✐ 01392 860860 ⚭ fursdon.co.uk ☉ gardens Apr–Sep 14.00–17.00 Wed & Thu; house guided tours Jun–Aug 14.30 & 15.30 Wed & Thu; booking recommended

A few miles south of Bickleigh lies Fursdon House, home to the Fursdon family since at least 1259. Today it is David and Emily Fursdon and their children who live here and, twice a week in the summer, they invite visitors in to see their family home.

The Fursdon family bought the land during the reign of Henry III and the house has been much changed over the 760 years of their ownership.

---

1 Knightshayes, the former home of entrepreneur Sir John Heathcoat-Amory. 2 Tiverton Museum of Mid Devon Life. 3 Horse-drawn barge along the Grand Western Canal. ▶

It is now largely a 17th-century Regency house with a Georgian façade Many of the rooms are panelled and have their original fireplaces; the dining room, which is primarily Georgian, has one wall of Tudor panelling, while the library, often used as a ballroom, has impressive floor-to-ceiling bookcases. Historic England describe Fursdon as 'a good example of a modestly scaled gentleman's house', which somewhat understates its grandeur – that said, though it is large it does feel modest and lived in.

"Surrounding the house are hillside gardens with terraced beds displaying a variety of annuals and perennials."

The small **museum** inside the house has a copy of the family tree; imagine being able to trace your ancestors (who lived in the very same house you do now) back to 1259. In one corner there is a collection of dresses that have been passed down through the family since the 18th century.

Surrounding the house are four acres of hillside gardens with terraced beds displaying a colourful variety of annuals and perennials. The vine-clad pavilion and the thatched dovecote offer great places to sit and enjoy the view over the Exe Valley to Dartmoor. Across the lane is the meadow garden, designed as a memorial to Harriet Fursdon who died in 1821. The garden is currently being renovated into a wildlife sanctuary with a woodland walk, a pond and a host of wildflowers.

A small **tea room** in the Coach Hall serves highly praised cream teas, cakes and ice cream.

¶¶ FOOD & DRINK

The Bistro Restaurant & Bar Bickleigh Mill, EX16 8RG ✆ 01884 855419 ◷ 10.00–17.00 daily & evenings Thu–Sat. A very popular lunch-time stop for coaches so can get crowded, but the food is good, served in a delightful outside area by the river. The menu is traditional, with a good selection of specials each day.

Fisherman's Cot Bickleigh EX16 8RW ✆ 01884 855237. A beautiful riverside pub. Choose it for the superb location and classic pub food.

4 CRUWYS MORCHARD

This hamlet lies a few miles west of Tiverton but we have linked it with Bickleigh because it was one of the residents of the manor here, Sir Alexander Cruwys, who had the altercation on Bickleigh Bridge which resulted in his remorse-ridden ghost's yearly appearance (page 234). The Cruwys family *is* Cruwys Morchard.

Robert de Cruwys arrived here in 1175, only a century after his countryman, William the Conqueror, and the family have been here ever since, residing in the big house next to the church which features in *England's Thousand Best Churches* 'for family longevity alone'. For several centuries the family provided the church rectors – 42 in all – and the graveyard is full of their memorials.

Of special interest inside the church are the box pews with the names of parishioners inscribed on them. They were rented out to local families for 6d a year to help pay for the repairs after a catastrophic fire nearly demolished the church in the 17th century. Curiously – but perhaps significantly – the only monument in the church is hidden behind the organ. Could that be because it commemorates a John Avery, not a Cruwys?

✳ ✳ ✳

🚶 A BUS-ASSISTED WALK: BICKLEIGH TO TIVERTON

❊ OS Explorer map 114 or download the map & directions from the online PDF of the East Devon Way; start: Bickleigh Mill; about 4 miles; easy

One of the few stretches of the **Exe Valley Way** (EVW) to be on footpaths rather than lanes, this delightful walk takes you through meadows and woodland, following the right-hand bank of the Exe. It is often very muddy, so you'll need boots.

Park in the overflow carpark at Bickleigh Mill, and walk past the mill, turning left behind the building, just before a house named Millhayes. The footpath is signposted. From here it's simply a case of following the EVW signs, sometimes through woods and sometimes through meadows. In April, when I walked it, the woods were full of bluebells, wild garlic and wood anemones, along with the occasional early purple orchids. The meadows, sloping down to the river, were equally alluring. The only place you may get confused is shortly after a private suspension bridge when the path divides and there are no waymarkers. Turn right, leaving the river, and head uphill through the woods, rather than continuing straight on. Once the path levels out again it can be very muddy, particularly around gates where cows have gathered. The next place you could go wrong is when the broad track goes right, uphill, but the waymarked EVW goes straight ahead to another muddy kissing gate. At the far end of this field turn left and head towards the waterworks where there is a confusion of signs. Follow the path between the waterworks and the hedge and you will soon emerge on a lane.

From here to Tiverton it's over a mile of lane walking, a little dull after the delightful footpath you've been on, but so it goes. Collipriest Road meets St Andrew's Street where you turn left and use the footbridge to cross the main road. Follow signs to the museum and the bus station, and enjoy a coffee or snack while waiting for the half-hourly number 55 bus back to Bickleigh.

If doing the walk in reverse – and the advantage is that you can then have lunch at Bickleigh Mill – park in Tiverton's multi-storey carpark near the Phoenix Centre and get a map of the town from the TIC. Then it's easy enough to find St Andrew's Street. The EVW is signposted at the top of Collipriest Road which runs parallel to the river. Cross the bridge at Bickleigh to take the bus back to Tiverton.

✱ ✱ ✱

TIVERTON & AREA

From its birth near Simonsbath in Exmoor down to Exmouth and the sea, the Exe has shaped the history of Devon. Though too shallow to carry much cargo, the river drove the wool mills at Tiverton and these days provides some very pleasant views and walks or bike rides along the Exe Valley Way.

5 TIVERTON

🏠 **Brambles Bed and Breakfast** (page 250) 🏰 **Castle Barton** (page 250)
Tourist Information Beck's Sq, EX16 6PJ 🕾 01884 256295 𝌆 tivertonmuseum.org.uk

This very pleasant town tends to escape the attention of visitors despite its several attractions. It has a pedestrianised Fore Street, an excellent covered market, a fascinating church and perhaps the best museum in the county conveniently situated next to the short-stay carpark and bus station.

Textiles and faith have been the main movers and shakers here. The town's prosperity grew from its situation at the meeting of two rivers, the Exe and the Loman (the name means 'Town of Two Fords'). The water drove the textile mills and faith drove the construction of the many churches in and around the town. Two are notable: **St George's** on St Andrew Street (how confusing), an elegant Georgian church in the Wren style best viewed from the outside – it is often closed – and **St Peter's**, near the castle (𝌆 stpeterstiverton.org.uk). In 2021 the latter underwent a major restoration, still ongoing when I visited, so the kneelers, which were such a feature when I first wrote about this church, may be less visible. A few years ago you opened the door to a blaze of colour. The kneelers, made by the church's Tappissers Group, were displayed as in an art gallery, resting on the shelf that normally carries hymn books. They encompass a whole range of subjects, from birds, flowers and butterflies to local landscapes, all meticulously stitched and a joy to see. They were all made for a purpose, in memory either of a person, reflecting their lives and character, or of an event such as the Millennium, or Golden Jubilee. Other appealing features in the church are the decoratively carved capitals above the pillars and a richly carved font. It's also worth taking a close look at the organ, dedicated in 1696. An erudite and fascinating leaflet available in the church describes this in detail, explaining that it may have been built at the same time as the one in St Paul's Cathedral by the great masters of organ

"The walls are like a medieval bestiary: monkeys, lions, dogs, dragons, all mixed in with angels."

building, the German Christian Schmidt and, later, John Snetzler. It is housed in a splendid wooden case with carvings attributed to Grinling Gibbons. Organs are an accepted part of church services these days but just after the Restoration the concept of using instrumental music in worship was controversial, leading the Reverend John Newte to plead for an organ to 'Regulate the untenable Voices of the Multitude'.

Outside the church, on the exterior walls of the Greenway chapel, recently restored to its former glory, are carvings which Simon Jenkins in *England's Thousand Best Churches* describes as 'an encyclopaedia of English maritime history'. John Greenway was a wealthy 15th-century merchant venturer, widely travelled, who decorated the exterior of his chapel with carefully carved ships, all different, all armed. But these aren't the only images; the walls are like a medieval bestiary: monkeys, lions, dogs (maybe), dragons, monster gargoyles, all mixed in with angels and the odd bishop or two. It's well worth walking right round the building to admire them.

Every now and then the church holds a Tower Open Day (check their website) which is well worth booking for the opportunity to climb the circular stone staircase to the top of the 99ft tower, pausing at two levels to learn about the bells and bell ringing, and the clock. The view of the town from the top of the tower is impressive, and you will descend knowing a lot more about the history and technique of Devon bell ringing. Recommended.

Tiverton Castle

Park Hill, EX16 6RP ℘ 01884 255200 ⊘ tivertoncastle.com ⊙ Easter Sun–end Oct
14.30–17.30 Thu, Sun & bank hols

Just north of the church is this castle, built in 1106 by the first Earl of Devon in motte and bailey style with a moat, long since filled in. It remained the seat of the Earls of Devon for many centuries, with its most illustrious inhabitant being Princess Katherine Plantagenet, daughter of Edward IV, who was related to a goodly number of kings, including Richard III. In 1495 she married William Courtney, who became Earl of Devon. When the earl died in 1511 she continued to enjoy a lavish lifestyle in the castle until her own death in 1527. It is said that the splendour of her funeral at St Peter's has never been surpassed.

During the Civil War the castle was occupied by both sides in turn, suffering considerable damage, before being besieged and falling to Sir Thomas Fairfax, commander of Oliver Cromwell's Parliamentarians.

Richard Pococke, travelling in Devon in 1750, reported seeing this appealing inscription in the chapel attached to the castle:

Ho, ho, who lies here?
Tis I, the Earl of Devonshire,
With Kate my wife, to me full dear,
We lived together fifty-five year.
That we spent we had,
That we left we lost.
That we gave we have.

Which earl this was, and when he lived, we may never know.

If you are staying in the area it's well worth planning a visit to coincide with one of the open days. Since it's privately owned, visitors are allowed to sit on chairs, try on armour, test the weight of a cannon ball, and generally get the feeling of what it must have been like living – and fighting – in a place like this. Children will love the garderobes (toilets) which, had they lived in the olden days, they would have had to clean out.

Tiverton Museum of Mid Devon Life

Beck's Sq, EX16 6PJ ℘ 01884 256295 ⊘ tivertonmuseum.org.uk ⊙ check website

Lots of little museums in Devon depict rural life, so I was a bit sceptical when a visitor told me that the one at Tiverton was her favourite place in the county. I can now see why. It's a wonderful museum, conveniently incorporating the tourist information centre. There really is something here for everyone: 15 galleries displaying a huge range of everyday things that our grandparents or great grandparents would have been familiar with. Steam-train enthusiasts will spend a happy time sitting in the cab of *The Tivvy Bumper*, a Great Western Railway locomotive that once ran through pre-Beeching countryside round Tiverton, and those who like even older transport can examine Britain's most comprehensive collection of wagons. One of them has a

"The museum is particularly family friendly, running all sorts of craft activities, as well as handling sessions."

horse story: in 1904 a man called Alf Wyatt won a bet that he could drive a wagon, loaded with barley, from Netherexe to Exeter, a distance of about seven miles. Nothing exceptional in that, you might think, but his team of three horses had no reins to guide or slow them. They responded to their master's voice, and arrived safely at the brewery despite the danger of the city's tramcars. That's in the outhouses. Inside there are toys, lacemaking, agriculture, cooking, public health … if it was used during the last few centuries, it'll be here. I was particularly taken by the barrel piano. These barrel pianos provided a nice little business for Canon Algernon Ogle Wintle, who bought them in the early part of the 20th century, renovated them and resold them under his name. A visitor to the museum remembers Canon Wintle from his childhood near Bury St Edmunds. He recalls a rotund, grumpy man with a workshop full of barrel pianos: 'Ladies of the village used to trundle them up to his house, with the pins pulled out ready for him to put in the latest tunes.'

The museum is particularly family friendly, running all sorts of craft activities, as well as handling sessions so children can learn more about the exhibits. There are opportunities for dressing up and play areas for younger children. Adults have a choice of evening talks or day outings.

Heathcoat Factory

West Exe St, EX16 5LL ⊘ heathcoat.co.uk

I would never have thought that a visit to a textile factory would be 'absolutely fascinating' but I was assured, during my visit to St Peter's church tower, that this was not to be missed if one happened to be in Tiverton when a tour was on offer.

John Heathcoat was born in Derbyshire in 1783, and at an early age showed a talent for understanding machinery. The invention which made his fortune was a mechanised lace-making machine – understandably not popular in lace-making centres such as Honiton. These days they make a huge range of textiles in their Tiverton factory, but their speciality is coming up with solutions to the challenges of the aerospace industry. In 2020 they created the lightest and toughest parachute fabric yet made for the Mars space probe *Perseverance.*

ᵀ¶ FOOD & DRINK

FrouFrou Bistro 43 Gold St, Tiverton EX16 6QB ✆ 01884 250544. ⊙ 17.00–23.30 Tue–Sat. A classy restaurant with a French slant, housed in a 17th-century building.
The Independent Coffee Trader 17 Gold St, Tiverton, EX16 6QB ✆ 01884 798055. A wide range of coffees and excellent cakes.

6 THE GRAND WESTERN CANAL

It was indeed a grand idea: build a canal to link the Bristol Channel with the English Channel, thus avoiding the long and hazardous journey around the Cornish peninsula. It would also be ideal for transporting coal from South Wales into the heart of Somerset and Devon.

Work began in the early 19th century and the first section from Tiverton to the limestone quarries of Westleigh was completed in 1814. But already the project had run into trouble; it had proved far more expensive than envisioned to make the deep cuttings necessary to ensure a level route through Devon's hilly countryside.

The next section to Taunton was eventually completed in 1838, no doubt to vociferous complaints about the waste of money, and then fizzled out, all thought of reaching either the English or the Bristol Channel abandoned. For a while, however, it carried enough coal and limestone to be profitable, but the arrival of the railway was the final nail in the coffin. Goods could be carried more cheaply by rail. The section from Lowdwells to Taunton was sold off, and the rest of the canal was gradually abandoned to its fate. In the 1960s a proposal to fill in the now leaking, weed-choked canal and build a road had the required effect. A campaign to save the canal gathered strength until Devon County Council gained ownership in 1971 and declared it a Country Park, investing sufficient money to dredge and reline it so it once again could transport boats, including the famous horse-drawn barge, the *Tivertonian.* In 2005 it was declared a Local Nature Reserve and is now one of the region's leading tourist attractions. It has an informative visitor centre, 11 miles of tow path for walking or cycling, and calm waters for canoeing. Canadian canoes and rowing boats can be hired near the entrance.

Horse-drawn barge trips

The Wharf, Canal Hill EX16 4HX ✆ 01884 253345 ◈ tivertoncanal.co.uk ◷ Apr–Oct

It's about as slow and tranquil as you can get. Well-tended gardens sloping down to the canal give way to open meadows and huge trees standing with their feet in the water. Mallards coast by, looking up expectantly for titbits, and moorhens scurry around the reedy edges.

Only three horse-drawn barges remain in England, and this is the last in the West Country, operated as a step back in time with staff dressed in Victorian costume. The 2½-hour journey is a good mix of information and relaxation. Come early so you can watch the horse being prepared for its job of pulling the barge.

The shire horses are for show rather than historical accuracy. Once a barge is moving, very little effort is involved in keeping it going, so ponies or even donkeys would have been used in the past; you can tell

POSSESSIONING DAY (1887)

The following is an extract from the Tiverton Gazette, 16 August 1887.

Friday last, was what is termed 'possessioning day' at Cullompton, when possession is taken of the Town Lake, which ceremony takes place every seven years. Some are apt to think that it is quite often enough, considering some of the pranks that are practised; for instance: strangers passing through the town, walking or riding, are subjected to attack from a set of youths, and so-called men, who throw sand and water over them as they are passing by. This sort of thing began about one o'clock. After a while they made for the source of the stream, where refreshments were provided. After the repast, the party made their way down stream to get into the town, and there to insult anybody who was so unfortunate to pass by. Towards the close of the evening one youth was served rather badly by a 'gentleman' who had been almost drenched. This 'gentleman' used his stick rather freely and the youth became insensible. However he soon recovered consciousness and was taken home. Some persons had to be escorted through the street by a policeman.

(Visitors to Cullompton today may be relieved to know that the ceremony seems to have been discontinued after this particular occasion.)

that from the low height of the bridges. We learned about the special tack needed to protect the horses from the sideways pull of the rope: coloured bobbins (rollers) to stop the traces chafing the horse's sides and looby pins which instantly release the rope from the towing mast in case of any emergency such as a horse bolting.

The canal is only a few feet deep but full of fish: tench, perch, rudd, bream and pike to name a few. Kingfishers may be spotted in the early morning or evening. Most trips are mid morning or afternoon, going to the East Manley aqueduct, built by Brunel, which gives an indication as to why the project ran out of money: it's a magnificent engineering feat. If music is your thing, then there are night trips with a jazz band. A licensed bar on board serves a wide range of old-fashioned drinks and ales. If you're still hungry when you disembark, the **Canal Tea Rooms** by the wharf carpark has outdoor seating, a good menu of light lunches and teas with a huge choice of cakes.

7 KNIGHTSHAYES

EX16 7RH ⊘ gardens 10.00–17.00 daily; house, shop & café 11.00–16.00 daily; booking recommended for guided tours of the first-floor rooms; National Trust

Just nine miles north of Tiverton is Sir John Heathcoat-Amory's Gothic revival country house, which has been in the care of the National Trust since 1972. Sir John's grandfather revolutionised lace making with his invention of a mechanised bobbin; their factory still stands in Tiverton (page 241) and can be seen from the terrace of this impressive home.

The approach to Knightshayes is through a parkland of ancient and notable trees including a 400-year-old champion holly, two huge redwoods and a 300-year-old turkey oak. A trail runs around these trees, one of three such paths in the grounds – pick up an excellent trail map from reception. William Burges designed the house in 1869; he had a reputation for dramatic houses and churches and there is something both majestic and ecclesiastical about the architecture of Knightshayes with its turrets and leaded windows. Burges also had extravagant plans for the interior, but the house took longer than expected to build and the cost had escalated. Burges was fired and John Crace was employed to create a more modest and less expensive interior.

Walking around the house, it still seems quite extravagant, with a minstrel's gallery over the hall, leather wallpaper, wood-panelled ceilings and intricately carved stone corbels holding up the roof beams. However, the original Burges designs, displayed in many rooms, are in another league – exuberantly over-the-top by anyone's standards. In every room the ceiling is an elaborate work of art and quite overpowering, so much so that the family had many boarded over or painted white. The National Trust has carefully reinstated them.

Outside, the gardens are equally impressive. The 2½-acre walled kitchen garden is not to be missed; on a south-facing slope, it has a heated wall for exotic fruits and a terrace of banana trees, canna lilies and palm trees. Of course, Burges embellished it with turrets on each corner of the wall. Today, the garden grows fruit and vegetables for the on-site café and Tiverton's pannier market, as well as having its own small vineyard. In front of the house, the terrace overlooks the formal garden with extensive views across the surrounding countryside. A ha-ha wall preserves the uninterrupted view while keeping the sheep out of the garden. Box hedges cut into bizarre animal topiary link this garden to the woodland garden. Here, a myriad of trails lead in all directions allowing one to wander, blissfully lost or, if you prefer, to find one of the many sunny benches for a little relaxation and time to take in the view.

After exploring, enjoy a little refreshment in The Stables **café** – the vegan pasty is highly recommended – or visit the **shop and plant centre**; there is even a second-hand bookshop.

8 SAMPFORD PEVERELL

🏠 **The Globe Inn** (page 250)

This is a pleasant village of white-washed houses and two pubs, the Globe (✎ 01884 821214) – which also has a bicycle hire place (page 228) – and the Merriemeade (✎ 01884 820270).

The **church** was built with the help of the mother of Henry VII, Lady Margaret of Beaufort. The Grand Western Canal sliced through part of the rectory garden and the former south wing, so the company paid for its rebuilding, and that of a second rectory, in 1836. Even before the excitement of the canal, the village experienced a notable event, with a householder much bothered by a poltergeist. This achieved such notoriety that the crowds became more bothersome than the ghost and he shot one (a man, not a ghost) 'in self defence'. Eventually the supernatural goings on turned out to be a gang of smugglers concealed behind a false wall.

ACCOMMODATION

The places to stay included here have been listed either with an eye to their location, because they are special or unusual in some way, or because they encapsulate the Slow approach. Inclusion doesn't necessarily mean they are the best in the area – just places we stayed in, visited or had recommended to us. An internet search will reveal many more. When booking a place to stay, bear in mind that most accommodation is cheaper off season or if you stay several nights, and as a rule self-catering places can only be let for four days or more. Campsites run the gamut of possibilities – from a meadow that's only open in August, to glamping in luxury. Indeed, glamping has become

SELF-CATERING AGENCIES & PROVIDERS

Blue Chip Holidays ⬙ bluechipholidays.co.uk. Southwest specialists.

Canopy & Stars ⬙ canopyandstars.co.uk. Sawday's glamping selection.

Classic Cottages ⬙ classic.co.uk. West Country specialists.

Classic Glamping ⬙ classicglamping.co.uk

Devon Farms ⬙ devonfarms.co.uk. Stay on a working farm.

Devon Holiday Cottages ⬙ devonholidaycottages.com. Devon for all budgets. You can book direct with the owner.

Exmoor Holidays ⬙ exmoor-holidays.co.uk

Helpful Holidays ⬙ helpfulholidays.co.uk

Holiday Cottages ⬙ holidaycottages.co.uk

The Landmark Trust ⬙ landmarktrust.org.uk. This charitable organisation is quite different from the other accommodation providers listed here. Their role is to rescue historic buildings in danger of dereliction, restore them, and rent them out to holidaymakers. There are no televisions or telephones.

Quality Unearthed ⬙ qualityunearthed.co.uk. Glamping.

Quirky Accommodation ⬙ quirkyaccom.com. Self explanatory; includes boats & treehouses.

Toad Hall Cottages ⬙ toadhallcottages.co.uk. West Country specialists.

Unique Homestays ⬙ uniquehomestays.com. Aimed at the upper end of the market.

one of the most popular ways of enjoying a rural holiday. Suggestions vary from tree houses to gypsy caravans.

In Devon, by far the most popular holiday accommodation is self-catering. The box opposite lists some agencies alphabetically.

Note that sat nav is often unreliable here, and there may not be a mobile phone signal, so always check the accommodation provider's directions in advance.

The hotels, inns and B&Bs featured in this section are indicated by 🏠 under the heading for the town or village nearest their location. Self-catering is indicated by 🏚, campsites by ⚑ and glamping by ⚑.

For detailed descriptions of the following places, go to ✂ bradtguides. com/midnorthdev.

1 NORTHWEST DEVON: THE CORNISH BORDER TO THE RIVER TORRIDGE

Hotels

Hartland Quay Hotel Hartland
✂ hartlandquayhotel.co.uk. Thirteen rooms, on the SWCP so perfect for walkers. Page 38.
New Inn Hotel Clovelly ✂ thenewinnclovelly. co.uk. Eight small but comfortable rooms in the heart of the village.
Hoops Inn Horns Cross ✂ hotelsnorthdevon. co.uk. Thirteen en-suite rooms. A picturesque, thatched 13th-century inn set in 2.5 acres near the North Devon coast between Clovelly and Bideford.

Self-catering

Downe Cottages Hartland ✂ downecottages. com. Nine cottages, sleeping two to eight people.Situated on Hartland Peninsula overlooking the Atlantic and Lundy Island. Set in seven acres of grounds and all sharing a lovely spa, for relaxing after a long day's walking, and a gym, for those who need even more exercise.
Bridge Cottage Peppercombe
✂ landmarktrust.org.uk. A tiny thatched cottage near a secluded beach. Sleeps three.

Camping & glamping
Koa Tree Camp Welcombe ✂ koatreecamp.com. Log cabins & geodomes.
Loveland Farm Hartland
✂ lovelandfarmcamping.co.uk. Glamping at its best. Six geodesic domes and three tipis; also a campsite run on sustainable principles.

2 NORTH DEVON'S SEASIDE

B&Bs & hotel
Pack o' Cards Combe Martin ✂ packocards.co.uk. World-famous hotel folly. Page 90.
The Smugglers Rest Mortehoe
✂ thesmugglersrest.co.uk. A classy B&B near the beach and coast path. Page 74.

Self-catering
The Linhay Butterhills, near Braunton.
✂ butterhillsescapes.co.uk; see ad, page 93. An off-grid hideaway sleeping two.
Mary's Cottage Near Combe Martin
✂ indicknowle.co.uk. A secluded cottage on a working farm. Sleeps six.
Pickwell Manor Georgeham, near Woolacombe ✂ pickwellmanor.co.uk. Three bespoke treehouses in the woods. Two are designed for couples who want the ultimate

romantic treetop retreat and a third sleeps four as a family hideout.

West Challacombe Manor Near Combe Martin. ⟨ nationaltrustcottages.co.uk. Sleeps five. Possibly haunted. Page 92.

Camping & glamping
North Morte Farm Caravan & Camping Park Mortehoe ⟨ northmortefarm.co.uk. Within a stone's throw of the coast path and the best beaches.

3   LUNDY ISLAND

The Landmark Trust is responsible for all Lundy's accommodation, which is listed on its website with full descriptions and photos ⟨ landmarktrust.org.uk/lundyisland.

4   BARNSTAPLE & INLAND NORTH DEVON

B&B & hotel
Broomhill Art Hotel Muddiford ⟨ broomhill-estate.com. Comfortable and surrounded by art. Page 124.

Hollamoor Farm Tawstock ⟨ devonhorsebedbreakfast.co.uk. A 300-year-old farmhouse welcomes two- and four-footed visitors.

Self-catering
Anderton House Goodleigh (east of Barnstaple) ⟨ landmarktrust.org.uk. Exceptional modern architecture. Sleeps five.

Rosemoor House Great Torrington ⟨ rhs.org.uk. The former home of Lady Anne Berry, situated in RHS Garden Rosemoor. Page 137.

Glamping
Fisherton Farm's Vintage Vardos Near Atherington, Umberleigh ⟨ fishertonfarm. com. Gypsy caravans on a farm.

Woodland Retreat Langtree, Great Torrington ⟨ canopyandstars.co.uk. A treehouse in a woodland setting. Sleeps four.

5   DEVON'S EXMOOR

Hotels & Inns
The Hunter's Inn Heddon Valley ⟨ thehuntersinnexmoor.co.uk. The most famous inn on Exmoor, now owned by the National Trust. Page 159.

The Old Rectory Hotel Martinhoe ⟨ oldrectoryhotel.co.uk. Award-winning luxury country hotel with 11 rooms.

B&Bs
Highcliffe House Lynton ⟨ highcliffehouse. co.uk; see ad, page 27. Luxury B&B and the best views on Exmoor.

Orchard House Lynmouth ⟨ orchardhousehotel.co.uk. A good value B&B in a lovely location.

Shoulsbarrow Farmhouse Challacombe ⟨ shoulsbarrowfarm.co.uk. A warm welcome and two double rooms.

Self-catering
New Mill Farm Barbrook ⟨ outovercott.co.uk. Four holiday cottages on a 100-acre sheep farm with riding stables.

Treetops Woody Bay ⟨ hideaways.co.uk. A lovely retreat giving easy access to the beach.

Camping & glamping
Westland Farm Bratton Fleming ⟨ westlandfarm.co.uk. Glamping in a yurt, shepherd's hut or drover's hut. Also camping.

6 WEST MID DEVON: RUBY COUNTRY

B&Bs & hotels

The Devil's Stone Inn Shebbear ✆ 01409 281210. This 400-year-old former coaching inn has five en suite-bedrooms, each different and reflecting the inn's history. Page 187.

Forda Farm Thornbury ⬧ fordafarm.com. A small two-bedroom B&B on a working sheep and beef farm.

The George Hatherleigh ⬧ thegeorgeinhatherleigh.com. Once a courthouse, The George was beautifully restored after being burnt to the ground in 1980 and now offers four-posters and some accessible rooms. Page 181.

Half Moon Inn Sheepwash ⬧ halfmoonsheepwash.co.uk. A 16th-century traditional inn with 13 en-suite rooms and exclusive salmon and trout fishing on the Torridge. Page 189.

Self-catering

Belvedere Tower Hatherleigh ⬧ holidaycottages.co.uk. A 1879 folly once used as a lookout and now a tiny one-room romantic holiday home for two with a private decked area on the roof. Page 184.

The Cow Shed Exbourne ⬧ classic.co.uk. Situated on an historic farmstead, this two-bedroom detached cottage on the edge of the village has great views over the farm's meadows and beyond.

Easter Hall Park Petrockstowe ⬧ easterhallpark.co.uk. A wonderful two-bedroom log cabin at this equestrian centre. Page 186.

Lemon Cottage Hatherleigh ⬧ airbnb.co.uk. A late-medieval terraced cottage that sleeps four; inside it is all low beams, inglenook fireplace and slightly wonky floors.

Syncocks Farm Petrockstowe ⬧ cottages.com. Dating from the 1350s, this beautifully restored, thatched farmhouse has a large landscaped garden and sleeps eight.

Camping & glamping

Hideaway Camping Higher Melbury ✆ 01837 871777 ⬧ hideawaycamping.co.uk. Thirteen camping pitches in a large field with a communal campfire, plus quirky glamping options that include igloos, an owl pod and a double decker bus that sleeps six.

Ten Acres Vineyard Camping Winkleigh ⬧ tenacresvineyardcamping.co.uk. A unique, small campsite with some glamping tents and its own vineyard and wine store, overlooking Devon's rolling countryside.

Wild Spaces East Panson ⬧ wildspacesgypsycaravan.co.uk. Two beautifully restored gypsy caravans, each set in its own field, with their own wood-burning stove and adjacent private bathroom.

7 THE HEART OF DEVON

B&Bs & hotels

The Fox & Hounds Eggesford ⬧ foxandhoundshotel.co.uk. A former coaching inn set in six acres of gardens that stretch down to the River Taw.

The George South Molton ⬧ thegeorgesouthmolton.co.uk. A beautiful, 18th-century town house with 12 bedrooms, a coffee lounge and a bar, in the centre of South Molton.

The New Inn Coleford ⬧ thenewinncoleford.co.uk. A 14th-century thatched inn constructed from cob with seven double bedrooms, all very individual.

Warrens Farm B&B Yeoford ⬧ warrensfarm.co.uk. Three traditional en-suite rooms on a working farm, surrounded by lovely gardens and wonderful views.

Self-catering

Hidden Chapel Zeal Monachorum EX17 6DG ⬧ hostunusual.com. A stunningly converted 19th-century congregational chapel that sleeps six.

Holly Water East Village
⌂ hollywaterholidays.co.uk. See ad, page 225.
Holly Water extends over 35 acres, offering two
luxury shepherds' huts and the Beehive tree
house, sleeping two and four, respectively.
Wheatland Farm ⌂ wheatlandfarm.co.uk.
Despite its name, this is really a nature reserve
rather than a farm, with four lodges sleeping
from four to eight people and a cottage
sleeping four. Page 216.

Camping & glamping
Orchard Retreat Cheriton Fitzpaine
⌂ theorchardretreat.co.uk. See ad, page 224.
A great base for a family holiday, with three
yurts, a cider barn and a cottage set in 15 acres.
Upcott Roundhouse Cheriton Fitzpaine
⌂ upcottroundhouse.co.uk. This amazing,
cathedral-like home, lit by candles and a central
fire, offers an opportunity to experience Iron-
Age living; sleeps from four to ten.
Welcombe Meadow High Bickington
⌂ welcombemeadow.co.uk. Luxurious
glamping in safari-style tents, sleeping six.

8 THE EXE VALLEY

B&B & Hotels
Brambles Bed and Breakfast Whitnage
⌂ bramblesbedandbreakfast.co.uk. An
unassuming, friendly and comfortable B&B in
a small village.

The Globe Inn Sampford Peverell ⌂ the-
globeinn.co.uk. A traditional inn in the heart
of the village with six simple, comfortable
rooms; the perfect place for visitors using public
transport.

Self-catering
Castle Barton Tiverton ⌂ tivertoncastle.com.
Part of historic Tiverton Castle, this cottage
was built as a farmhouse in the 1840s; three
bedrooms, an open fireplace in the sitting
room, and a private, self-contained garden.
Page 240.
Fursdon Cottage Cadbury ⌂ fursdon.co.uk.
Set in the grounds of Fursdon House, this
former gardener's cottage provides peaceful
accommodation surrounded by flowers and
birdsong. Page 234.
Silverton Park Stables Silverton
⌂ landmarktrust.org.uk. An extraordinary
place offering accommodation for up to 14
people in converted stables, with gorgeous
views over the Devon countryside.

Glamping
Exe Valley Glamping ⌂ exevalleyglamping.
com. A peaceful and very comfortable retreat
on a 150-acre farm adjoining the River Exe.

INDEX

Entries in **bold** refer to major entries; those in *italics* indicate maps.

INDEX OF ADVERTISERS

In the beginning

It all began in 1974 on an Amazon river barge. During an 18-month trip through South America, two adventurous young backpackers – Hilary Bradt and her then husband, George – decided to write about the hiking trails they had discovered through the Andes. *Backpacking Along Ancient Ways in Peru and Bolivia* included the very first descriptions of the Inca Trail. It was the start of a colourful journey to becoming one of the best-loved travel publishers in the world; you can read the full story on our website (www. bradtguides.com/ourstory).

Getting there first

Hilary quickly gained a reputation for being a true travel pioneer, and in the 1980s she started to focus on guides to places overlooked by other publishers. The Bradt Guides list became a roll call of guidebook 'firsts'. We published the first guide to Madagascar, followed by Mauritius, Czechoslovakia and Vietnam. The 1990s saw the beginning of our extensive coverage of Africa: Tanzania, Uganda, South Africa, and Eritrea. Later, post-conflict guides became a feature: Rwanda, Mozambique, Angola, Sierra Leone, Bosnia and Kosovo.

Comprehensive – and with a conscience

Today, we are the world's largest independently owned travel publisher, with more than 200 titles, from full-country and wildlife guides to Slow Travel guides like this one. However, our ethos remains unchanged. Hilary is still keenly involved, and we still get there first: two-thirds of Bradt guides have no direct competition.

But we don't just get there first. Our guides are also known for being more comprehensive than any other series. We avoid templates and tick-lists. Each guide is a one-of-a-kind expression of an expert author's interests, knowledge and enthusiasm for telling it how it really is.

And a commitment to wildlife, conservation and respect for local communities has always been at the heart of our books. Bradt Guides was championing sustainable travel before any other guidebook publisher.

Thank you!

We can only do what we do because of the support of readers like you – people who value less-obvious experiences, less-visited places and a more thoughtful approach to travel. Those who, like us, take travel seriously.

TRAVEL TAKEN SERIOUSLY